THE COMPLETE IDIOT'S GUIDE® TO

QuickBooks 2012

by Barbara Harvie

ALPHA

A member of Penguin Group (USA) Inc.

This book is dedicated to all entrepreneurs who are willing to take that risk and follow their dreams of owning a small business.

ALPHA BOOKS

Published by the Penguin Group

Penguin Group (USA) Inc., 375 Hudson Street, New York, New York 10014, USA

Penguin Group (Canada), 90 Eglinton Avenue East, Suite 700, Toronto, Ontario M4P 2Y3, Canada (a division of Pearson Penguin Canada Inc.)

Penguin Books Ltd., 80 Strand, London WC2R 0RL, England

Penguin Ireland, 25 St. Stephen's Green, Dublin 2, Ireland (a division of Penguin Books Ltd.)

Penguin Group (Australia), 250 Camberwell Road, Camberwell, Victoria 3124, Australia (a division of Pearson Australia Group Pty. Ltd.)

Penguin Books India Pvt. Ltd., 11 Community Centre, Panchsheel Park, New Delhi—110 017, India

Penguin Group (NZ), 67 Apollo Drive, Rosedale, North Shore, Auckland 1311, New Zealand (a division of Pearson New Zealand Ltd.)

Penguin Books (South Africa) (Pty.) Ltd., 24 Sturdee Avenue, Rosebank, Johannesburg 2196, South Africa

Penguin Books Ltd., Registered Offices: 80 Strand, London WC2R 0RL, England

International Standard Book Number: 978-1-61564-117-8
Library of Congress Catalog Card Number: 2011905822

13 12 11   8 7 6 5 4 3 2 1

Interpretation of the printing code: The rightmost number of the first series of numbers is the year of the book's printing; the rightmost number of the second series of numbers is the number of the book's printing. For example, a printing code of 11-1 shows that the first printing occurred in 2011.

Printed in the United States of America

Most Alpha books are available at special quantity discounts for bulk purchases for sales promotions, premiums, fund-raising, or educational use. Special books, or book excerpts, can also be created to fit specific needs.

For details, write: Special Markets, Alpha Books, 375 Hudson Street, New York, NY 10014.

Publisher: *Marie Butler-Knight*
Associate Publisher/Acquiring Editor: *Mike Sanders*
Executive Managing Editor: *Billy Fields*
Development Editor: *Jennifer Moore*
Senior Production Editor: *Janette Lynn*
Copy Editor: *Krista Hansing Editorial Services, Inc.*

Cover Designer: *Kurt Owens*
Book Designers: *William Thomas, Rebecca Batchelor*
Indexer: *Tonya Heard*
Layout: *Ayanna Lacey*
Proofreader: *John Etchison*

Contents

Introduction

Nothing is more rewarding than starting and running your own business. It's exhilarating, scary, daunting, and satisfying all at the same time. You learn something new every day, face new challenges, solve new problems, build confidence, and, best of all, get to work for the best boss in the world—you! While you may be full of passion and purpose for the more creative side of your business, you probably have some trepidation about the "back office": all that accounting and paperwork.

QuickBooks to the rescue! That's where this book comes in, too. It guides you through learning about QuickBooks without having to delve too much into the accounting. QuickBooks takes care of all the behind-the-scenes financial mysteries. I also try to tell you the "why" behind what you're doing; this isn't just a step-by-step guide that you blindly follow without knowing why QuickBooks is asking you to do something or understanding the effect of what you're doing.

Rash Assumptions

Sometimes it seems like QuickBooks comes in more varieties than ice cream. But I'm assuming you're running QuickBooks Pro 2012 for the PC. **This book talks only about QuickBooks Pro 2012 for the PC.** You can still use this book if you use a different flavor of QuickBooks, but your version may have more features (or different features) that this book doesn't cover.

Another assumption I've made is that you are a true small business: either you're a sole proprietor or you have only a few employees. As such, I'm assuming you haven't purchased one of the many QuickBooks add-ons for payroll services; you use the do-it-yourself payroll method.

You're a businessperson, not an accountant. In fact, you prefer to think about accounting as little as possible. I'm also assuming that you have a trusted accountant you can turn to for questions that only your accountant can answer based on his or her knowledge of your business.

Finally, I'm assuming that you've read the excellent installation instructions that came with your QuickBooks software to install QuickBooks before diving into this book.

Book Organization

I've organized this book into eight parts:

Part 1, Getting Started, walks you through setting up your company file using either the Express Start or the EasyStep Interview. It covers gathering your paperwork to prepare for setting up your company file. It also explains how to navigate in QuickBooks and shows how QuickBooks is laid out. And although you don't need to know accounting, a chapter is devoted to the very basic concepts you'll run across in QuickBooks.

Part 2, Setting Up Your Business Lists, gives you step-by-step instructions on how to add things to lists (lists are the backbone of QuickBooks), such as your customer list, vendor list, products and services list, and so on.

Part 3, Money Coming In, explains how you can track the sales you make to customers, create estimates, create invoices or statements, and use sales receipts. It explains how customers pay you and how you can handle overdue payments from customers.

Part 4, Money Going Out, shows you how to pay bills and how to track and pay sales taxes.

Part 5, Managing Inventory, shows you how you can track, purchase, and receive inventory in QuickBooks Pro. It also covers reporting on inventory and counting inventory.

Part 6, Day-to-Day Banking Tasks, explains how to use bank registers, deposit money, and reconcile your bank accounts.

Part 7, Managing Your Business, talks about actions you may have to perform from time to time in your business. It covers topics such as tracking time and mileage, tracking payroll, and recording owner's equity. It also includes some minor miscellaneous tasks, such as writing off bad debt, tracking petty cash, and making journal entries. Not all businesses will need to do these.

Part 8, How Is Your Business Doing? shows you how to run reports—such as a Profit and Loss report—to monitor several key areas of your business. It also covers some important tasks you'll need to perform at year's end.

Extras

Throughout the book, you'll find sidebars that contain extra stuff you should know about.

> **DEFINITION**
>
> These sidebars define terms used in QuickBooks that you may not be familiar with.

> **QUICKTIP**
>
> These sidebars show you little tricks and tips for getting the most out of QuickBooks.

> **BEHIND THE SCENES**
>
> These sidebars explain what QuickBooks does with the information you provide—for example, how it handles the accounting side of things so you don't have to.

> **NUMBERS HAPPEN**
>
> These sidebars point out some pitfalls to watch out for that may cause problems if done incorrectly.

Acknowledgments

I am grateful to the talented and dedicated editorial staff at Penguin Group who helped bring this book to small business owners who need a guide to working with QuickBooks. Special thanks go to Mike Sanders for being this book's champion. And many thanks go to the thorough and talented editors who helped usher this book through production and publication: Jennifer Moore, my development editor; Krista Hansing, my copy editor; and Janette Lynn, my production editor. For her incredible index, a special thanks to Tonya Heard.

A huge thank you goes to Carole Jelen of Waterside Productions for being my helpful agent.

Many thanks to the Beta team at Intuit (especially Bryan Ruff and Lesley Kew) who provided me with access to the beta version of QuickBooks Pro 2012.

And I could not have completed this book without the help of Kelli O'Rourke Wall, my technical reviewer. Kelli brings many years of experience in helping small business owners run their businesses, and has run a couple of successful small businesses of her own. Her attention to detail is legendary, and that gave me peace of mind on the technical accuracy of the book. She also brings business insight from having solved many problems of small business owners. Kelli is a Certified QuickBooks ProAdvisor and is currently consulting with several small businesses.

Special Thanks to the Technical Reviewer

The Complete Idiot's Guide to Quickbooks 2012 was reviewed by an expert who double-checked the accuracy of what you'll learn here, to help us ensure that this book gives you everything you need to know about Quickbooks. Special thanks are extended to Kelli Wall.

Trademarks

All terms mentioned in this book that are known to be or are suspected of being trademarks or service marks have been appropriately capitalized. Alpha Books and Penguin Group (USA) Inc. cannot attest to the accuracy of this information. Use of a term in this book should not be regarded as affecting the validity of any trademark or service mark.

Getting Started

Before you can dig in and start using QuickBooks, you have to set up your company file, which is what QuickBooks calls the file that holds all your company data. The chapters in this part show you the first steps in creating your company file and offer a quick tour of QuickBooks Pro 2012.

Chapter 1 helps you get organized and tells you what information you need and then walks you step-by-step through the process of creating your company file. Chapter 2 orients you to QuickBooks by providing an overview of how to navigate the program and make use of QuickBooks Centers. Chapter 3 explains how QuickBooks stores your information in lists and forms. It also explains how you can customize QuickBooks by setting the Preferences to suit the way you like to work. Chapter 4 gives you a quick and dirty overview of the principles of accounting. And finally, Chapter 5 covers the basics of printing checks and forms and e-mailing forms to your customers.

Setting Up Your QuickBooks Company File

In This Chapter

- Getting organized for setting up your company file
- Determining the start date of your company file
- Using Express Start
- Going through the EasyStep Interview

QuickBooks tries to make setting up your company file as easy as possible using "interviews." By answering a series of questions, you tell QuickBooks a lot about your company and set up some of the features you'll need. I'm not going to lie to you—setting up QuickBooks can take a bit of time. But the more you do up front, the more you ensure that your accounting will be correct—and that you will save time in the long run. So put on a pot of coffee or tea and get started!

Opening and Exiting QuickBooks

If you haven't yet installed QuickBooks, follow the excellent instructions that came in the box. And the first things you need to know are how to open QuickBooks and how to quit when you are done for the day.

After you install QuickBooks, you'll see a QuickBooks icon on your desktop. You double-click that icon to open QuickBooks, or you go to the Start menu, point to **All Programs**, point to **QuickBooks**, and then click **QuickBooks Pro**.

To quit QuickBooks, go to the **File** menu and click **Exit**.

Creating a QuickBooks Company File

QuickBooks offers four ways to set up your company file:

- Use Express Start to answer a few basic questions about your business. This is the quickest way to set up your company file, using QuickBooks-recommended settings. See the next section, "Starting Express Start."

- Use Advanced Setup (called the EasyStep Interview) to fine-tune your company settings and provide more details about your business. This method takes a little longer and is good to use if you want to customize the settings.

- Set up your company file manually.

- Convert from another software program.

Setting up your file manually is more for experts and accountants, so I won't be talking about that here. If you need to convert your data from another software package, check Appendix B for how to use QuickBooks help, and use the Search tool to search for "convert."

Starting Express Start

Use Express Start to quickly set up your company file using default settings based on your company type and industry. You can always change these settings later if you find they don't work for you. QuickBooks assumes today is the start date of your company file and you don't need to enter historical transactions. If you don't want to use today as your start date, you'll need to skip this section and follow the instructions in "Starting the EasyStep Interview" later in this chapter.

To start Express Start, follow these steps:

1. On the Welcome page QuickBooks displays when you first start it, click the **Express Start** button (see Figure 1.1). If you don't see the Welcome page, you may see the No Company Open page. On that page, click **Create a New Company**. You can also go to the File menu and click **New Company**.

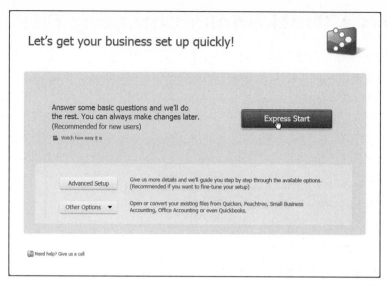

Figure 1.1: *Starting Express Start.*

2. In the **Company Name** field (see Figure 1.2), type your company name.

Figure 1.2: *Tell QuickBooks about your business.*

3. Next to the Industry field, click **"Help me choose."**

4. On the Select Your Industry window (see Figure 1.3), choose the industry that best fits your business and click **OK**.

Figure 1.3: *Choose the industry that best matches your business.*

5. In the Company Type field, click the down arrow and choose the type that corresponds to your company (see Figure 1.4). Click **"Help me choose"** to read explanations of each type.

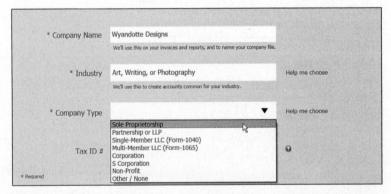

Figure 1.4: *Choose the type of company so QuickBooks can choose tax settings for your business.*

6. In the Tax ID # field, type either your EIN number or your Social Security number, if you don't have an EIN. (If you have employees, you must enter the EIN number.)

7. Click **Continue**.

8. In the next screen (see Figure 1.5), enter your company contact information.

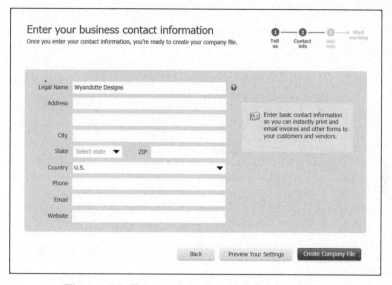

Figure 1.5: *Enter your company contact information.*

9. To see the default settings QuickBooks has set up for your company file, click **Preview Your Settings**. In the next screen (see Figure 1.6), click the tabs to review the settings. Click **OK** when finished.

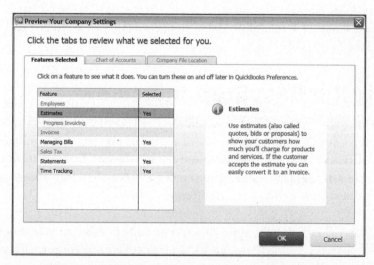

Figure 1.6: *Click the tabs to review your company settings.*

10. Click **Create Company File**.

11. On the QuickBooks Setup window (see Figure 1.7), click **Start Working**.

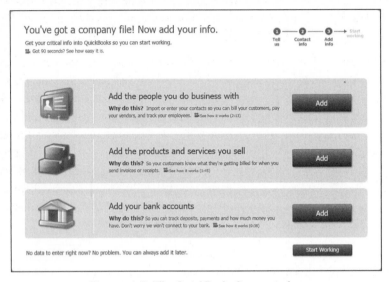

Figure 1.7: *The QuickBooks Setup window.*

You can use the QuickBooks Setup page (Figure 1.7) to start entering customers, vendors, products, services, and bank accounts. QuickBooks Setup provides a way for you to import your contacts, add bank accounts in a spreadsheet-like format, and add products and services. Later chapters cover instructions for completing those tasks, so I'm not going to cover the steps here. To add customers, see Chapter 6; to add vendors, see Chapter 7; to add products and services, see Chapter 9; and to add bank accounts, see Chapter 8.

Starting the EasyStep Interview

If you did not use Express Start, you can use the EasyStep Interview to set up your company file. Before you begin, you need to decide on the start date to use for your QuickBooks file, and you'll need all those pieces of paper from your past, piled in one of those color-coded plastic bins from the office store or strewn about in piles in your office. The next two sections explain in more detail.

Deciding on the Start Date

Before you can start using QuickBooks for keeping your financial records, you need to choose a date to use as the starting point for entering your business transactions into QuickBooks. Whichever date you choose, you'll need to enter all historical transactions from the start date to today.

If you're lucky, you've just started your business today and you can choose today as your start date, without having to enter historical transactions. But if you've been in business already, you have a couple choices: you can start your business records in QuickBooks based on the start of the current fiscal year or you can choose any other date you like. Beginning with the current fiscal year enables you to see and report on transactions for the entire year. Say that your fiscal year starts in January, and it's currently June. You would set your start date to January 1 and enter all your historical transactions from January 1 to the present day. Choose any date, like the first of the month or quarter—or even today, if keeping records of historical transactions isn't important to you.

Gathering What You'll Need

You're going to need some basic information about your company, including some easy stuff like your name, address, EIN number, and sales tax information. You'll also need your bank account information and your account balances, to bring your company up-to-date with your start date. (Chapter 11 explains how to enter the opening balances.)

Here's what you'll need to do:

- Reconcile all your bank accounts. You need the reconciled balance, not the balance currently shown in your check register.

- Make a list of all deposits and withdrawals that haven't cleared since you reconciled the account.

- Total all the unpaid invoices you haven't collected from your customers as of your QuickBooks start date. These invoices must be dated *before* your start date. (In Chapter 11, you'll enter these unpaid invoices to get your accounts receivable balance.)

- Gather any unpaid bills you owe to vendors. (In Chapter 11, you'll enter these unpaid bills to determine your accounts payable balance.)

- Find the balances for all your assets, including fixed assets (the current value and the depreciation).

- Find the balances for all your liabilities, including mortgages and loans.

- List the names, cost, and count of items you hold in inventory (if you track inventory).

- If you do payroll, you'll need names of your employees and all their information, including deductions and salary.

- Be sure to have last year's tax return handy, too.

You don't need all this information right away, but as long as you're getting organized, you can start to prepare. You'll need these before you actually start using your company file on a day-to-day basis.

Now that you've gathered the information you need and are on your third espresso, you can begin to set up your company file. The EasyStep Interview makes it fairly painless.

To start the EasyStep Interview, follow these steps:

1. On the Welcome page QuickBooks displays when you first start it, click the **Create a New Company File** icon. If you don't see the Welcome page, you may see the No Company Open page. On that page, click **Create a New Company**. You can also go to the File menu and click **New Company**.

2. Click **Advanced Setup** (see Figure 1.8).

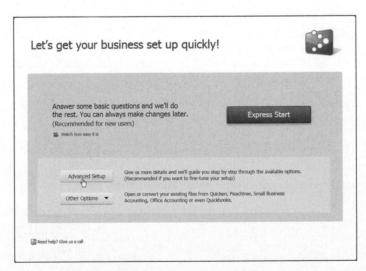

Figure 1.8: *Starting the EasyStep Interview.*

You can step away from the interview at any time: just click the **Leave** button at the bottom left of the interview page. If you haven't saved the company file yet and you click Leave, you will lose what you've entered so far. If you've saved the company file, clicking Leave closes it and takes you to the No Company Open page. To return to the EasyStep Interview at a later time, select the company in the No Company Open page and click **Open**. The interview picks up where you left off.

Entering Your Company Information

For the first page of the interview (see Figure 1.9), you need to supply your company name and address, phone, fax, e-mail address, and website address.

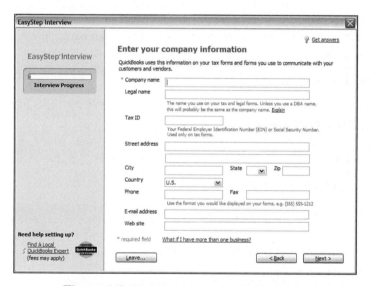

Figure 1.9: *Entering your company information.*

Even though only the company name is required, it's a good idea to provide as much information as possible. QuickBooks uses this information to automatically fill out some of the fields on your forms, such as invoices and tax forms.

Follow these steps to fill out the company information page:

1. Click in the **Company Name** field and type your company name.

2. If you have a legal name (the name associated with your Federal Employer Identification Number [EIN]), type the legal name. If you are a sole proprietor and you use your Social Security number instead of the EIN, your legal name is your name, not the name of your company.

3. In the Tax ID field, type either your EIN number or your Social Security number, if you don't have an EIN. (If you have employees, you must enter the EIN number.)

4. Fill in the remaining fields for your address, phone, fax, e-mail, and website. Enter the information as you want it to appear on your forms. QuickBooks uses this information to prefill fields on forms, which means you don't have to keep typing it in.

5. Click **Next** to continue.

QUICKTIP

If you're a sole proprietor, it's a good idea to apply for a Federal Employer Identification Number (EIN) even if you don't have employees. Using your EIN instead of your Social Security number helps keep your business finances and personal finances separate. When you get the EIN, you can update your company information by choosing **Company Information** from the **Company** menu.

Choosing Your Industry

Next, you need to indicate the type of business you're in. Figure 1.10 shows the Select your Industry page.

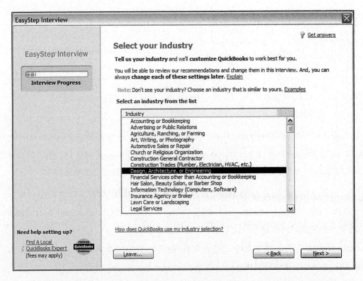

Figure 1.10: *Choose the best match for your type of business.*

On this page, choose the industry that matches or comes close to the type of business you have. QuickBooks uses this information to choose the types of accounts this type of business typically uses, as well as to recommend certain features of QuickBooks that this type of business uses.

Not all industry types are listed, so if you don't see yours, try to choose one that is similar. For example, if you're a freelance personal chef, choose Special Food Services and Catering. Or you can scroll to the bottom of the list and choose "General Product-based Business" or "General Service-based Business."

Choosing Your Company Organization Type

Next, you select the legal entity (sole proprietor, LLC, and so on) for your business. Figure 1.11 shows the legal entity choices. QuickBooks uses this information to choose the relevant tax form so that it can attach the tax lines to associated accounts.

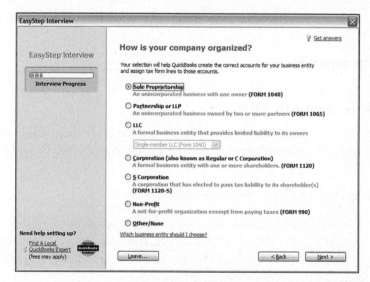

Figure 1.11: *Choose the legal entity for your business.*

If you're the only owner of the business and you plan on reporting business income along with your personal taxes, choose Sole Proprietor. If you're in business with a friend or relative and are splitting the business profit, you are likely a Partnership. If you've filed legal business formation papers, you may be an LLC, Corporation, S Corporation, or Non-Profit.

Entering Your Fiscal Year

On the next page, choose the month for the start of your *fiscal year.*

DEFINITION

The **fiscal year** is a 12-month period used for calculating your company's yearly financial reports. People usually choose January as the start of the fiscal year, to match the income tax year.

Setting Up the Company File Administrator

Setting up a company file administrator is optional but recommended. Whenever someone opens your company file, QuickBooks asks for the password. This is important if you plan to store customer credit card numbers. Also, certain actions (like setting QuickBooks Preferences) can be performed by only an administrator). If you don't set up an administrator, anyone using your company file can go in and change preferences.

Enter the password and click **Next**.

Saving the Company File

QuickBooks asks you to choose a location to save your company file to. Click **Next** and either choose the location or accept the location suggested. Click **Save**.

Customizing Your Company File

In the next few screens, QuickBooks asks you questions about how your business operates, such as whether you charge sales tax. In asking these questions, QuickBooks is setting preferences that determine which features you'll need. You can change the preferences at any time; this is just to get you started.

Click **Next** to start answering the questions; these are fairly simple questions, so I won't go into detail here. QuickBooks provides pretty good explanations as you proceed through the questions and offers recommendations based on your business type.

Before you answer the Start Date question, refer back to the tips about your start date at the beginning of this chapter. You can also consult your accountant about which date to use.

Setting Up Income and Expense Accounts

When you reach the Review Income and Expense Accounts screen (see Figure 1.12), you'll want to go through the list to see which accounts QuickBooks recommends for your business (those accounts have a check mark next to them).

Use the scrollbar to review all the accounts listed. If you find one that you want to use that doesn't have a check mark, click in the check mark column. Likewise, if you find one that you don't want to use, click the check mark to remove it. You can always add accounts later, if you change your mind.

Figure 1.12: *Review the income and expense accounts QuickBooks recommends.*

QUICKTIP

Scroll down the list of accounts until you reach the bottom. Notice the account called "Ask my accountant." Keep that account to use when you're not sure about which account to use; it will be easier than trying to fix a mistake later.

Click **Next**, and whoopee! You're done with the initial company file setup.

On the final screen, click **Go to Setup**.

You can use the QuickBooks Setup page (see Figure 1.13) to start entering customers, vendors, products, services, and bank accounts. QuickBooks Setup provides a way for you to import your contacts, add bank accounts in a spreadsheet-like format, and add products and services. Later chapters cover instructions for completing those tasks, so I'm not going to cover the steps here. To add customers, see Chapter 6; to add vendors, see Chapter 7; to add products and services, see Chapter 9; and to add bank accounts, see Chapter 8.

> **NUMBERS HAPPEN**
>
> If you use QuickBooks Setup for adding bank accounts, it's better *not* to enter the opening balances. We'll be doing that in a more accurate way in Chapter 11.

Figure 1.13: *QuickBooks Setup offers a fast way to get started.*

What's Next

You need to take a few steps before you can start using QuickBooks for real. You need to enter historical transactions, enter account balances, add customers and vendors, and add inventory (if you track inventory).

The chapters that follow show you how to do this.

The Least You Need to Know

- Use Express Start to let QuickBooks build your company file and set up the features you'll need based on a few questions you answer. QuickBooks uses today as your company file start date.

- Use the EasyStep Interview to fine-tune your company settings and provide more details about your business. This method takes a little longer and is good to use if you want to customize the settings and enter historical transactions.

- Even though QuickBooks sets up features and preferences based on your answers in the Express Start and EasyStep Interview, you can always change them later.

- Use the QuickBooks Setup page to import your contacts, add bank accounts in a spreadsheet format, and add products and services.

- If you need to convert your data from another software package, check Appendix B for instructions on how to use QuickBooks help. Use the Search tool to search for "convert."

Navigating QuickBooks Pro

In This Chapter

- Starting QuickBooks
- Opening your company file
- Using the Home page
- Using QuickBooks Centers
- Using the QuickBooks Calendar
- Closing QuickBooks

QuickBooks is designed to make it as easy as possible to navigate the program. The Home page displays icons that take you to the different features to perform your business tasks, and it shows you the flow of those tasks with workflow arrows. But QuickBooks is also very flexible; you don't need to perform the tasks in any particular order. QuickBooks Centers organize related business segments, such as your customers and vendors. The QuickBooks Calendar gives you a visual view of to-do items, transactions, and other tasks.

Opening QuickBooks

When you installed QuickBooks, QuickBooks asked if you wanted an icon on your desktop. Assuming that you did, you can double-click that icon to open QuickBooks. Alternatively, you can click the Start menu, point to **All Programs**, point to **QuickBooks**, then click **QuickBooks Pro 2012**. QuickBooks opens the same company file you were using when you left QuickBooks. If you set up an Admin password during the EasyStep Interview, you need to enter the password before opening the file.

About the Home Page

The QuickBooks Home page gives you a visual overview of your business (see Figure 2.1). It's divided into logical sections: vendors, customers, employees, company, and banking. Icons that represent tasks (such as entering bills and paying bills) appear in the appropriate sections, and the workflow arrows show the progression of related tasks. The icons you can see vary depending on some of your answers to the questions when you set up your company file (see Chapter 1). For example, if you said you don't want to use estimates, you won't see the Estimates icon. Clicking most of the icons on the Home page takes you directly to the window for that task.

Other icons appear on your Home page as you turn on a feature in QuickBooks Preferences. For example, if you turn on inventory tracking, inventory-related tasks show up in the Vendors section. As your business changes over time, you can customize the Home page so that the tasks and workflows match your current business needs.

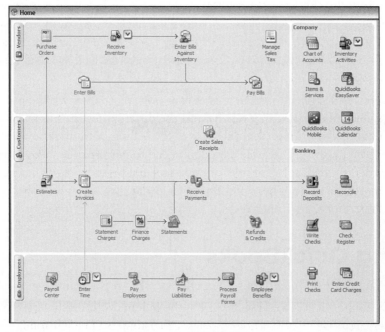

Figure 2.1: *The Home page.*

Navigating with Menus and Icons

QuickBooks makes it easy for you to find your way around using menus and icons. Figure 2.2 shows you the menu bar and the navigation bar.

Figure 2.2: *The menu and navigation bars.*

Use the menu bar to access all of QuickBooks' features and tasks.

Use the navigation bar to quickly go to one of the QuickBooks Centers or the Home page.

You can also customize the navigation bar to provide one-click access to the features you use the most.

As you work in QuickBooks, you may find you have a bunch of windows open at the same time but can't see them all. To view a list of all the windows you have open, go to the **View** menu and click **Open Window List**. In the list, click a window to jump back and forth between windows you're using, or click the **Close** button to close any of the windows you're not using.

About QuickBooks Centers

QuickBooks organizes your company information into centers. Those centers store information and transactions, and provide a central place to perform related tasks and generate reports. Each center is summarized in the following sections.

You open a center by clicking its icon in the navigation bar, clicking the buttons on the left edge of the Home page, or selecting it from the menus.

Customer Center

The Customer Center (see Figure 2.3) is the hub for your customers; here you can find anything you want to know about your customers. The Customer Center is basically a list of your customers and jobs, and it includes transactions such as invoices, received payments, sales receipts, and statement charges. Chapter 6 covers using the Customer Center in more detail.

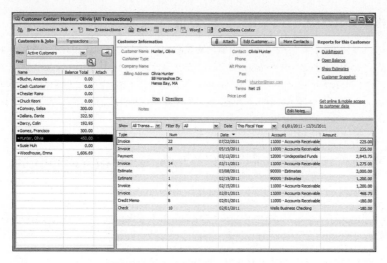

Figure 2.3: *The Customer Center.*

Lead Center

The Lead Center (see Figure 2.4), like the Customer Center, is the hub for your prospective customers. You can keep track of your interactions with prospective customers, such as phone calls, follow-up tasks, e-mails, and meetings. You can take notes to document your interactions and associate the notes with the customer. Chapter 6 covers using the Lead Center in more detail.

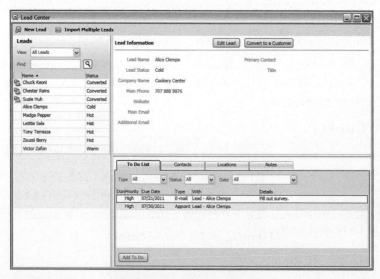

Figure 2.4: *The Lead Center.*

Collections Center

Inside the Customer Center is the Collections Center (see Figure 2.5). The Collections Center provides a central area to help you collect money that customers owe you. It lists customers with overdue or almost-due invoices and gives you a quick way to send e-mail reminders. Chapter 15 covers the Collections Center in more detail.

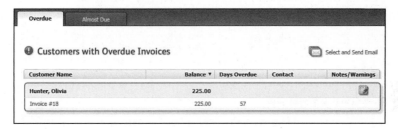

Figure 2.5: *The Collections Center.*

Vendor Center

Like the Customer Center, the Vendor Center (see Figure 2.6) is the hub for your vendors. Here you can find anything you want to know about your vendors, including transactions. Chapter 7 covers the Vendor Center in more detail.

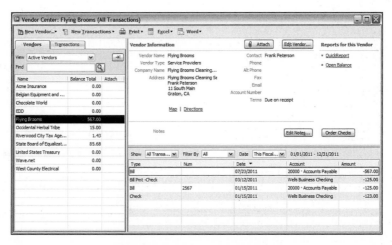

Figure 2.6: *The Vendor Center.*

Employee Center

The Employee Center stores information about your employees and their transactions (see Figure 2.7). If you don't have employees or you don't track time, you won't see the Employee Center. Chapter 26 covers the Employee Center and payroll in more detail.

If you subscribe to one of the payroll services, the Employee Center also includes the Payroll Center, where you can perform all your payroll tasks.

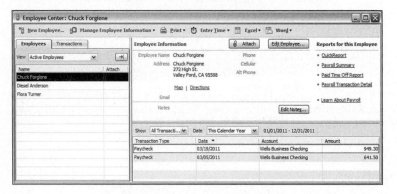

Figure 2.7: *The Employee Center.*

Report Center

The Report Center provides quick access to all QuickBooks reports (see Figure 2.8). The Report Center has three views: list view, grid view, and carousel view. Chapter 29 covers the Report Center in more detail.

Other Centers

QuickBooks provides two other centers: the Doc Center (which appears if you signed up and paid for the QuickBooks Attached Documents service) and the App Center. In the App Center, you can find web-based applications from Intuit Workplace Apps. Additional fees may apply.

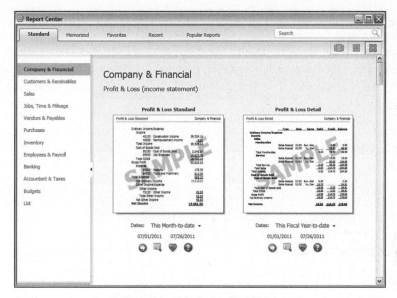

Figure 2.8: *The Report Center.*

Using the QuickBooks Calendar

The QuickBooks Calendar can save you time by giving you a quick visual view of upcoming transactions, overdue transactions, and upcoming to-do items and other tasks.

To open the calendar, click the **Calendar** icon in the Tool Bar (to the right of the Home icon), or in the Company section of the Home page, click **QuickBooks Calendar.** Figure 2.9 shows the weekly view of the Calendar.

You can change the calendar view by clicking the view icons next to the Today button: Daily, Weekly, or Monthly. The calendar shows the dates on which purchase orders, invoices, or bills were created or are due. It also shows all your to-do items by the date they are due. To narrow what the Calendar shows (for example, show only To-Do items or show only bills), choose a filter from the Show menu at the top of the Calendar.

You can quickly navigate to a transaction or to-do item by expanding the list below the calendar and double-clicking the transaction. Figure 2.10 shows an expanded list.

Figure 2.9: *The QuickBooks Calendar Weekly View.*

Figure 2.10: *Double-click a transaction or to-do item to quickly navigate to the original form.*

The collapsible side panel to the right of the Calendar helps you stay on top of transactions and to-dos: it lists all the things that are overdue (it's like having your very own taskmaster). Figure 2.11 shows an expanded list.

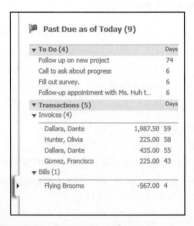

Figure 2.11: *Stay on top of your overdue items.*

Viewing a List of Your To-Do Items

In addition to viewing your to-do items in the Calendar view, you can see a list of all your to-do items related to customers, vendors, and leads all in one place.

To open the To-Do List, click the **Company** menu and click **To Do List**. Figure 2.12 shows the To Do List.

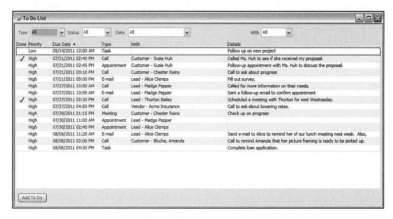

Figure 2.12: *View all your to-do items in one place.*

Use the menus at the top of the To Do List to filter what the list shows. Double-click a to-do item to make changes to it. To add a to-do item that is not associated with a customer, vendor, or lead, click the **Add To Do** button.

Closing QuickBooks

QuickBooks saves your work as you go, so you don't need to save your company file before you leave the program. To quit QuickBooks, go to the **File** menu and click **Exit**.

The Least You Need to Know

- Use the Home page to navigate to your common business tasks.
- The menus give you access to all of QuickBooks' features and tasks.

- Customize the navigation bar to provide one-click access to the features you use the most.
- Use the centers to find all the information relevant to your customers, vendors, and employees.
- Use the QuickBooks Calendar to see at a glance all the to-do items and transactions that are due on a particular date and keep on top of past-due items.

Basic Concepts

In This Chapter

- Using QuickBooks lists
- Understanding preferences and how they work
- Using QuickBooks forms

QuickBooks is easy to learn in one sense because, although it has many features, they tend to work the same way throughout the program. Lists store information you use regularly. Preferences turn features on or off, depending on how you run your business. Forms are similar, in that they have fields with menus populated with the items you put into your lists.

About QuickBooks Lists

Lists store information you use every day in your business, such as customers, vendors, products, services, and more. After you set up a list, you use the information to fill out forms, which helps ensure accuracy, saves you a lot of time, and prevents typing mistakes.

Navigating to Lists

Depending on the type of list, you can get to a list in two ways.

You'll find the Customer:Job List, Vendor List, and Employee List in the QuickBooks Centers (Customer, Vendor, and Employee). QuickBooks Center buttons are located at the top of the window in the navigation bar (see Figure 2.2). Click a

Center button to display the list. Chapters 6, 7, 24, and 28 cover working with the centers in detail.

Most other lists, such as the Item List, are shown in the Lists menu. To open a list, go to the **Lists** menu and click the list you want to open. There's also a To Do List that shows upcoming tasks; you can find this list under the Company menu.

How Lists Work

QuickBooks uses the information in your lists to prefill your forms, simplify data entry, track related financial transactions, and prepare useful reports. The more detail you provide, the better QuickBooks is able to help.

Common Tasks

Tasks associated with lists include adding to a list, editing a list, deleting from a list, and merging items in lists. This section describes tasks related to working with all lists, to help you avoid repeating this information for each list.

To add to a list, follow these steps:

1. Go to the **Lists** menu and click the list you want to open. (For this example, I opened the Price Level list.)

2. Click the button on the lower left of the list to open the menu (see Figure 3.1).

3. Click **New**. (You can also press **Ctrl+N** from the list without opening the menu.)

4. Fill in the fields and click **OK** to save the new list item.

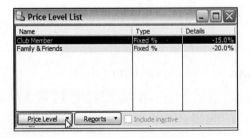

Figure 3.1: *Click New from the Price Level menu to add to the list.*

To edit an item in the list, follow these steps:

1. Go to the **Lists** menu and click the list you want to open.

2. Click the item in the list you want to edit.

3. Click the button to the lower left of the list (see Figure 3.2).

4. Click **Edit**. (You can also double-click the item to edit it or select the item and press **Ctrl+E** from the list without opening the menu.)

5. Change the information.

6. Click **OK** to save the changes.

Figure 3.2: *Click Edit to change an item on the list.*

To sort a list by the column headings, follow these steps:

1. Go to the **Lists** menu and click the list you want to open.

2. Click the column heading that you want to sort by. Click it again to reverse the sort.

To delete an item from a list, follow these steps:

1. Go to the **Lists** menu and click the list you want to open.

2. Click the item in the list you want to delete.

3. Click the button to the lower left of the list.

4. Click **Delete**. (You can also press **Ctrl+D** from the list without opening the menu.)

5. Confirm that you want to delete it.

If what you want to delete has a balance or has been used in a transaction, you can't delete it. Instead, you can make it inactive. Making something inactive doesn't delete it; it just hides it, to make your lists easier to manage.

To make an item in a list inactive, follow these steps:

1. Go to the **Lists** menu and click the list you want to open.

2. Click the item in the list that you want to make inactive.

3. Click the button to the lower left of the list.

4. Click **Make Inactive.**

To see inactive items in a list, follow these steps:

1. Click the button to the lower left of the list.

2. Click **Show Inactive** (or click the **Include Inactive** check box). See Figure 3.3.

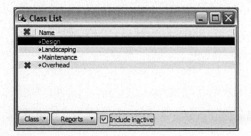

Figure 3.3: *Inactive items appear with an X next to the name.*

Many of the lists have an Activities menu that you can use to quickly perform a task, such as create an invoice or purchase order.

What appears on the Activities menu varies depending on the list. Figure 3.4 shows the Activities menu for the Item List.

Some lists have a Reports menu, to let you quickly generate reports related to the list.

For some lists, such as the Customer:Job list and Vendor list, you can change what the list displays by changing the view of the list (see Figure 3.5), filtering the list of transactions (see Figure 3.6), or changing the date range (see Figure 3.7).

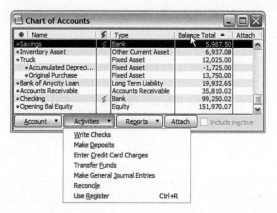

Figure 3.4: *The Activities menu for the Chart of Accounts list.*

To change what you see in the Customer:Job or Vendor list, click the **Customer & Jobs** tab or **Vendors** tab and then click the **View** menu.

Figure 3.5: *Change what the list shows by choosing one of the preset views or choosing Custom Filter to create your own view.*

To filter a list of transactions, click the **Filter By** menu arrow and choose what you want to see.

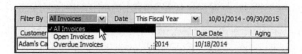

Figure 3.6: *Change what the list shows by filtering it.*

To change the date range, click the **Date** menu arrow and choose a new date range.

Figure 3.7: *Change what the list shows by choosing a new date range.*

About QuickBooks Preferences

Another key concept to understand about QuickBooks is how to set preferences so you can customize the program to fit the way you like to work. A lot of the major preferences were set for you when you set up your company file, so you might not even need to change them.

Examples of preferences you can set include the default date to use for new transactions, the color scheme, and which icons to show on the Home page, among many others. Preferences are covered in the appropriate chapters throughout this book.

To view the preference options, follow these steps:

1. Go to the **Edit** menu and click **Preferences**.

2. Click the **My Preferences** tab to set preferences that affect only you.

3. Click the **Company Preferences** tab to set preferences that affect all users of your company file (see Figure 3.8 for an example). (Only an Admin user can change Company Preferences.)

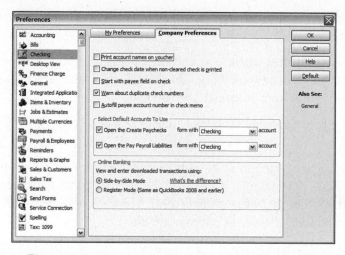

Figure 3.8: *The Company Preference settings for Checking.*

About QuickBooks Forms

QuickBooks uses forms such as invoices, estimates, credit memos, purchase orders, and sales receipts to track your purchase and sale transactions as you run your business. Figure 3.9 shows an example of a form.

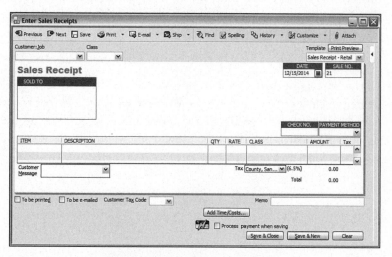

Figure 3.9: *Blank sales receipt form.*

Although the forms have different fields, they all work the same way, as described here:

- Menus on forms enable you to choose items from the lists you've set up. After you choose something, QuickBooks fills out much of the form with the information from your lists.

- The first menu choice on these menus is **<Add New>**, which allows you to add an item, such as a new customer, to the associated list as you work.

- If you start typing in a field, QuickBooks gives you a list of customized options—for example, if you type the letter J, QuickBooks shows you the entries from the list that start with J. You can continue to type to narrow the list and then choose the appropriate entry.

- Pressing **Tab** moves you from one field to the next. Pressing **Shift+Tab** moves you to the previous field.

- QuickBooks automatically fills in the date based on preferences you've set. When the cursor is in a date field, pressing **+ (Plus key)** increases the date and pressing **– (Minus key)** decreases the date. To change the date back to today's date, press **T**. You can also click the little calendar icon to choose a date from the calendar.

- At the top of forms are two buttons: **Previous** takes you to the previous saved form in sequence; **Next** takes you to the next saved form in sequence or to a new, blank form.

- Other buttons appear at the top of various forms to give you easy access to certain tasks, such as **Save, Print, Send, Find, Spelling,** and **History**.

- At the bottom of forms are two buttons: **Save & Close** saves the current form and closes the window. **Save & New** saves the current form and opens a new, blank form. If a button is highlighted in blue, it is tied to the Enter key on your keyboard. So if **Save & New** is highlighted in blue, pressing **Enter** saves the form and opens a new one.

The Least You Need to Know

- Use the information stored in your lists so that QuickBooks can prepopulate forms, to ensure accuracy, save time, and prevent typing mistakes.

- You can delete items from a list if there are no associated transactions. If what you want to delete has a balance or has been used in a transaction, you can't delete it, but you can make it inactive.

- Use Preferences to customize QuickBooks to match the needs of your business and the way you like to work.

- Use forms—invoices, estimates, credit memos, purchase orders, and sales receipts—to track the purchases and sales your business makes.

Accounting Principles for Poets

In This Chapter

- Using cash basis or accrual basis
- Understanding accounts payable and accounts receivable
- Understanding double-entry bookkeeping
- Learning about the basic account types
- Reading financial statements to track profitability

The beauty of QuickBooks is that you don't need to know much about accounting. QuickBooks takes care of all the accounting transactions behind the scenes. This is good for me because I like to think of myself as "too creative" or "too sensitive" for accounting. Sure some accountants can get pretty creative, but I don't have the time or a burning desire to really understand accounting—and maybe you don't, either. But you do need to know a few principles if you want to keep your business going.

Accounting? Why Bother?

One word: IRS. You also need to make sure you track all your expenses to get the maximum deductions.

Cash or Accrual?

One of the first decisions you need to make about your business is which accounting method to use: cash accounting or accrual accounting. The accounting method determines how and when you report income and expenses for tax purposes. Certain types of businesses are required to use accrual-basis reporting when preparing tax documents, namely those that carry inventory. For help in determining which accounting method to use, go to the IRS website at www.irs.gov/publications/p538/ar02.html#d0e1026. And to keep the IRS happy, you must use the same method year after year unless you get IRS approval to change it.

Using the cash basis method, you report income when you receive a payment instead of when you bill a customer. You report expenses when you pay bills.

Using the accrual basis method, you report income as soon as you bill a customer, instead of when you actually receive the money. You report expenses when you receive a bill, not when you pay the bill.

About Accounts Receivable and Accounts Payable

Accounting uses accounts to track the money coming into and the money going out of a business, and QuickBooks creates two essential accounts for you: Accounts Payable and Accounts Receivable. Accounts Payable (also known by the abbreviation A/P) is a liability account that manages outstanding bills; the account balance increases when bills are recorded and decreases when bills are paid. Accounts Receivable (abbreviated as A/R) is an asset account that manages incoming payments; the balance increases when payments are received and decreases when refunds or credit memos are recorded. Whenever you record a transaction, QuickBooks takes care of accounting for the transaction in the appropriate account behind the scenes.

Understanding Double-Entry Bookkeeping

QuickBooks is a double-entry accounting system. This means that every transaction has two sides: where the money comes from and where the money goes. All transaction entries must be in balance. The two sides of a transaction are called debit and credit—and *every* transaction has a debit and a credit. This is where my poet's brain gets easily confused. It's sometimes mistakenly believed that a debit is a reduction of funds and a credit is an increase. But that's not always the case. Whether a debit increases or decreases an amount or a credit increases or decreases an amount depends on the type of account the transaction goes through. If you really care, the following table explains how a debit or credit affects each account type. Because you're smart and you're using QuickBooks, though, you don't really need to know. QuickBooks takes care of all the debits and credits for you, to keep your accountant happy.

Debits and Credits.

Account Type	Debit	Credit
Asset	Increases	Decreases
Liability	Decreases	Increases
Equity	Decreases	Increases
Income	Decreases	Increases
Expense	Increases	Decreases

Let's say you sell a shovel to a customer. When you record the invoice in QuickBooks, the sale is recorded as a Credit (increase) to an income account and the same amount is recorded as a Debit (increase) to the asset account called Accounts Receivable. When you receive payment from the customer, the money moves from the Accounts Receivable account (an asset account) with a credit (decrease) and into your checking account (another asset account) using a debit (increase). QuickBooks *posts* the transactions on both sides: the debit and the credit.

DEFINITION

In accounting, the word **post** is a verb that basically means to record the transaction to an account.

Say you go to the local big-box office store and purchase a new printer. You write a check for the cost of the printer. That transaction reduces (credits) your checking account but increases (debits) your Office Equipment expense account.

The Basic Five

QuickBooks uses accounts to track the money going into and out of your business. These accounts are collectively called a *chart of accounts*.

Many accounts can fall into the following five basic types of accounts:

- Asset
- Liability
- Equity
- Income
- Expense

Asset, liability, and equity accounts are categorized as balance sheet accounts. Income and expense accounts are categorized as profit and loss accounts. Stay with me here—try not to glaze over.

Balance Sheet Accounts

A balance sheet in accounting is the primary financial statement that shows the value of your business at any point in time. Bank accounts, equipment, buildings, and money owed to you are all considered assets. Loans, credit card debt, and money you owe are considered liabilities. Retained earnings, owner's equity, and capital investments are considered equity accounts. Each balance sheet account has its own *register* that QuickBooks maintains. You can see account balances by looking at your chart of accounts (see Figure 4.1).

DEFINITION

In QuickBooks, a **register** stores a list of transactions made in the account, much like a paper checkbook register.

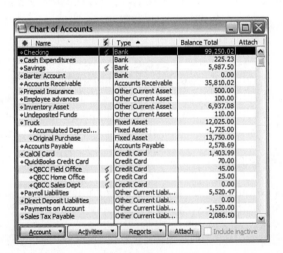

Figure 4.1: *The balances of the chart of accounts appear in the Balance Total column.*

Profit and Loss Accounts

Income and expense accounts are considered profit and loss accounts. Income accounts (sometimes called revenue accounts) track money the business has earned, such as income from sales or interest. Expense accounts track money used to run the business. QuickBooks sets up several expense accounts for you, based on the type of business. You can track expenses like office supplies, advertising, and insurance. Income and expense accounts do not have their own register like the balance sheet accounts do, but you can view a report for each income and expense account to see a list of transactions.

If you track inventory, you'll need to know about a certain type of expense account called Cost of Goods Sold (COGS, for short). If you keep goods and materials in inventory, such as items you purchase from others and then resell or materials you use when selling your services, those goods and materials have value. QuickBooks tracks their value in an Inventory Asset account, but as you sell these items, QuickBooks keeps track of the value of the item that you sold in the COGS account. The inventory chapter (Chapter 18) talks about this more.

At the end of the fiscal year of a business, the balances in income and expense accounts are moved to a retained earnings equity account. At the beginning of the next fiscal year, the balances in your income and expense accounts are set to zero.

Tracking Your Business Profitability

QuickBooks uses reports to help you determine whether your business is profitable. Two of these, the balance sheet and profit and loss statement, are the primary financial statements that give you the overall financial picture of your business.

The Balance Sheet

In a balance sheet, QuickBooks uses the information in asset accounts to determine the monetary value of what your business owns and uses the information in liability accounts to determine what your business owes. Equity accounts show the business owner's stake in the business. The equity is all of your assets minus your liabilities; equity is sometimes called *net worth*. The balance sheet gives you a detailed picture of your assets, liabilities, and equity at any point in time (see Figure 4.2).

Summary Balance Sheet

Modify Report... | Memorize... | Print... | E-mail | Export... | Hide Header | Collapse | Refresh

Dates: This Fiscal Year-to-date | As of 12/15/2014 | Columns: Total only | Sort By: Default

6:46 PM
12/15/14
Accrual Basis

Larry's Landscaping & Garden Supply
Summary Balance Sheet
As of December 15, 2014

	Dec 15, 14
ASSETS	
Current Assets	
Checking/Savings	105,462.75
Accounts Receivable	35,810.02
Other Current Assets	7,647.08
Total Current Assets	148,919.85
Fixed Assets	12,025.00
TOTAL ASSETS	160,944.85
LIABILITIES & EQUITY	
Liabilities	
Current Liabilities	
Accounts Payable	1,879.57
Credit Cards	1,473.99
Other Current Liabilities	6,086.97
Total Current Liabilities	9,440.53
Long Term Liabilities	29,857.03
Total Liabilities	39,297.56
Equity	121,647.29
TOTAL LIABILITIES & EQUITY	160,944.85

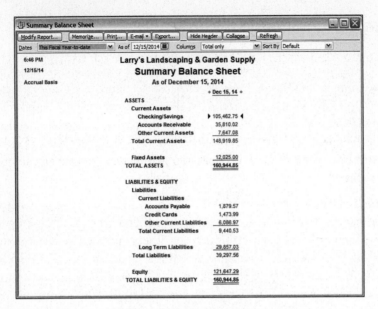

Figure 4.2: *The balance sheet.*

The Profit and Loss Statement

The profit and loss statement (also sometimes referred to as an *income statement;* see Figure 4.3) shows you detailed revenues and expenses over a period of time. You can tell whether you have a profit or loss for the time period you specify.

Modify Report... | Memorize... | Print... | E-mail | Export... | Hide Header | Collapse | Refresh

Dates: This Fiscal Year-to-date | From 10/01/2014 | To 12/15/2014 | Columns: Total only | Sort By: Default

6:50 PM
12/15/14
Accrual Basis

Larry's Landscaping & Garden Supply
Profit & Loss Prev Year Comparison
October 1 through December 15, 2014

	Oct 1 - Dec 15, 13		$ Change		% Change	
Tools and Misc. Equipment		0.00		735.00		100.0%
Uncategorized Expenses		0.00		0.00		0.0%
Utilities						
Gas and Electric	414.09		10.33		2.5%	
Telephone	170.76		-20.80		-12.2%	
Water	71.55		9.62		13.5%	
Total Utilities		656.40		-0.85		-0.1%
Total Expense		1,222.65		46,313.14		3,787.9%
Net Ordinary Income		1,884.43		12,057.92		639.9%
Other Income/Expense						
Other Income						
Misc Income		0.00		762.50		100.0%
Interest Income		0.00		91.11		100.0%
Total Other Income		0.00		853.61		100.0%
Net Other Income		0.00		853.61		100.0%
Net Income		1,884.43		12,911.53		685.2%

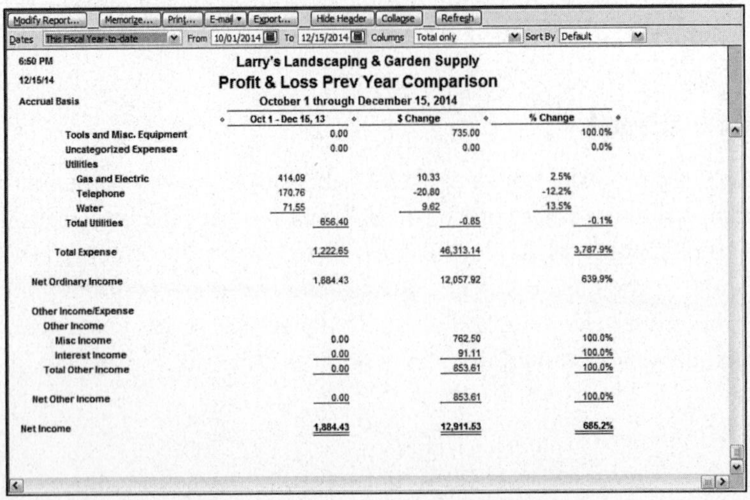

Figure 4.3: *The profit and loss statement.*

The Least You Need to Know

- Talk to your accountant about whether to use cash basis or accrual basis for your business.
- Don't sweat the double-entry credit/debit thing; QuickBooks takes care of that for you.
- A balance sheet gives you an overall picture of the health of your business.
- A profit and loss statement tells you whether you're making money or losing money.

Printing and E-mailing in QuickBooks

In This Chapter

- Setting up your printer
- Printing checks and forms
- Sending e-mail
- Customizing e-mail

We're not living in a paperless world yet, so at times you'll need to print checks, invoices, and other documents generated by QuickBooks. This chapter explains how to set up your printer to print documents and how to e-mail documents.

Setting Up for Printing in QuickBooks

These instructions assume that you've already set up and connected your printer according to the manufacturer's directions. The steps here tell you how to get set up to print specific QuickBooks documents, such as checks and forms.

Setting Up Check Printing

During the course of your business, you'll want to print checks if you're paying a bill by mail. When you print checks, you must use checks that are designed for QuickBooks.

Checks come in three styles: voucher, standard, and wallet (see descriptions in step 4 later in this section). Note that you can also use all check styles for handwritten checks.

To set up your printer to print QuickBooks-compatible checks, follow these steps:

1. Go to the File menu and click **Printer Setup**.

2. Click **Check/PayCheck** from the menu, as shown in Figure 5.1.

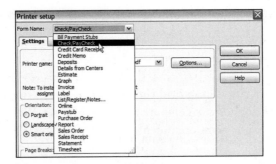

Figure 5.1: *Setting up your printer for check printing.*

3. In the Printer Setup for Checks window, choose the printer name and printer type you are using.

4. Click the appropriate button for the style of check you're using (see Figure 5.2).

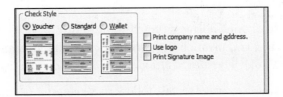

Figure 5.2: *Choosing the check style.*

Voucher: Checks that are business sized (that fit in a #10 envelope) but print one to a page and include two detachable stubs to use for payroll and accounts payable. QuickBooks supports voucher checks with the check portion at the top only.

Standard: Checks that are business sized (that fit in a #10 envelope), generally printed three checks to a page.

Wallet: Smaller, wallet-sized checks, with a perforated stub on the left edge that you can detach for record-keeping. Prints three checks to a page.

5. If you select Standard or Voucher and they are not preprinted with your name, address, and logo, click the **Print Company Name and Address** check box and the **Use Logo** check box. (For best results, your logo should be square. To add your logo, click **Logo**, click **File** to locate the logo, and then click **OK**.)

6. If you select Wallet, choose the type of wallet check from the **Wallet Check Type** menu that appears: Traditional or Check 21.

7. To print a signature on your Standard or Voucher check (if you have an image of your signature), click the **Print Signature Image** check box, click **File** to locate the image, and then click **OK**.

8. If your check doesn't print just as you'd like it, click the **Align** button to tweak the alignment of the data in the fields.

9. Click **OK** to save the printer setup for checks.

The Printer Setup window has two additional tabs: one for changing fonts and another for printing a partial page of checks using the portrait orientation or printing a single check using your printer's envelope feeder. To learn about those tabs, click the tab name and then click the Help button.

Setting Up Form Printing

You can print forms, such as invoices, estimates, and purchase orders, on Intuit pre-printed forms, on your letterhead stationary, or on blank sheets of paper.

To set up your printer to print forms, follow these steps:

1. Go to the File menu and click **Printer Setup**.

2. Click the form you want to print from the menu, as shown in Figure 5.3.

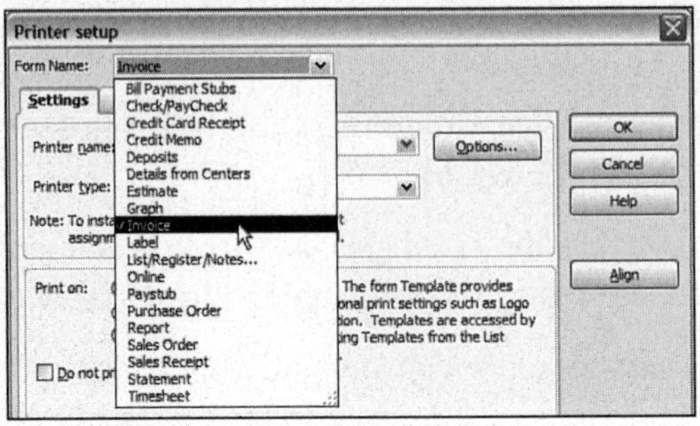

Figure 5.3: *Choose the form to set up.*

3. Choose the printer name and printer type you are using.

4. The options available vary depending on the type of form you are printing. For invoices, purchase orders, estimates, credit memos, and sales receipts, choose one of the following options:

    Intuit Preprinted Forms: Use for forms designed specifically for QuickBooks. The fields on the preprinted forms match the placement and field names of the forms in QuickBooks.

    Blank paper: Use to have QuickBooks print your business name and address at the top of the page, as well as fill in the field names and the information in the fields.

    Letterhead: Prints just like the blank paper setting, but without printing your business name and address. It also leaves room for your letterhead.

5. For Blank Paper and Letterhead, if you want to print lines around the fields on the form, make sure the **Do Not Print Lines Around Each Field** option is not checked. Printing lines around the fields makes the form easier to read.

6. If the check doesn't print just as you'd like it, click the **Align** button to tweak the alignment of the data in the fields.

7. Click **OK** to save the printer setup for the form type you chose in step 2.

The Printer Setup window has two additional tabs for checks: one for changing fonts and another for printing a partial page of checks. Click the tab and click **Help** for more information.

Printing Checks

QuickBooks offers three ways to print checks: printing one at a time as you write each one, printing a single check, or printing several checks in a batch.

Printing Checks as You Write Them

These steps assume that you have already set up your printer for printing checks. You can print checks one at a time or in a batch. Follow these steps to print a single check.

To print a check right after you write it, do this:

1. After writing a check in the Write Checks window, click the **Print** icon at the top of the window.

2. Make sure the printed check number QuickBooks shows you is the correct number to print. For example, if you used one of your checks as a handwritten check, QuickBooks doesn't know that and assumes the next number in sequence. Check the number on the check in the printer and change the check number in the Print Check dialog box to match it, if needed (see Figure 5.4).

Figure 5.4: *The Print Check window.*

3. Click **OK**.

4. In the Print Check window, click **Print**.

5. If the check printed correctly, click **OK** to confirm.

Printing Checks in a Batch

Instead of printing checks one at a time right after you create the check, you can prepare several checks at once and then print them in a batch. In the Write Checks window, fill out the check and click the **To Be Printed** check box. When you click **Save & New**, QuickBooks puts the checks in a printing queue for when you're ready to print.

These steps assume that you have already set up your printer for printing checks.

To print several checks in a batch, follow these steps:

1. After writing and saving all the checks in the Write Checks window, you can do one of the following:

   - In the Write Checks window, click the arrow next to the **Print** icon at the top of the window and choose **Print Batch**. Figure 5.5 shows the Select Checks to Print window.

   - If you want to print the checks later, click **Save & Close** in the **Write Checks** window. Then go to the **File** menu, click **Print Forms**, and click **Checks**. (Or, on the Home page in the Banking section, click the Print Checks icon.)

Figure 5.5: *Choose the checks you want to print.*

2. Make sure the correct bank account to use for these checks appears in the Bank Account field.

3. Make sure the check number shown in the First Check Number field matches the number of the first check in the printer. Change the number to match, if needed.

4. By default, all the checks are selected to be printed. If you don't want to print certain checks yet, click the check. The check mark is cleared for this print run. (The next time you print checks in a batch, that check will still appear in the Select Checks to Print window.)

5. Click **OK**. Then in the Print Checks window, click **Print**.

When you pay vendors, you use the Pay Bills window. Those checks also appear in the Select Checks to Print window. See the section titled "Paying Bills" in Chapter 16.

Reprinting Checks

If after printing you notice that some of the checks didn't print correctly—maybe they got wrinkled, your printer was running low on ink or printed askew, or you smudged your checks with chocolaty fingers—you can reprint those checks.

After printing, QuickBooks asks you whether the checks printed correctly in the dialog box titled "Did Checks Print OK?" Click **OK** if everything printing correctly. If you had problems, click the **Reprint** field for the checks that didn't print correctly, to put a check mark in it (or click **Select All** to reprint all the checks), and click **OK**. Those checks will appear in the Select Checks to Print window the next time you print.

BEHIND THE SCENES

What about the check numbers, you might ask? QuickBooks assumes that the check number is preprinted on the check and can't be used again. When QuickBooks reprints the checks, it starts with the next check number in sequence from the last printed check.

Printing Transaction Forms

QuickBooks uses forms such as invoices, estimates, credit memos, purchase orders, and sales receipts to track your purchase and sale transactions as you run your business. You might need to send paper copies of these transactions to your vendors and customers. (E-mailing forms is covered later in this chapter.)

As with checks, you can print a transaction right after you enter it, or you can print transactions in a batch.

Printing Transaction Forms as You Enter Them

These steps assume that you have already set up your printer for printing forms, as described earlier in this chapter.

As a precaution against theft, note that QuickBooks saves the transaction before printing so that you have a record of the transaction.

To print a transaction after you enter it, follow these steps:

1. After filling in a transaction form and before saving it, click the **Print** icon at the top of the window.

2. In the Print One <<Form>> window (see Figure 5.6), click **Print**.

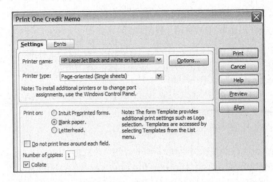

Figure 5.6: *The Print One Credit Memo window.*

3. Check the Print On setting (Intuit Preprinted Forms, Blank Paper, or Letterhead) and change the setting, if needed. (See "Setting Up Your Printer for Forms," earlier in this chapter.)

4. For Blank Paper and Letterhead, if you want to print lines around the fields on the form, make sure the Do Not Print Lines Around Each Field option is unchecked. Printing lines around the fields makes the form easier to read.

5. If the form doesn't print just as you'd like it, click the **Align** button to tweak the alignment of the data in the fields.

6. Click **OK** to save the printer setup for the form type you chose in step 2.

Printing Transaction Forms in a Batch

Instead of printing forms one at a time, you can click Save & New in the transaction window. Later, you can print all the forms in a batch.

These steps assume that you have already set up your printer for printing forms.

To print transaction forms in a batch, follow these steps:

1. Instead of printing each form one at a time as you create them, click to check the **To Be Printed** check box and then click **Save & New**.

2. After entering and saving all the forms, click **Save & Close**.

3. When you're ready to print, go to the **File** menu, click **Print Forms**, and then click the type of form you are printing.

4. In the Select <<Form>> to Print window (see Figure 5.7), by default, all the forms are selected to be printed. If you don't want to print certain forms yet, click the relevant check marks to remove those forms for this print run. (The next time you print forms of this type in a batch, those forms will still appear in the Select <<Form>> to Print window.)

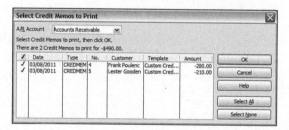

Figure 5.7: *Click the check mark to remove a form from this print run.*

5. Click **OK** and then, in the Print <<Form name>> window, click **Print**.

6. Confirm that the forms printed correctly, and click **OK**. If some did not print correctly, fix the problem with the printer and repeat from step 3.

E-mailing Forms

When you complete an estimate, invoice, credit memo, sales receipt, or purchase order, you can e-mail it to the customer. On the form, click the **To Be E-mailed** check box. When you e-mail a form, QuickBooks creates a PDF and attaches it to an e-mail.

You can send the e-mail using any compatible web e-mail service, such as Outlook, Hotmail, or Gmail, among others.

To e-mail an invoice as you create it, follow these steps:

1. Click the **Envelope** icon (or click **Send**) on the toolbar and click **E-mail Invoice**, as shown in Figure 5.8.

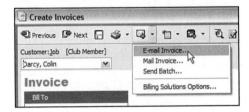

Figure 5.8: *Choices when e-mailing an invoice.*

2. If you don't have the customer's e-mail address on file, QuickBooks asks you to enter it in the **To** field.

3. In the Send Invoice window (see Figure 5.9), make sure **Web Mail** is selected in the Send By setting and enter the e-mail address. The other two options are available only if you pay extra for the add-on or service.

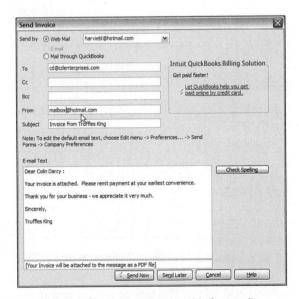

Figure 5.9: *Review the e-mail before sending.*

4. Review the e-mail, make any changes, and click **Send Now**.

QUICKTIP

To change the default text that appears for the e-mail, go to Edit and click **Preferences**. Click **Send Forms** and, on the Company Preferences tab, choose the form from the Change Default For menu, then type the new text. Click **OK**.

To e-mail other forms (estimates, purchase orders, credit memos, and so on), follow the preceding steps, but choose **Send** instead of E-mail invoice from the E-mail icon menu.

To e-mail several forms in a batch, follow these steps:

1. On each form, click the **To Be E-mailed** check box to put a check mark in it. Then save the form as usual.

2. When you're ready to e-mail the forms, go to the File menu and choose **Send Forms**.

3. From the Select Forms to Send window (see Figure 5.10), select the invoices you want to e-mail. (To remove one from the list, click it and click **Remove**.)

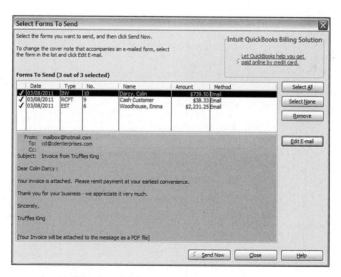

Figure 5.10: *Choose the forms to send.*

4. Select the form and review the text of the e-mail. If you want to change what the text says, click **Edit E-mail**. For example, QuickBooks might have addressed the person by first name and last name, but if that sounds too formal, you can change it. Click **OK** to save the changes.

5. Repeat step 4 as needed for each form.

6. When you are ready to send the forms, click **Send Now.**

The Least You Need to Know

- You can print forms, such as invoices, estimates, and purchase orders, on Intuit preprinted forms, on your letterhead stationery, or on blank sheets of paper.

- You can print checks and forms one at a time or in a batch.

- You can e-mail forms using a compatible e-mail program. QuickBooks creates a PDF of the form and attaches it to the e-mail message.

- You can customize the text of the e-mail in Send Forms preferences.

Setting Up Your Business Lists

Your company file is built around QuickBooks lists—lists of your customers, vendors, accounts, products and services, and so on. The more you set up in your lists before using QuickBooks day-to-day, the easier it will be to use QuickBooks to run your business.

Customers are key to the success of your business, so keeping good customer records is important. In Chapter 6, you begin the process of entering information about your customers and tracking individual customer jobs. You can also track prospective customers using the Lead Center. Similarly, Chapter 7 covers what you need to know about entering your vendor information so you can use QuickBooks to track vendor bills and payments.

Chapter 8 unveils your chart of accounts, which is a list of all your business accounts. QuickBooks stores the financial data from all your transactions in your chart of accounts.

Chapter 9 is all about items, which are a crucial part of your QuickBooks business records. Items represent the products and services you sell, as well as other things that appear on a sales form, such as sales tax, discounts, subtotals, and shipping.

In Chapter 10, you learn about the remaining QuickBooks lists, many of which make working within QuickBooks a little easier. You may find you don't need to use all the lists, but it's nice to know they're available.

Chapter 11 helps you perform the final, major step of setting up your company file: entering historical transactions and account balances.

Working with the Customers and Jobs List

In This Chapter

- Understanding customers and jobs
- Using the Customer Center
- Adding customers
- Adding jobs for customers
- Tracking prospective customers

I like nothing better than adding a new customer to the QuickBooks Customer Center, for two reasons. First, it means I actually have a customer who happens to wander into my off-the-beaten-path art gallery. Second, new customers buy things from the gallery. By keeping their information, such as e-mail address, mailing address, and even shopping preferences, I have a way to stay in touch with them. I can lure them back to my gallery with events or sales announcements, or to let them know that I have new work by their favorite artist.

About Customers and Jobs

In QuickBooks, the term *customer* is used loosely to apply to all kinds of situations—your business may refer to them as clients, patients, collectors, club members, donors, visitors, or even animals, if you're a veterinarian. But then you might have a bit of trouble trying to send a bill to a chicken.

The term *job* refers to projects, and they are associated with a customer. If you're a building contractor and you're remodeling a house, you could create jobs for each phase of the project, such as Kitchen Remodel or Master Bath Remodel. For a legal business, a job could be a case; for an insurance business, a job could be a policy. You can use jobs to keep track of larger orders by breaking down the order into smaller chunks, which can help you get a better handle on your income and expenses. You also use jobs if you do multiple projects for one customer, treating each project as a single job.

Not all businesses use jobs. A retail store might not have any use for them, and QuickBooks doesn't care whether you use them. But by using jobs, you can track expenses and income by job. You can figure out which jobs are the most profitable for your business.

DEFINITION

Job is just another word for a project.

About Customer Types

Using customer types in QuickBooks gives you a way to group your customers, to analyze different segments of your business. For example, an olive oil producer with a retail store might have three types of customers: retail, wholesale, and restaurant. The restaurant uses these three types because the prices and options vary for each type. The price for restaurants is lower because they buy in bulk quantities. The company also wants to track how its retail customers heard about the retail outlet, so it creates subtypes of the retail customer type: drive-by, website, other customer, and ad. If the company runs a report and learns that 80 percent of the customers are drive-by, it may rethink spending $600 a month on the ad in the tourist magazine.

You find out about adding customer types while creating a customer record later in this chapter. To add several customer types in bulk, see Chapter 10.

About Job Types

Wait ... there's more. You can also categorize your jobs. For a project-based business, grouping jobs by type helps you report on profitability. For example, you can group and subtotal the Job Profitability Report by type to see which jobs are bringing in the most money.

For example, a graphic designer works with several different companies on multiple projects. For each project with a company, the designer creates a job associated with the company just for that project. He can then analyze his profits by the type of work he created job types for: web design, brochures, logos, business cards, and annual reports.

Later in this chapter, you learn about adding job types while creating a customer record. To add job types in bulk, see Chapter 10.

About the Customer Center

The Customer Center is where you can find all the information about your jobs and customers. It's basically a list of your customers and jobs, and it includes transactions such as invoices, received payments, sales receipts, and statement charges. You can view what your customers purchased from you, invoices they've paid, how much they owe you, and their contact information. You can find anything you want to know about your customers in the Customer Center. From the Customer Center, you can …

- Add a new customer or job.

- Edit a customer or job.

- Write and store notes about a customer or job.

- Add a new transaction for a customer.

- View some or all of a customer's transactions.

- Generate reports.

Chapter 13 covers adding and viewing transactions, and Chapter 29 discusses generating reports.

QuickBooks offers lots of options for navigating. For example, you can open the Customer Center (shown in Figure 6.1) in four ways:

- From the Home page, click the vertical **Customers** button (see Figure 2.1). (That's my personal favorite.)

- Click the **Customer Center** icon in the navigation bar (see Figure 2.2).

- Click the **Customers** menu in the Menu bar (see Figure 2.2) and click **Customer Center**.

- Press **Ctrl-J**.

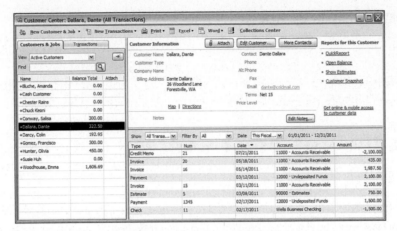

Figure 6.1: *The Customer Center.*

On the left side of the Customer Center (see Figure 6.1) are two tabs: Customers & Jobs and Transactions. When you select a customer or job on the Customers & Jobs tab, the right side of the Customer Center shows the basic information for the customer or job, as well as any associated transactions. You can change the way transactions are shown by filtering the list and choosing the date range. Chapter 3 talks about using lists in general, and you can find information on filtering and choosing a date range there.

The Transactions tab (see Figure 6.2) lists your transactions by type: invoices, statement charges, sales receipts, received payments, credit memos, and refunds. When you select a transaction type on the Transactions tab, the right side of the Customer Center shows all the transactions of that type.

You can change the transactions shown by filtering the list (for example, to show only open invoices), changing the date range, and choosing a column to sort by. Chapter 3 explores how you can change what a list shows.

Now it's time to start adding customers.

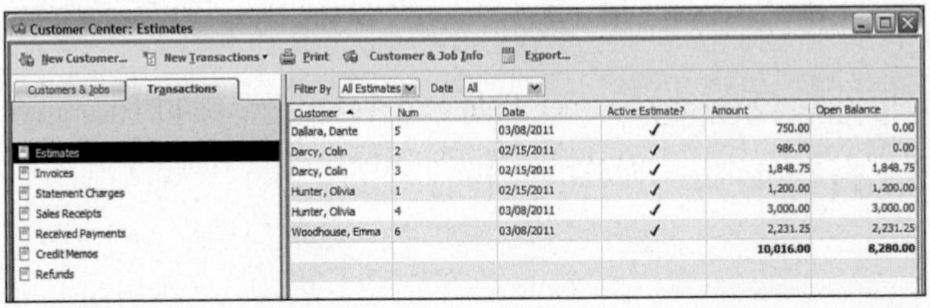

Figure 6.2: *The Customer Center showing invoice transactions.*

Adding Customers

You can approach the task of setting up customers in two ways. You can add customers to your list one after the other so you'll have all your customers set up before you begin using QuickBooks, or you can add them when you start to add transactions. In any Customer field on a transaction form, you can choose **<Add New>**.

One advantage of creating your customer records beforehand is that QuickBooks can take the information from the customer record and prefill some of the fields on a form, such as the billing and shipping addresses and the customer's preferred payment method.

As an alternative to adding customers one-by-one, you can use the Add/Edit Multiple List Entries window. In the Customer Center, click **New Customer & Job**, then click **Add Multiple Customers:Jobs**. This opens a spreadsheet-like view where each row represents a customer. You can copy and paste customer information from another contact software product, but before pasting, customize the columns in the window to match the columns and the order of the columns you used in the spreadsheet. If you've stored your customers in an Excel spreadsheet, you can import them. Click the **Excel** button and choose **Import from Excel**.

QUICKTIP

Create records for each of your customers and enter as much information about them as you can, to speed data entry down the road.

To add a customer, follow these steps:

1. Open the Customer Center using one of the methods listed earlier in this chapter.

2. Click the **New Customer & Job** button at the top left of the Customer Center and then choose **New Customer** from the menu. Figure 6.3 shows a blank customer record.

3. In the Customer Name field, type the customer's name as you want it to appear in the Customers & Jobs list.

4. Leave the Opening Balance field and As Of date blank. (QuickBooks fills it in as you enter transactions for the customer.)

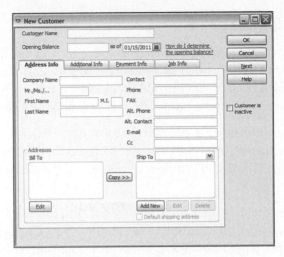

Figure 6.3: *The Customer Record window.*

What you enter in the Customer Name field is for your own convenience—it's more like a code or identifier. The name doesn't appear on any forms the customer would see, so let your imagination go. Each customer name must be unique, and the name just helps you distinguish one customer from another. For example, if you have two customers with the same name, you can tell them apart by the way you enter the name, like Dante Dallara Designs and Dante Dallara Second St.

QUICKTIP

If you want your customers alphabetized by last name in lists and reports, type the name that way in the Customer Name field for every customer (for example, Dallara, Dante).

This is important: However tempting it might be to enter the customer's balance, leaving the Opening Balance and As Of fields blank makes your records more accurate, especially if you plan to issue multiple invoices or track multiple jobs with the customer. QuickBooks can calculate the amount the customer owes you based on any invoices you create for the customer. If you enter the total amount the customer owes you, including all outstanding invoices, you can't later determine how the amount was arrived at—worse, you may find that you can't collect if you can't tell the customer what you provided and when. Even worse, when the customer actually does pay you, you won't be able to accept payments against specific invoices. And this will screw up your accounts receivable.

The customer record has four tabs for storing customer information, as follows:

- Address Info
- Additional Info
- Payment Info
- Job Info

Each tab is covered in detail next.

Entering Customer Address Information

To add address information for a customer, click the **Address Info** tab and fill in the fields. Figure 6.4 shows the Address Info tab.

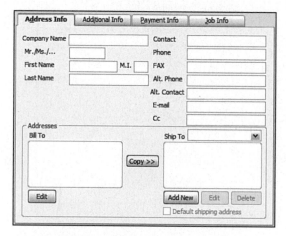

Figure 6.4: *The Address Info tab.*

- **Company Name:** This is the name that will appear on the form when you invoice the customer. If this customer is an individual, you can use his full name or leave the field blank.

- **Contact Fields:** Enter as much detail as you can about the customer or primary contact at the company. As you enter information in the fields, QuickBooks automatically fills in some of the other fields, which you can change, if needed. Be sure to enter an e-mail address to make it easier to e-mail invoices.

- **Bill To Address:** Enter the billing address to which your invoices will be sent. This address will appear on forms.

- **Ship To Address:** Click **Copy** if the shipping address is the same as the billing address. If the customer has a different shipping address, enter it. To add more than one shipping address, click **Add New**. In the Address Name field, replace the words "Ship to 1" with a store number or location to make it easier later on when choosing it. The first shipping address you enter is the one QuickBooks uses by default, meaning that the address will automatically appear in any shipping address field for that customer. At any time, you can choose a different shipping address from the Ship To menu on forms. To make a different address the default address, click **Edit** and make sure a check mark appears in the Default Shipping Address check box (see Figure 6.5).

Figure 6.5: *The Add Ship To Address window.*

Continue with the next section to add more information for the customer.

Filling in the Additional Info Tab

On the Additional Info tab (see Figure 6.6), you can add details about the customer, such as customer type, payment terms, price level, sales tax information, and more. All the fields on this tab are optional, but filling them out can save a boatload of time when you create invoices and other forms. These fields can also help you create more detailed and meaningful reports because you can base a report on the values entered.

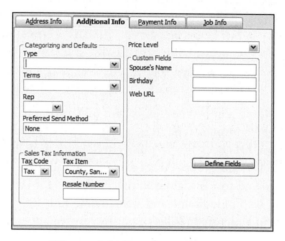

Figure 6.6: *The Additional Info tab.*

A lot of the menu choices on this tab (for example, the Type menu and Price Levels menu) come from other QuickBooks lists. This is sort of a chicken-and-egg situation. Do you fill out those other lists before adding customers? Or do you want to add to those lists as you go? It probably just depends on how organized you are. If you're the type of person who arranges clothes in your closet by color, set up all those lists before you start. If you're more like me, a go-with-the-flow type of person, you might prefer setting up the lists as you go.

The following steps show how you can add to these lists on the fly, but if you prefer to set them up first, follow the steps in Chapter 10.

To fill in the Additional Info tab, follow these steps:

1. On the customer record, click the **Additional Info** tab (see Figure 6.6).

2. From the Type menu, choose a customer type that you've already set up or choose **<Add New>**. As a reminder, the customer type is used to categorize customers for sorting or reporting (for example, Retail or Wholesale customers).

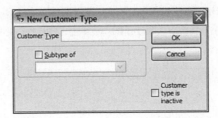

Figure 6.7: *The New Customer Type window.*

3. If you're adding a new type (see Figure 6.7), type a name for the category. If you want the customer type to be a subtype of a broader customer type, click the **Subtype Of** check box to put a check mark in it, and choose the overall type or click **<Add New>**. As an example, a building contractor deals in both commercial and residential buildings. Subtypes for the Residential customer type could be Single Home and Apartment. This lets you group related customers in a hierarchy (like an outline) instead of seeing them all in a flat, unindented list.

4. Click the **Terms** menu and either choose one of the payment terms QuickBooks provides or click **<Add New>** to add your own terms.

5. If you have sales reps, click the **Rep** menu and choose the person to associate this customer with (or click **<Add New>**). Assigning reps is useful if you pay commissions or if you want to track who is mainly responsible for this customer.

6. Click the **Preferred Send Method** menu and choose one of the following options to indicate how this customer prefers to receive invoices, estimates, and statements:

    None: Choose this if you plan to print the documents and snail-mail them.

    E-mail: Choose this if you plan to e-mail the documents as PDFs. When you select this option and then create an invoice or other form for this customer, QuickBooks automatically puts a check mark in the E-mail check box. Chapter 5 provides an overview of e-mailing.

    Mail: Choose this if you plan to use a QuickBooks Add-On service for mailing.

7. If you enabled the Sales Tax preference (either during the EasyStep Interview or in Preferences), fill out the following sales tax information for this customer:

    For taxable customers: Choose a tax item (which specifies a percentage) or click **<Add New>**. See Chapter 10 for how to set up sales tax items.

    For nontaxable customers: Either choose **Out of State** or choose **Non** from the Tax Code menu and then enter the customer's resale number. Be sure to get that resale number so that if the friendly tax auditors stop by for a chat, you can convince them that the tax burden falls on your customer, not you.

8. Choose the price level that determines how much this customer will pay for your products or services. See Chapter 10 for information on setting up price levels. Using price levels is totally optional.

9. If you've created any custom fields, fill in those fields. An example of a custom field is a birthday so that you can send birthday greetings, or a renewal date so that you can remind a customer that it's time to renew a membership.

Filling in the Payment Info Tab

The Payment Info tab (see Figure 6.8) stores your customer's financial information, such as account number, credit limit, and credit card information.

To fill in the Payment Info tab, here's what to do:

1. On the customer record, click the **Payment Info** tab.

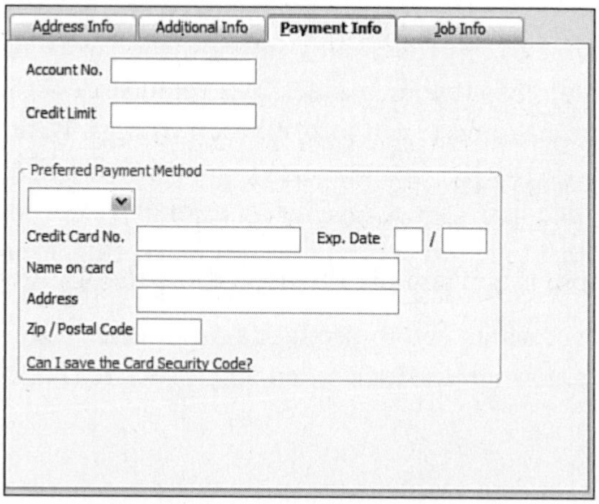

Figure 6.8: *The Payment Info tab.*

2. If you assign account numbers to your customers, type this customer's number in the optional Account Number field.

3. In the optional Credit Limit field, type the amount of credit you are willing to give this customer. When the customer is about to exceed this limit, QuickBooks warns you. However, you get to decide whether to proceed with the order, reject the order, or ship it collect on delivery (COD).

4. In the Preferred Payment Method field, choose the customer's preferred payment method or choose **<Add New>**. This payment method appears automatically on the Receive Payments window when you receive a payment from this customer.

5. If the customer's preferred payment method is a credit card, use the fields provided to fill out the credit card information. Entering this information is optional, but if you do enter it, it automatically appears in the Receive Payments window.

QUICKTIP

If you leave the Credit Limit field blank, you are saying that this customer can keep buying from you no matter what he already owes you. If you type a zero (0) in the Credit Limit field, you're saying that this customer can't buy anything. This could come in handy for a deadbeat client.

Filling in the Job Info Tab

The Job Info tab helps you keep track of the status of a single project you're working on for a customer. Use this tab when you don't track multiple jobs for a customer.

It took me a long time to figure out jobs and how they work in QuickBooks. First, you can totally ignore jobs if your business is a retail store—that's because you don't do projects for your customers; you just sell them things. Basically, when adding a new customer, fill out the Job Info tab (see Figure 6.9) if you're working with a client on one—and only one—project. Consider an example: a corporate client wants you to produce a one-time video to test how a viral marketing strategy might work. This is a one-time event because, if it goes well, the client will hire a staff videographer. However, if the client wants you to produce several videos over several months, you would then create a new job for each video and associate the jobs with this client.

If you fill out the Job Info tab for the one and only project and later decide to create other jobs for the customer, all is not lost. When you add another job to a customer with a job in the main customer record, QuickBooks moves that job tab out of the customer record and into a new job called Job 1.

To fill in the Job Info tab, follow these steps:

1. On the customer record, click the **Job Info** tab.

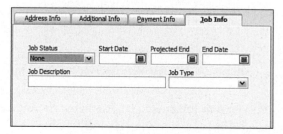

Figure 6.9: *The Job Info tab.*

2. Click the **Job Status** menu and choose the current status. The status is to help you keep track of a job. You can create a report for a customer and modify it to include a column for Job Status. Each time the job status changes, come back to the Job Info tab for the customer and change it.

3. In the Start Date field, type in the date you started the job (or click the calendar and choose the date).

4. In the Projected End Date field, type in the date the job is supposed to end (or click the calendar and choose the date).

5. In the End Date field, type in the date that the job actually ended (or click the calendar and choose the date).

    Keeping track of the dates helps you monitor how long a job takes and can help you better estimate future jobs. You can create a report for a customer and modify it to include a column for Start Date, Projected End Date, and End Date.

6. In the Job Description field, type a short description to help you distinguish this job from other jobs.

7. If you plan to categorize your jobs by job type, choose the job type if you've already set them up or click **<Add New>** (see Figure 6.10). As a reminder, the job type is used to categorize your projects for sorting or reporting (for example, Kitchen Remodel or Office Remodel).

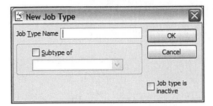

Figure 6.10: *The New Job Type window.*

8. If you're adding a new job type, give it a name. If you want the job type to be a subtype of a broader job type, click the **Subtype Of** check box to put a check mark in it, and choose the general type or click **<Add New>**.

QUICKTIP

Don't like the statuses QuickBooks has provided? You can change the status names in Preferences. Keep in mind that the statuses apply to all jobs, not just the one job on the Job Info tab.

Saving the Customer Information

After filling in all the tabs for the customer, you can do one of the following:

- Click **OK** to save the customer information and close the customer record.

- Click **Next** to save the customer information and open a new record to add another customer.

Adding Notes on a Customer or Job

Keeping notes on your customers is a great tool to market your business, provide better customer service, and make more sales.

You can add notes to a customer record to store quick reminders of promises you've made, meeting notes, or notes on phone calls. If a particular customer is crazy for your ylang-ylang lavender soap, you can jot it down and notify her of sales promotions or similar products.

You can't add notes until you've saved a customer record or job. Then you can go back and edit the customer record to add the note.

To add notes on a customer or job, follow these steps:

1. Open the Customer Center.

2. In the Customers & Jobs tab, double-click the customer or job and then click the **Notes** button. You can also click the customer or job once and then click the **Edit Notes** button on the right side of the window. See Figure 6.11.

3. If you want to keep track of the date of the note using today's date, click **Date Stamp** before you type the note. For other dates, you have to enter them manually.

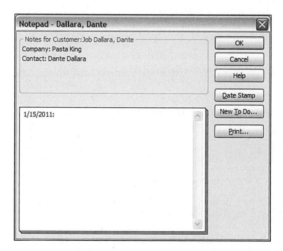

Figure 6.11: *The Notepad window.*

4. Type the note.

5. If you want to be reminded of a to-do item, click **New To Do**.

6. Type the to-do item and choose the date on which you want to be reminded. The to-do item then shows up on your To Do List. You'll see the reminder if you open QuickBooks that day and look at the To Do List.

7. Click **OK** and then, in Notepad, click **OK** again.

Adding Jobs

Jobs are associated with customers—in fact, you can't create a job without a customer. By using jobs, you can track job status, due dates, and income/expenses by job.

You can add a job in two ways:

- Add a single job to a customer by filling out the Job Info tab for that customer. Use this method when you will work with this customer on only one project.

- Select a customer in the Customer Center and add a job. This creates a new job record and associates it with the customer. Use this method when you plan to work with this customer on several jobs.

To add multiple jobs for a customer, follow these steps:

1. Open the Customer Center.

2. Click on the customer. Click the **New Customer & Job** button at the top left of the Customer Center and then choose **Add Job** from the menu. (You can also right-click the customer's name and choose **Add Job**.)

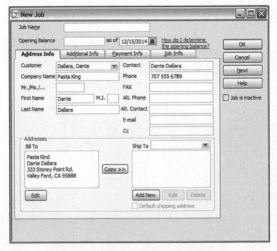

Figure 6.12: *The New Job window.*

3. In the Job Name field (see Figure 6.12), type a name for the job (up to 41 characters), keeping in mind that it will appear on customer invoices. You don't need to use the customer's name as part of the job name; QuickBooks adds the customer's name for you (for example, Anderson:Install Garage Door).

4. Click the **Job Info** tab if you want to add more details for the job.

   QuickBooks copies the information in the other tabs from the customer record. You can ignore the other tabs unless you need to change some of the information for this job. The changes affect this job only. For example, if you need to change the shipping address for this job, you can change it without affecting the customer's shipping address.

5. Fill out the Job Info tab following the steps in the preceding "Filling in the Job Info Tab."

6. To create another job for this customer, click **Next**; otherwise, click **OK** to save the job and close the job record.

Each time the job status or dates change, edit the job's Job Info tab.

To edit a job's status or dates, follow these steps:

1. In the Customer Center, double-click the job in the Customers & Jobs tab to open the job record.

2. Click the **Job Info** tab and change the status or dates.

3. Click **OK** to save the changes.

Tracking Leads

The Lead Center is where you can keep track of prospective customers (also known as leads). It lists current leads, as well as leads that have been converted to customers. You can keep track of your interactions with prospective customers, such as phone calls, follow-up tasks, e-mails, and meetings. You can take notes to document your interactions and associate the notes with the customer. From the Lead Center, you can …

- Add a new lead.
- Edit a lead.

- Convert a lead to a customer.

- Track the status of the lead (Hot, Warm, Cold, or Converted).

- Create to-do items for a lead.

- Write and store notes on a lead.

To add a lead, follow these steps:

1. Click the **Customers** (or **Company**) menu in the Menu bar and click **Lead Center**.

2. Click the **New Lead** button at the top left of the Lead Center. Figure 6.13 shows a blank lead record.

Figure 6.13: *The Add Lead window.*

3. In the Name field, type the lead's name as you want it to appear in the Leads list.

4. From the Status menu, choose **Hot**, **Warm**, or **Cold** to indicate how likely it is this lead will be converted to a customer in the near future.

5. Fill in as many of the fields on the form that you can. When you convert a lead to a customer, the information you enter here is transferred to the customer record.

6. Click the **Contacts** tab and enter detailed information on the contact(s) at the lead's company.

7. Click **OK** to save the lead record and return to the Lead Center.

> **QUICKTIP**
>
> You can enter multiple leads quickly by clicking the **Import Multiple Leads** button located at the top of the Lead Center. In the grid that appears, you can enter the leads manually or you can copy and paste from Excel.

Adding a To-Do Task for a Lead

After entering a lead, you can add to-do items to help you remember and track your interactions with that lead. To-do items can include calls, faxes, e-mails, meetings, appointments, and tasks. To add a to-do item for a lead, follow these steps:

1. Click the **Customers** (or **Company**) menu in the Menu bar and click **Lead Center**.

2. In the list of leads on the left, click to highlight a lead. Click the **Add To Do** button at the bottom of the window. Figure 6.14 shows the Add To Do window. QuickBooks prefills some of the fields for you.

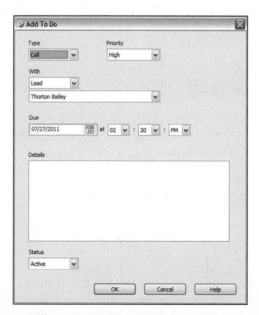

Figure 6.14: *The Add To Do window.*

3. From the Type menu, choose the to-do item type: **Call, Fax, E-mail, Meeting, Appointment**, or **Task**.

4. From the Priority menu, choose how urgent the to-do item is: **High, Medium**, or **Low**.

5. Enter the date and time that the to-do item is due or the date and time it occurred if you've already completed the to-do item.

6. In the Details field, type any information about the to-do item, such as results of the call or notes on a meeting.

7. Use the Status menu to indicate the status of the to-do item: **Active, Done**, or **Inactive**.

8. Click **OK** to return to the Lead Center. Figure 6.15 shows the To-Do item in the lead's record.

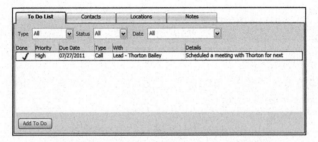

Figure 6.15: *The To Do List for a Lead.*

Adding Notes on a Lead

After entering a lead, you can keep notes on the lead, such as the source of the lead, personal information about the lead, and other relevant information you can use to help convert the lead to a customer.

To add a note for a lead, follow these steps:

1. Click the **Customers** (or **Company**) menu in the Menu bar and click **Lead Center**.

2. In the list of leads on the left, click to highlight a lead.

3. Click the **Notes** tab and then click **Add Notes**.

4. Click **OK** and the note is listed on the Notes tab for the lead.

Converting a Lead to a Customer

Success! A lead has become a new customer. To transfer the information you've kept on the lead to a customer record, highlight the lead in the Lead Center. Click **Convert to a Customer**.

QuickBooks creates a customer record for the lead. Go to the Customer Center to see it. You can then edit the record to fill out the customer-related fields (such as terms, price level, and sales tax information). The lead record remains in the Lead Center as well with the status of **Converted**.

The Least You Need to Know

- You don't have to set up all your customers (or other lists) at once. Throughout QuickBooks, you can add something on the fly by choosing **<Add New>** from menus where it appears.

- When adding a customer or job, you don't have to fill out all the fields. As long as you give the customer or job a name, you can save the record and come back later to change it.

- Customer and job types are optional features whose purpose is to group customers and jobs by type for reporting.

- If your business involves primarily selling products, you don't have to mess with jobs.

- QuickBooks lets you keep notes on customer preferences or ways to improve customer satisfaction.

- Keep track of prospective customers in the Lead Center. Create to-do items and add notes to document your interactions.

Working with the Vendors List

In This Chapter

- Understanding vendors and vendor types
- Using the Vendor Center
- Adding vendors
- Using the Prefill tab

Do you use a phone service for your business? Do you hire the occasional seasonal employee? Do you pay a tax agency sales tax? Do you sometimes hire a lawyer? Or a handyman to change the light bulbs? If you run a business, you're going to have vendors, and you'll need to pay those vendors for the services they provide.

About Vendors

In QuickBooks, the term *vendor* refers to people and companies from whom you buy goods and services to run your business. Vendors can include the office supply store, the utilities company, the cleaning service, manufacturers of goods you sell, and any tax agencies. Before you can pay your bills, you'll need to set up your vendors.

DEFINITION

In QuickBooks, a **vendor** is anyone (except your employees) to whom you pay money in the course of running your business.

About Vendor Types

Using vendor types in QuickBooks provides a way for you to group your vendors. QuickBooks provides a few standard vendor types, such as Tax Agency and Supplies. You might find it useful to categorize your vendors by geographical location or by industry. You can create reports or send e-mails by group.

Adding vendor types while creating a vendor record is covered later in this chapter. To add several vendor types in bulk, see Chapter 10.

Working with the Vendor Center

Chapter 2 briefly touched on the Vendor Center; this section shows you how to use it.

In the Vendor Center (see Figure 7.1), you can find details about your vendors and their transactions. This is basically a list of your vendors and transactions specific to that vendor. You also can view a list of transactions by type across all vendors, including purchase orders, item receipts, bills, bill payments, credit card activities, checks, and sales tax.

From the Vendor Center, you can do the following tasks:

- Add a new vendor
- Edit a vendor
- Write and store notes about a vendor
- Add a new transaction for a vendor
- View some or all of a vendor's transactions
- Generate reports

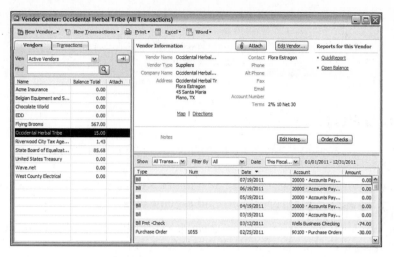

Figure 7.1: *The Vendor Center.*

QuickBooks offers the following three ways to open the Vendor Center:

- From the Home page, click the vertical **Vendors** button (see Figure 2.1).

- Click the **Vendor Center** icon in the navigation bar (see Figure 2.2).

- Click the **Vendors** menu in the menu bar (see Figure 2.2) and click **Vendor Center**.

On the left side of the Vendor Center are two tabs: Vendors and Transactions. When you select a vendor on the Vendors tab, the right side of the Vendor Center shows the basic information for the vendor and any associated transactions. You can change the way transactions are shown by filtering the list and choosing the date range. Chapter 3 covers using lists in general; you can find information on filtering and choosing a date range there.

The Transactions tab (see Figure 7.2) lists your transactions by type: purchase orders, item receipts, bills, bill payments, checks, credit card activities, and sales tax payments. When you select a transaction type on the Transactions tab, the right side of the Vendor Center shows all the transactions across all vendors.

Figure 7.2: *The Vendor Center Showing purchase orders.*

Adding Vendors

You can approach the task of setting up vendors in two ways. You can add vendors to your list one after the other so that you have all your vendors set up before you begin using QuickBooks, or you can add them on the fly when you start to add transactions. For example, if you're creating a purchase order for a vendor but you haven't yet entered the vendor, you can click the arrow in the Vendor field and choose **<Add New>**.

QUICKTIP

To enter vendors quickly, go to the Vendor Center and click **New Vendor**, then click **Add Multiple Vendors**. This opens a spreadsheet-like view, where each row represents a vendor. You can copy and paste vendor information from another contact software product. Or if you've stored your vendors in Excel, you can import them. Click the **Excel** button and choose **Import from Excel**.

To add a vendor, follow these steps:

1. Open the Vendor Center using one of the methods listed in the preceding section.

2. Click the **New Vendor** button in the top left of the Vendor Center and then choose **New Vendor** from the menu. Figure 7.3 shows a blank vendor record.

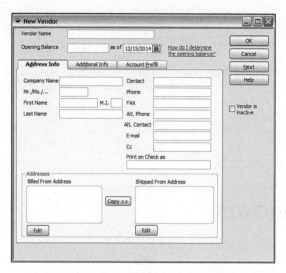

Figure 7.3: *The Vendor Record Window.*

3. In the Vendor Name field, type the vendor's name as you want it to appear in the Vendor list. This name is for your use only; it doesn't appear on purchase orders or bill payments. As an example, suppose that you get your phone and Internet service from the same vendor. You can use the Vendor Name field to distinguish between the two: Comcast Phone and Comcast Internet.

   QuickBooks uses this name to sort the Vendor list.

4. Leave the Opening Balance field and As Of date blank. It's better to have QuickBooks calculate the opening balance, which it gets after you enter the historical transactions for this vendor.

The vendor record has three tabs for storing customer information: Address Info, Additional Info, and Account Prefill.

Each tab is covered in detail in the following sections.

Entering Vendor Address Information

To add address information for a vendor, click the Address Info tab (see Figure 7.4). Fill in the fields on the tab.

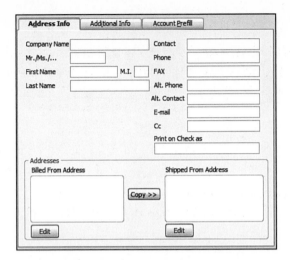

Figure 7.4: *The Address Info tab.*

- **Company Name:** Type the company name of the vendor. If this vendor is an individual, you can use the person's full name or leave the field blank.

- **Contact information fields:** Enter as much detail as you can about the company or the primary contact at the company. As you enter information in the fields, QuickBooks automatically fills in some of the other fields, which you can change if needed. Be sure to enter an e-mail address to make it easier to e-mail purchase orders.

- **Print on Check as field:** QuickBooks automatically uses the vendor name, but if you want it to appear differently on checks, you can change the name in this field.

- **Billed From Address:** Type the address where you send your payments. This address will appear on forms.

- **Shipped From Address:** Click **Copy** if the shipped from address is the same as the billed from address, or enter a different address.

Continue with the next section to add more information for the customer.

Entering Additional Information

On the Additional Info tab (see Figure 7.5), you can add details about the vendor, such as vendor type, payment terms, credit limit, tax information, and more. All the items on this tab are optional, but filling them in can save you time when you pay your bills. This tab can also help you create more detailed and meaningful reports because you can base a report on the values entered.

A lot of the menu choices on this tab (for example, the Type menu) come from other QuickBooks lists.

The following steps show how you can add to those lists on the fly, but if you prefer to set up those lists first, follow the steps in Chapter 10.

To fill in the Additional Info tab, follow these steps:

1. On the vendor record, click the **Additional Info** tab.

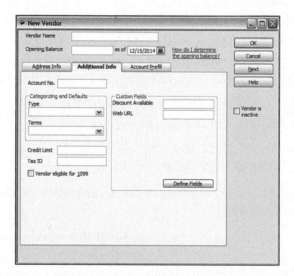

Figure 7.5: *The Additional Info tab.*

2. In the Account No. field, type the account number this vendor has assigned to you, if any. When you print a check to this vendor, QuickBooks puts the account number in the Memo field. (If you pay this vendor online, filling in the account number is required so that the vendor can identify you.)

3. From the Type menu, choose one of QuickBooks vendor types or choose **<Add New>**.

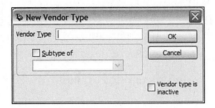

Figure 7.6: *The New Vendor Type window.*

4. If you're adding a new type (see Figure 7.6), enter a name for the type. If you want the vendor type to be a subtype of a broader vendor type, click the **Subtype Of** check box to put a check mark in it and choose the broader type, or click **<Add New>**.

5. Click the **Terms** menu and either choose one of the payment terms QuickBooks provides or click **<Add New>**. The vendor dictates the terms you need to follow when paying. When you enter a bill from this vendor, QuickBooks uses the terms to figure out when a bill is due.

6. If the vendor has set a credit limit, type in that amount. When you come close to the limit, QuickBooks gives you a warning.

7. If you send 1099-MISC forms to this vendor, fill in the Tax ID field with the vendor's Social Security number or EIN.

8. If you send 1099-MISC forms to this vendor, click the check box for **Vendor Eligible for 1099**.

9. If you've created any custom fields, fill in those fields. Examples of a custom field are a birthday (so that you can send birthday greetings) and a field to remind you what kind of discount you're eligible for with the vendor.

Choosing a Prefill Account

The Account Prefill tab (see Figure 7.7) saves you time and improves accuracy when using a vendor in a transaction. You assign up to three expense accounts to the vendor, and QuickBooks automatically displays the correct accounts when paying bills or writing checks to this vendor.

To fill in the Account Prefill tab, follow these steps:

1. On the vendor record, click the **Account Prefill** tab.

Figure 7.7: *The Account Prefill Tab.*

2. Choose up to three expense accounts for a vendor. For example, if you use the same provider for the phone and Internet, you can assign Utilities:Phone and Utilities:Internet expense accounts. When paying the bill, you can choose the appropriate account for split amounts.

Saving the Vendor Information

After filling in all the tabs for the vendor, you can do one of the following:

- Click **OK** to save the vendor information and close the vendor record.

- Click **Next** to save the vendor information and open a new record to add another vendor.

The Least You Need to Know

- You don't have to set up all your vendors (or other lists) at once. Throughout QuickBooks, you can add items on the fly by choosing **<Add New>** from menus where it appears.

- When adding a vendor, you don't have to fill out all the fields. As long as you give the vendor a name, you can save the record and come back later to change it.

- Use the Account Prefill tab to save time and improve accuracy when using a vendor in a transaction. You assign up to three expense accounts to the vendor, and QuickBooks automatically displays the correct accounts when paying bills or writing checks to the vendor.

- Vendor types are totally optional; their purpose is to group vendors by type for reporting.

Working with the Chart of Accounts List

In This Chapter

- Understanding the chart of accounts
- Tweaking the preset chart of accounts
- Deleting, hiding, or merging accounts
- Creating new accounts and subaccounts

Math was never my best subject, and I don't do numbers. Luckily for me, QuickBooks does. QuickBooks tracks your numbers (what you spend and what you receive) in various accounts, and all those accounts make up your chart of accounts. I'm not sure why it's called a "chart," but I think of it as a map to where your business is going and how it's doing getting there.

About the Chart of Accounts

When you set up your company file in Chapter 1, we recommended that you accept the chart of accounts QuickBooks suggested based on your industry. You also had the opportunity to fine-tune the chart of accounts, so you have some idea of what accounts you'll be using. The chart of accounts contains a complete list of your business accounts and their balances, to help you track the flow of money in your business. The chart of accounts shows you the money, inventory, and other assets that you own, as well as the expenses you have, debts you owe, and equity that you've built in your business.

Each of the accounts (except income and expense accounts) in your chart of accounts has its own register. QuickBooks enters transactions into these registers for you as you work. Each transaction has a debit and a credit (known as double-entry book-keeping), and all transactions must be in balance. Chapter 4 explains debits and credits in more detail.

About Account Types

The QuickBooks chart of accounts has balance sheet accounts (Bank, A/R, A/P, Asset, Liability, and Equity) and income and expense accounts. When you create a new account, you choose one of the following types of accounts:

Account Type	Description
Income accounts	Track the sources of your company's income, such as sales
Expense accounts	Track where your money goes, such as to rent or supplies
Bank	Use to create accounts for checking, savings, petty cash, and money market accounts.
Fixed Asset	Track major purchase items you own that would have to be sold to generate cash, such as automobiles, buildings, and equipment.
Loan	Track loans or lines of credit—what you owe to a lending institution or other source, such as a family member or investor.
Credit Card	Use to create an account for each credit card your business uses.
Equity	Use to create accounts to track owner's equity, owner's draws, capital investments, and capital stock.
Accounts Receivable	Track money your customers owe you on invoices. Most businesses need only the one A/R account QuickBooks sets up for you.
Accounts Payable	Track money you owe to vendors for purchases. Most businesses need only the one A/P account QuickBooks sets up for you.

Account Type	Description
Cost of Goods Sold	Track costs used to produce items you keep in inventory and sell. QuickBooks sets up one COGS account for you. Create additional COGS accounts as subaccounts to track costs for different types of inventory or costs for equipment rentals and purchases made on behalf of a customer.
Other Current Asset	Track the value of purchases that will be used up or converted to cash within a year, such as prepaid income taxes, security deposits, and supplies.
Other Current Liability	Track money you owe that you expect to pay off within a year, such as retainers and security deposits, sales taxes, and payroll taxes.
Long-Term Liability	Track money you owe that you do not expect to pay off within a year, such as mortgages, long-term loans, and lease payments.

What Is the Undeposited Funds Account?

QuickBooks creates a separate account called the Undeposited Funds account, meant to hold money received from customer payments until you're ready to fill out a deposit slip and take the payments to the bank. You learn more about this account in Chapter 21.

Using the Chart of Accounts

Even though QuickBooks has thoughtfully set up a chart of accounts based on your business type, you'll probably want to add new accounts to more accurately reflect your business, change account names, delete accounts you won't use, and tweak the preset accounts to suit your needs.

Opening the Chart of Accounts

To open the chart of accounts, follow these steps:

1. Go to the **Lists** menu (or Company menu) and click **Chart of Accounts** (or press **Ctrl+A**). Figure 8.1 shows the chart of accounts. If you haven't entered any transactions or balances yet, you won't see any balances in the Balance Total column.

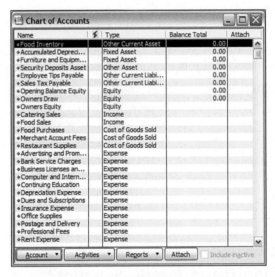

Figure 8.1: *The Chart of Accounts window.*

2. To view the register for an account, double-click it. (Note that not all accounts have a register; income and expense accounts do not, but you can view a list of the transactions by double-clicking the account.)

Numbering Your Accounts

QuickBooks refers to the accounts in the chart of accounts by name; however, you can use numbered accounts, if you prefer. Your accountant may prefer it for his or her convenience, but this is your business and your chart of accounts. Pros and cons accompany using account numbers, and you can decide what works best for you.

If you use account numbers, you can view and arrange accounts in a more logical order (such as balance sheet accounts first, then income and expense accounts). You can number your accounts and *subaccounts* to group related accounts together and determine the order in which they appear in the chart of accounts.

DEFINITION

Subaccounts break down a larger, more general account into smaller, more specific accounts. They're useful for giving you more detail on income and expense accounts.

Talk with your accountant to determine whether you should use account numbers. Before you assign account numbers, you must turn on the account numbering preference.

To turn on account numbering, follow these steps:

1. Go to the **Edit** menu and click **Preferences**.

2. In the Preferences window, click **Accounting** in the left panel. Click the **Company Preferences** tab. Figure 8.2 shows a partial screenshot of the Accounting Preferences.

Figure 8.2: *The Company tab of Accounting Preferences.*

3. Click the **Use Account Numbers** check box so that a check mark appears.

   QuickBooks automatically assigns numbers to the accounts in the preset chart of accounts and inserts the number before the account name. The accounts are listed in numerical order instead of alphabetically. Figure 8.3 shows the Chart of Accounts with account numbers.

4. Click **OK**.

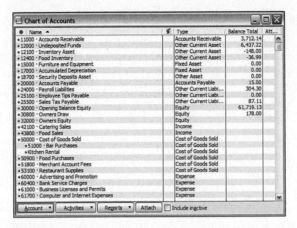

Figure 8.3: *The Chart of Accounts, with account numbers.*

Changing Account Names

You might need to change the name of an account if, for example, you have two checking accounts with the same bank—one for a checking account and another for an equity line. You can distinguish the accounts by matching the account names to the correct account.

To change a name of an account, follow these steps:

1. Go to the **Lists** menu and click **Chart of Accounts** (or press **Ctrl+A**).

2. Click once to select the account you want to rename, and then click the **Account** button in the lower left corner. Figure 8.4 shows the Account menu.

3. Choose **Edit Account**.

4. In the Account Name field, type the new name.

5. Click **OK**.

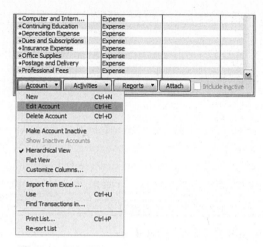

Figure 8.4: *The Account menu: Edit Account.*

Deleting Accounts

You may find that you don't end up using an account that QuickBooks has provided for you, and you want to delete it. This assumes that you haven't yet entered any transactions for that account; you can't delete an account that has any transactions associated with it or that isn't linked to a sales item or payroll item. (You can hide the account from the list, however—see the next section "Hiding Accounts.")

QUICKTIP

If you scroll down to the bottom of your Chart of Accounts, you'll see a fun account called Ask My Accountant. Don't delete this account; you can choose this account in transactions you aren't sure about and go over them later with your accountant, who can suggest the correct account.

To delete an account, follow these steps:

1. Go to the **Lists** menu and click **Chart of Accounts** (or press **Ctrl+A**).

2. Click once to select the account you want to delete, and then press **Ctrl+D** (or click the **Account** menu button and choose **Delete Account**).

3. Click **OK** to confirm that you want to delete the account.

If you delete an account by mistake, you can undo the deletion, but only if you do it right away. Before you take any other action, go to the **Edit** menu at the top of the window and choose **Undo Delete Account**.

Hiding Accounts

If you can't delete an account because transactions are associated with it, you can make the account inactive. This keeps the account for your records, but you won't have to look at it all the time in the Chart of Accounts or in menus throughout QuickBooks.

In the Chart of Accounts window, click to select the account you want to hide and choose **Make Account Inactive** from the Accounts menu. You'll no longer see the account in the Chart of Accounts, but you can view it again by putting a check mark in the **Include Inactive** check box at the bottom of the window.

Adding New Accounts

The first account you need to add is your checking account. As your business changes, you may find you want to add more accounts to the Chart of Accounts that QuickBooks set up for you. For example, you might need to create a new account for a savings account or a new credit card account. Other examples might include a fixed asset account to track the depreciation of new equipment, a long-term liability account to track a business loan, or an equity account to track the investment from a new business partner.

To add a new account, follow these steps:

1. Go to the **Lists** menu and click **Chart of Accounts** (or press **Ctrl+A**).

2. Click the **Account** button and choose **New** (or press **Ctrl+N**). (See Figure 8.5.)

Figure 8.5: *The Account menu: New.*

3. From the Choose Account Type window, select the type of account you want to add (see Figure 8.6). Click **Continue** to move to the next screen.

Figure 8.6: *The Choose Account Type window.*

4. Fill out the Add New Account window that appears. The fields in the window vary depending on the type of account. Figure 8.7 shows the Add New Account window for a bank account.

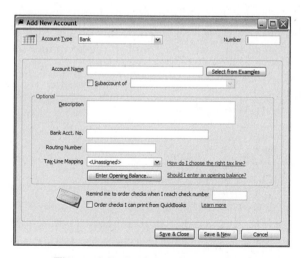

Figure 8.7: *The New Account window.*

5. If you've turned on the Account Numbers feature, enter the number in the Number field. If you don't know what to enter, ask your accountant. (This isn't the bank account number—it's the number assigned to accounts in your Chart of Accounts.)

6. The only required field is the account name. Enter a name, or click **Select from Examples** to choose from a list of suggested account names and descriptions. You only see the Select from Examples button if you created your company file using the QuickBooks 2011 or newer version.

7. (Optional) To make this account a subaccount of another account, click the **Subaccount Of** check box and then choose the main account.

8. (Optional) Type a description of the account.

9. (Optional) For bank or credit card accounts, type the account number and routing number.

10. If you need to assign a tax line, see the next section.

11. If the account you are adding is a balance sheet account (for example, a bank account), click the **Enter Opening Balance** button and type the opening balance. Locate your latest bank statement dated before your QuickBooks start date, and enter the ending balance.

    If this is a new account and the account doesn't have any money in it before your QuickBooks start date, create a transaction (such as a deposit or money transfer) that adds a starting amount to the account. (See Chapter 1.)

12. Click **Save & New** to save this account and add another one, or click **Save & Close**.

Choosing a Tax Line

If you want to make tax time less painful, you can assign a tax form line to an account. This way, you can generate a report at tax time showing you which amounts to enter for a particular tax line on a tax form. For example, suppose you've created an expense account for a business vehicle to help you track gas and repairs. For each subaccount, you could assign it to Sch. C: Car and Truck Expenses.

If the tax line feature has been turned on, you'll see a Tax Line Mapping menu. QuickBooks probably already assigned a tax form for your business based on your answers when you set up your company file.

If you don't see the Tax Line Mapping menu and you want to assign tax lines to your accounts, you'll need to tell QuickBooks which tax form you use.

To indicate your tax form, follow these steps:

1. Go to the **Company** menu and click **Company Information**.

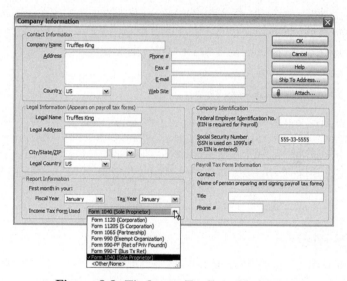

Figure 8.8: *The Income Tax Form Used menu.*

2. From the Income Tax Form Used menu (see Figure 8.8), choose the tax form you use when filing your taxes. Then click **OK**.

For the accounts QuickBooks set up for you based on your business type, QuickBooks also assigned tax lines. If you're adding new accounts, you'll want to assign tax lines to them.

To assign tax lines to income and expense accounts, follow these steps:

1. Open the Chart of Accounts (**Ctrl+A**).

2. In the list of accounts, click the account, click the **Account** menu button, and choose **Edit Account**.

3. Click the **Tax-Line Mapping** drop-down list and choose the tax line you want to associate with this income or expense account.

   If you see a tax line already assigned, QuickBooks has cleverly figured out which line to use and has preassigned it.

4. Click **Save & Close**.

> **NUMBERS HAPPEN**
>
> If the account you're adding will have subaccounts (see the next section), do *not* assign the same tax line to both the main account and the subaccount; assign tax lines to the subaccounts only.

Adding Subaccounts

Subaccounts give you a way to break larger accounts into more manageable chunks or to group related accounts. You can track related income or expenses separately, but keep them under a single main (or parent) account. For example, under the parent account Interest Expenses, you could have a subaccount for Loan Interest and another for Finance Charges.

Using Subaccounts

You add subaccounts just like you add any account (see the steps earlier in this chapter). When adding accounts, plan ahead and figure out the accounts to use as parent accounts and the accounts to use as subaccounts. Then when adding a subaccount, click the **Subaccount Of** check box to put a check mark in it, and choose the parent account as shown in Figure 8.9.

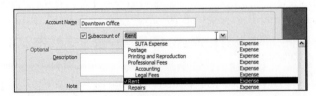

Figure 8.9: *Downtown Office is a subaccount of the parent account Rent.*

Viewing Subaccounts

Subaccounts appear in the Chart of Accounts list, indented under the parent account (see Figure 8.10).

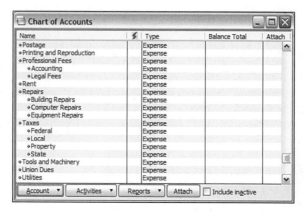

Figure 8.10: *The Chart of Accounts with subaccounts.*

If you've added subaccounts and you don't see them in the list, click the **Account** menu button at the bottom of the window and choose **Hierarchical View**.

The Least You Need to Know

- QuickBooks provides a predefined set of accounts based on your type of business and the tweaks you made when you set up your company file, but you can add new accounts or edit existing accounts at any time.
- Assign transactions you aren't sure how to handle to the built-in Ask My Accountant account. Later, you can go over these transactions with your accountant and assign the correct account.
- Mapping tax lines to income and expense accounts will make tax time a whole lot easier.
- Use subaccounts to group related income or expenses. This gives you more detailed reports.

Working with the Items List

In This Chapter

- Understanding items and item types
- Adding line items
- Adding subitems
- Editing items

In QuickBooks, you can't sell anything without setting up items. No matter what your business—whether you're a lawyer, an artisan chocolatier with a retail store, or a dog psychologist—you need to set up items for the products and services you sell. If you plan to use invoices, estimates, sales receipts, billing statements, or credit memos, you need items.

About Items

Think of items as representing things you sell and things you purchase. Do you sell products that you buy from others for resale? Do you sell services, such as pet sitting or psychic readings? Whether you run your business from your office, a retail store, or online, you need items to track what you sell and the income from the sales.

Items also represent things you buy from vendors and the expenses for those purchases. For example, you can set up an item for cleaning services, office equipment repairs, or office supplies.

Here's the lowdown on what items do: basically, the items you set up are linked to accounts in your chart of accounts so that QuickBooks can accurately track your income and expenses behind the scenes. When you set up an item (for example, something you sell), you enter your cost of the item and associate an account where the cost should be posted. You also enter the price at which you sell the item and the income account where the amount should be posted.

BEHIND THE SCENES

When you select an item when creating a transaction, QuickBooks posts an entry to the account you associated with the item. QuickBooks also posts another entry to the appropriate offset accounts.

Items also include things you use in the course of selling, such as shipping, and things you use to do calculations, such as sales tax, discounts, subtotals, and markups. Basically, items are what appear on invoices, sales receipts, and purchase orders; you can't fill out a form without items. This chapter covers setting up all items except sales tax items and inventory items. Chapter 17 covers using sales tax in QuickBooks, and Chapter 18 covers inventory items.

How to Use Items

When you create an invoice for a customer, you list the things you've sold in the line item area of the invoice. Figure 9.1 shows an invoice that contains a couple items in the line item area.

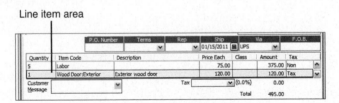

Figure 9.1: *The line item area on an invoice.*

For example, imagine that a dog shrink provides psychological counseling for both dogs and their owners. She does a short half-hour consultation for $55 and an hour's consultation for $100. She also does quick 15-minute follow-up consultations for $25 to address one specific question the owner might have. She needs to create three service items in QuickBooks: one for the half-hour session, one for the hour session, and another one for the quick question. No shipping is involved, so she doesn't need a shipping item; likewise, she doesn't sell any products, so she doesn't need any inventory items.

When you purchase products from a vendor, you use a purchase order and include items (see Figure 9.2).

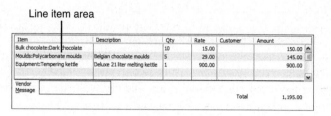

Figure 9.2: *The line items on a purchase order.*

The next section explores the different item types, which will hopefully clarify how to use items.

About Item Types

QuickBooks categorizes items into ten types, described in this section. Think about your business and your items thoughtfully before you dive in and create items. Choosing the incorrect item type can easily wreak havoc with your books, and you don't want to pay your accountant for the hours it will take to straighten things out. Here are the item types and when to use them:

Service. Services you provide to your customers, such as consulting by project or by the hour; and for services you purchase, such as professional fees for your accountant and lawyer.

Inventory part. Products you buy, stock on your shelves, and then resell to your customers. (Note that you must turn on the inventory preference to see this item type. See Chapter 18.)

Noninventory part. Products that you buy but you don't track as inventory. These can be things you buy for a particular job, and you plan to pass on the expense for them to the customer; these also can be things you buy as part of running your business, such as packing supplies or those cheap pens that have your business contact information on them.

Other charges. Charges you include on invoices or purchase orders, such as shipping, handling, delivery fees, retainers, service charges for late payments or bounced checks, and so on.

Subtotal. Total of all the items on the lines above it. For example, you can create a subtotal and then apply a discount to those items. You can also have more than one subtotal on an invoice. For example, if you provide both services and products, you can create a subtotal for the services and then create another subtotal for the products, to calculate the sales tax on just the products, not the services.

Discount. Calculating a discount on the item immediately above it (or on a subtotal) by a percentage or fixed dollar amount. You can create several discount items: one for wholesalers, one for family and friends, another for volume purchases, and another for special holiday promotions. Note that you can't use a discount item on purchase orders.

Group. Associating several items (that are already in your Item List) together to make entering line items quicker and easier. For example, instead of listing the individual items you sell in a gift basket for picnics, you can group all the items you sell in the gift basket so that you have to enter only one item.

Payment. Recording payments received from customers at the time of sale—for example, a down payment or deposit. This item reduces the amount owed on the invoice.

Sales Tax. Calculating a single sales tax for each tax authority you pay. (You must turn on the sales tax preference to create a sales tax item.) See Chapter 17 for how to set up sales tax items.

Sales Tax Group. Calculating more than one sales tax for a customer (such as state, county, and local taxes). (You must turn on the sales tax preference to create a sales tax item.) See Chapter 17 for how to set up sales tax items.

Issues to Consider

A big question is looming: which types of items do you use in your business, whether you're selling items, buying items, or using items in the course of running your day-to-day business? A bit of preplanning will save you time and agony later, and you'll thank me for making you think about this now.

Keep in mind that items (except Discount items) can be used on both invoices and purchase orders. For example, a contractor who builds decks and patios might create a noninventory part item for decking materials with "two sides." One side would be an expense when purchased and would be assigned to an expense account; the other side would be assigned to an income account when the cost is passed on to the customer.

Consider the following when planning for items:

- Do you provide services to customers? What are they? How do you charge for them—by the hour or by the project? How much do you charge? Is the service taxable? Which account do you want to use to track the income when selling a service, or the expense when buying a service?

- Do you sell products? Do you want to track each product individually, or can you use a "generic" item (for example, Standard Doorknobs and Deluxe Doorknobs)? Keep in mind that if you sell products on behalf of your customers, based on a project, and you don't keep those products in stock, you don't need to track them as inventory.

- Do you buy things from vendors that you don't want to track as inventory? You still want to track this as expenses, but you don't need to track quantities.

- Do you charge shipping? Handling fees? Service charges? Do clients hire you and pay you a retainer fee? Do you sell gift certificates? All these are "other charge" types of items.

- Do you offer discounts? Are your discounts by percentage or a fixed dollar amount? Or do you offer both? The discount items subtract from the total on an invoice.

- Do you accept deposits or down payments?

- Do you charge sales tax? Do you need to charge any county and local taxes?

QUICKTIP

The number of items—including inventory and sales tax items—you can have in QuickBooks is limited to 14,500. Once you use an item in any transaction, you can't delete it. So if you sell handcrafted stuffed pigs and each one is unique, you don't want to track each individual pig. Instead, you'd want to create items based on the sizes of pigs: 2-inch pigs, 5-inch pigs, 10-inch pigs, and so on.

About Subitems

Using subitems lets you divide a larger item category into smaller, related ones. This helps you track sales and purchases on reports in more detail. For example, an animal-sitting service company in a rural area might have a parent item called

Animal Sitting, with subitems with different prices based on the difficulty of handling the animal: Chicken Sitting, Cow Milking, Horse Exercising/Stable Maintenance, and so on.

The subitems must be the same type as the parent item—you can't have an inventory part item as a subitem to a service item.

Adding Items

When you figure out the items you'll need, you add them to the Item List. The process for adding items is the same for all item types. The following steps describe the initial process, and the sections that follow describe the steps for each specific item type. Figure 9.3 shows the Item List.

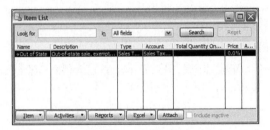

Figure 9.3: *The Item List.*

To add an item, follow these steps:

1. Open the Item List by going to the **Lists** menu and clicking **Item List**, or click the **Items & Services** icon on the Home page in the Company section.

2. Click the **Item** button at the bottom left of the list and click **New**. Figure 9.4 shows the Item menu.

3. Depending on the type of item, follow the steps in the appropriate sections that follow.

Note that not every business tracks inventory; Chapter 18 covers creating inventory part items.

Figure 9.4: *The Item Window menu.*

Adding Items for Services, Noninventory Parts, and Other Charges

The steps for adding service, noninventory parts, and other charge items are almost identical, so I'm lumping them together here.

To add a service, noninventory part, or other charge item, follow these steps:

1. Follow the steps in the preceding section to start adding an item.

2. In the New Item window, choose **Service**, **Noninventory Part**, or **Other Charge** from the Item Type menu.

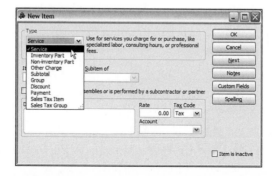

Figure 9.5: *The New Service Item window.*

3. Click in the Item Name/Number field and type a unique identifier for the item. When you create an invoice or purchase order, this is the name you will see as a choice on the line item menu.

4. (Optional) To make this item a subitem, click the **Subitem Of** check box to put a check mark in it, and then choose the parent item. For example, a home stager might use two different cleaning services—one for cleaning rugs and the other for repairing and cleaning furniture. Both of those could be subitems of Cleaning.

5. (Optional) If you purchase this noninventory part item from a vendor and the vendor has a part number, click in the Manufacturer's Part Number field and type the number. This is useful when writing a purchase order for the item because the vendor will know exactly what you want to order.

6. For now, ignore the This <Item> Is Used in Assemblies or Is Performed by a Subcontractor or Partner check box. (That's explained later in this section.)

7. Click in the Description field and type the description you want to appear on the form for the item.

8. In the Rate or Price field, type the rate for the service or price for the noninventory part.

9. From the Tax Code menu, choose whether this item is taxable. (You'll see the Tax Code menu only if you charge sales tax.)

10. From the Account menu, choose the income account to use to track the income from the sale of this item, or choose the expense account to use to track the purchase of this item.

11. Click **OK** to save the item, or click **Next** to save the item and create another one.

In some cases, you may want to use an item on both invoices and purchase orders. We're getting back to that check box we ignored earlier.

To use an item on both invoices and purchase orders, follow these steps:

1. Follow the preceding steps until step 6.

2. If you plan to use this item on both invoices and purchase orders, click in the **This <Item> Is Used in Assemblies or Is Performed by a Subcontractor or Partner** check box. This expands the New Item window to include

description, price, and account information for both purchases and sales. See Figure 9.6. (Note that assemblies are not available in QuickBooks Pro; Premier and Enterprise editions use assemblies.)

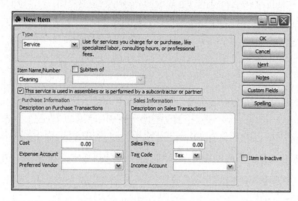

Figure 9.6: *The New Service Item window, with both purchase and sales information.*

For Purchase Information:

a. Click in the Description field for Purchase Information and type the description you want to appear for purchase transactions.

b. Click in the Cost field for Purchase Information and type the cost of the item, or leave it blank and fill in the cost on the purchase order (or when you enter the vendor's bill and pay with a check).

c. From the Expense Account menu, choose the expense account you want to post the cost to.

d. If you have a preferred vendor for this item, choose the vendor name.

For Sales Information:

a. Click in the **Description** field and type the description of this item you want to appear on invoices.

b. Click in the **Sales Price** field and type the hourly rate or flat fee you charge for this item. (You can change the rate, if needed, when you create an invoice, or you can leave the rate blank and type a rate when you create an invoice.)

    c. From the Tax Code menu, choose whether this item is taxable. (You'll see the Tax Code menu only if you charge sales tax.)

    d. From the Income Account menu, choose the income account to use to track the income from the sale of this item.

3. Click **OK** to save the item, or click **Next** to save the item and create another one.

Adding Other Items

To keep this guide from having more pages than *War and Peace*, I describe only the fields or information unique to each type of the remaining items.

Other Charge: In the **Amount or %** field, type a fixed amount (such as 5 for $5) or a percentage. You must include the percentage sign (as in 10%).

Subtotal: Give the item a name, such as *Subtotal*. Add it to an invoice. QuickBooks subtotals all the line items above it (or up to a previously entered subtotal). You must use a subtotal item if you want to apply a discount or other charge to several items on an invoice.

Group: Give the group a name and choose the items (up to 20) to include in the group and the quantity of each item (see Figure 9.7). Groups are handy for saving time (you choose the group on an invoice instead of each individual item) and keeping the invoice from becoming too cluttered for your customer. To print all the items in the group on an invoice and packing slip, click the **Print Items in Group** check box. Your customer will see all the items listed on the invoice. Leave the check box empty to print only the group name, not the individual items.

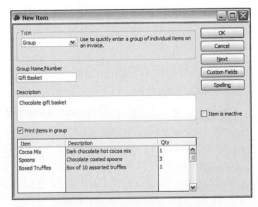

Figure 9.7: *The New Group Item window.*

Discount: You can create as many discount items as you need, but discounts can be used only on invoices, not purchase orders. Figure 9.8 shows the New Discount Item window. In the **Amount or %** field, type a positive, fixed amount (such as 5 for $5) or a percentage to be subtracted from the invoice. You must include the percent sign (such as 10%). Alternatively, if the amount of your discount varies, you can leave the Amount or % field blank, and enter the discount on the invoice or sales receipt directly. QuickBooks applies the discount to the line item directly above it. To apply the discount to several line items, create a subtotal first and then add the discount line item. Choose the income or expense account to post to. If you choose an income account, the discount amount shows up as negative income. If you choose an expense account, your expenses are increased. Either way, your profit ends up the same. In the Tax Code field, choose the option to tell QuickBooks to apply the discount before or after calculating sales tax. (Consult your accountant or local tax agency to see which method you should use.)

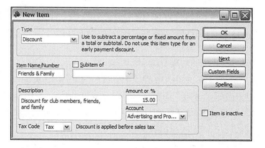

Figure 9.8: *The New Discount Item window.*

Payment: Use payments to record a partial payment that will be subtracted from the invoice total. Figure 9.9 shows the New Payment Item window. From the Payment Method menu, choose the payment method for this payment item. This way, you can group payments by payment method when you deposit the payments (all checks, all Visa, and so on). To do this, you need to create a payment item for each payment method. Next, click a button to indicate how you want QuickBooks to deposit the payment item: group with other undeposited funds (with this method, you record the deposits when you're ready using the Make Deposits window) or deposit to a specific account, such as checking. When you choose an account and you receive a customer payment, QuickBooks immediately creates a transaction in the selected account; you don't have to record the deposit manually by using the Make Deposits window. For example, if you create a Payment by Credit Card item, you can choose the account your credit card payments are normally deposited to.

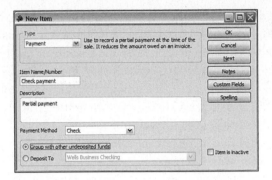

Figure 9.9: *The New Payment Item window.*

Editing Items

You can make changes to items you've set up. If you already used the item in a transaction, that transaction isn't affected. But the next transaction you make using the edited item will have the new changes.

To change an existing item, open the Item List and double-click the item you want to change. Make the changes and click **OK**. If a field (such as the Item Type) is gray, you can't change the item's type. An item's type can be changed only if the item is a Noninventory Part, an Other Charge item, or an Inventory Part.

If you change an item's price, it doesn't affect existing transactions that use that item.

For information on deleting or hiding items in a list, see Chapter 3.

The Least You Need to Know

- Items represent things you sell; services you sell; and things you purchase.
- Items also include things you use in the course of selling, such as shipping, and things you use to do calculations, such as sales tax, discounts, subtotals, and markups. Basically, you can't fill out a form without items.
- An item (except a Discount item) can be used on both invoices and purchase orders.
- Use subitems to divide a larger item category into smaller, related categories. This helps you track sales and purchases on reports in more detail.

Working with Other Lists

In This Chapter

- Setting up the Price Level list
- Getting the Currency list ready
- Understanding classes
- Getting started with the Fixed Asset Item list
- Setting up Profile lists

QuickBooks is built around lists, which help you enter data, keep accurate records, generate detailed reports, and quickly fill out forms. Previous chapters talked about the Customer List, Vendor List, Items List, and Chart of Accounts List. This chapter covers all the other types of lists; some you may never need to use, but they're available if and when you need them.

Setting Up the Price Level List

Price levels make it easy to apply different rates on sales receipts and invoices so that you don't have to manually figure out the percentage increase or decrease. On a sales receipt, invoice, or credit memo, you can apply price levels to service, inventory, and noninventory part items. You must turn on the Price Level feature in Preferences before setting up the list.

For each price level you create, you give it a name and set the percentage increase or decrease. You can create up to 100 price levels to use on sales forms. And although you could create a price level just for your mother, called Mom, you can potentially run out of price levels. In this case, it would work better to create a price level for a group of customers, such as Family or Preferred.

Price levels are different from discount items. Price levels are custom prices aimed at a group of customers or a particular customer or job. Discount items are used as needed on a customer's invoice or sales receipt (such as a discount for early payment or a discount for an annual sale). Customers can see the discount being applied but cannot see the price level name.

QUICKTIP

Customers don't see the price level name on the sales form. You might find it amusing to name the price level High Maintenance or Jerk Markup, but it's probably more practical to aim for clarity and politeness over amusement value.

To turn on the Price Level feature, follow these steps:

1. Go to the **Edit** menu and click **Preferences**.

2. In Preferences, click **Sales & Customers** in the left panel of the window and click the **Company Preferences** tab. (See Figure 10.1.)

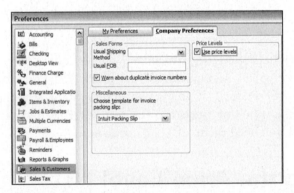

Figure 10.1: *The Company Preferences tab for Sales & Customers.*

3. Click the **Use Price Levels** check box to put a check mark in it.

4. Click **OK**.

To create price levels, follow this list:

1. Go to the **Lists** menu and click **Price Level List** (see Figure 10.2).

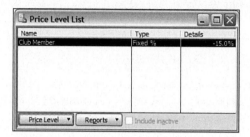

Figure 10.2: *The Price Level List window.*

2. At the bottom of the window, click **Price Level** and then click **New**. See Figure 10.3.

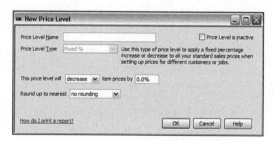

Figure 10.3: *The New Price Level window.*

3. Type a name for the price level. For example, you could call it Preferred or Wholesale, or you could include the percentage in the name, as with 10% Discount or 20% Markup.

4. The Price Level Type can be only a fixed percentage in QuickBooks Pro, so leave the type as is.

5. In the field **This Price Level Will**, choose **Decrease** if you want the price level to discount the price, or choose **Increase** if you want the price level to mark up the price.

6. In the percentage field, enter the percentage amount to use (for example, 15 or 10.5). Always enter the percentage as a positive number.

7. In the **Round Up to Nearest** field, choose the rounding method you want to use (see Figure 10.4). Sometimes the price level can cause the resulting amount to get funky, like with fractions of cents. Using rounding, you can round the amount to pennies, nickels, dimes, quarters, half-dollars, and dollars.

QUICKTIP

If you like prices to end in .99, choose **1.00 minus .01** so all the prices end in .99. Or if you want prices to end in 9, choose **.10 minus .01** and you get .19, .29, .39, and so on.

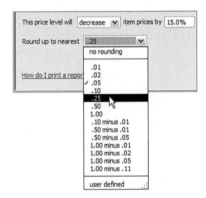

Figure 10.4: *The Rounding menu.*

8. Click **Next** to create another price level, or click **OK** if you're finished.

You assign a price level to a customer on the Additional Info tab of the customer record (see Figure 10.5).

Figure 10.5: *Assigning a price level to a customer.*

Setting Up the Currency List

If you deal with multiple currencies in your business, you can set up a list of currencies. You must turn on the Multiple Currencies feature in Preferences before you set up the list. Then you can choose which currencies to use. However, before you turn on multiple currencies, make a backup of your company file. Once you turn on multiple currencies, you can't turn it off.

To turn on multiple currencies, follow these steps:

1. Go to the **Edit** menu and click **Preferences**.

2. In Preferences, click **Multiple Currencies** in the left panel of the window and click the **Company Preferences** tab (see Figure 10.6).

3. Click the button next to Yes, I Use More Than One Currency.

4. Choose the currency you want to use by default (the "home" currency).

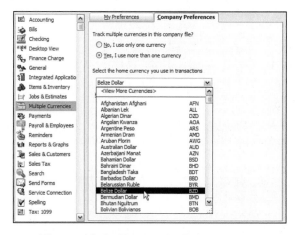

Figure 10.6: *Choosing the "home" currency.*

5. Click **OK**.

QuickBooks closes the company file and reopens it to add the currency features. Then you can assign a specific currency to bank accounts, customers, and vendors. When you create a transaction for the account, customer, or vendor, QuickBooks uses the currency you've assigned.

To open the currency list, follow these steps:

1. Go to the **Lists** menu and click **Currency List**.

2. Activate the currencies you'll need so they'll appear in lists: click the currency once, and then click the **Currency** menu button and choose **Make Currency Active** (see Figure 10.7).

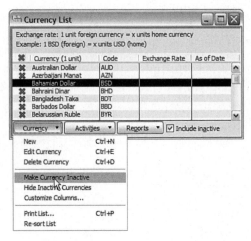

Figure 10.7: *The Currency list.*

You can assign a currency to a customer, vendor, or bank account by opening the customer or vendor record and choosing the currency to use (see Figure 10.8).

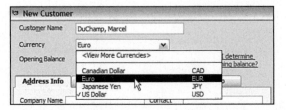

Figure 10.8: *Assigning a currency to a customer.*

Setting Up Classes

Classes let you classify your transactions by segment of your business (for example, by department, location, or service or product lines). Then you can track the segment's income and expenses. For example, imagine that a business builds outdoor pizza ovens, sells pizza-baking tools, and gives private pizza-cooking lessons. This business could use classes (Oven Construction, Pizza Tools, and Lessons) to keep track of trends and identify which segment of the business is the most profitable.

Using classes is a totally optional feature, and you may decide that you don't need the level of detail they can provide. You must turn on Use Class Tracking option in Preferences before you set up classes.

To turn on class tracking, follow these steps:

1. Go to the **Edit** menu and click **Preferences**.

2. In Preferences, click **Accounting** in the left panel of the window and click the **Company Preferences** tab.

3. Click the **Use Class Tracking** check box to put a check mark in it.

4. To make sure you use classes consistently, click the **Prompt to Assign Classes** check box. When you try to save a transaction without a class assigned, QuickBooks warns you.

5. Click **OK**.

To create classes, follow these steps:

1. Go to the **Lists** menu and click **Class List**.

2. From the Class menu button, click **New**.

3. Type a name for the class.

4. To make this class a subclass, click the **Subclass Of** check box and then choose the parent class.

5. Click **OK** to save the new class, or click **Next** to save the class and add another one.

You assign a class when you create a transaction (see Figure 10.9).

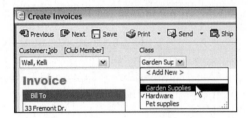

Figure 10.9: *Assigning a class to a transaction.*

Setting Up the Fixed Asset List

Fixed assets are things like vehicles, equipment, and furniture that you use for your business. You keep a list of these items so you can track *depreciation*, the initial cost to purchase the item, the cost of repairs or upgrades, and the loss or gain if you ever sell it. Tracking the cost of fixed assets affects the worth of your business and the size of your tax bill.

> **DEFINITION**
>
> **Depreciation** is used to expense the price of a fixed asset over time (not just the year it was purchased), since fixed assets generally have long-term value when operating a business.

To add a fixed asset, follow these steps:

1. Go to the **Lists** menu and click **Fixed Asset Item List**.

2. From the Item menu button, click **New**. Figure 10.10 shows the New Fixed Asset window.

3. In the Asset Name/Number field, type an identifier for this asset. This name will appear on reports, so give it a name that will distinguish it from other fixed assets.

4. Choose the asset account for this fixed asset. (Each fixed asset can have its own account.) If you haven't yet set up an account for this fixed asset, choose **<Add New>**.

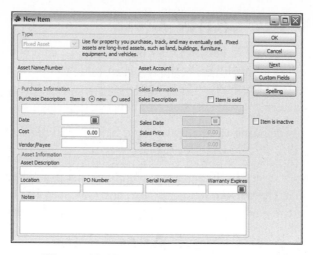

Figure 10.10: *The New Fixed Asset window.*

5. Type a description of this purchase and indicate whether the item is new or used.

6. In the Date field, enter date you purchased this fixed asset, or choose the date from the calendar.

7. In the Cost field, type the purchase price of the asset.

8. In the Vendor/Payee field, type a description of the vendor or person you purchased the item from.

9. In the Asset Description field, describe the asset.

10. In the Location field, type the location where this asset was placed into service; if the item is real estate, type the address.

11. In the PO Number field, type the purchase order number you used to purchase the item, if applicable.

12. In the Serial Number field, type the serial number of the asset.

13. In the Warranty Expires field, enter a date or choose the date from the calendar.

14. Enter any optional notes.

15. Leave the sales information blank until you actually sell the fixed asset.

16. Click **OK** to save the fixed asset, or click **Next** to save the fixed asset and add another one.

Setting Up the Other Lists

You can set up several other lists in QuickBooks to make data entry faster and easier. Adding to these lists basically works the same, so I don't want to waste your time tediously going through each list. In the following sections, I briefly describe each list so that you can determine whether you can benefit from setting it up.

Some of the lists, including the Items List and Sales Tax Items List, also are covered in other chapters.

All these lists work basically the same way: open the list from the **Lists** menu, click the menu button at the bottom left of the list, and choose **New**. Fill in the fields and click **OK** to save the new item, or click **Next** to add another item of the same type.

The Other Names List

The Other Names List stores people or companies that are not a customer, vendor, or employee, even though you write checks for them. When you add them to the Other Names List, they appear as a selection in the Name field on checks. For example, you could add business partners or co-owners to the Other Names List.

The Customer & Vendor Profile Lists

The Profile Lists are all lists related to customers and vendors, such as customer type or sales rep. You open these lists the same way: go to the **Lists** menu, go to **Customer & Vendor Profile Lists**, and then click the list you want. The purpose of each list is as follows:

Sales Rep List: Stores your sales reps so that you can associate the rep with a particular sale. This way, you can track their income. On sales forms, you can choose a sales rep from the Rep menu.

Customer Type List: Provides a way to categorize your customers, such as by their location, how they heard about you, or their type of business. You can generate reports by customer type to view the income you've received by type.

Vendor Type List: Provides a way to categorize your vendors, such as by consultants, service providers, or suppliers. You can generate reports to see expenses by vendor type.

Job Type List: Provides a way to classify your jobs. A graphic designer might classify jobs by web design, brochures, logos, business cards, and annual reports.

Terms List: Provides both customer and vendor payment terms. QuickBooks already has several common payment terms for you, such as Net 15. You can use these terms on an invoice, a purchase order, or a vendor bill.

Customer Message List: Provides common messages you might want to use on a customer invoice in the Customer Message area. Examples include "Thank you for your business" and "We appreciate your prompt payment."

Payment Method List: Stores a list of payment methods you can use on customer invoices or sales receipts. QuickBooks provides a bunch of common payment types already in the list.

Ship Via List: Stores the shipping methods you use in the Via field on invoices. QuickBooks already supplies several common shipping methods in the list. Note that you can set a default shipping method (which appears automatically on invoices, but you can change it) in Sales & Customers Preferences.

Vehicle List: Keeps a list of vehicles you set up for use in your business, which is useful for tracking mileage. Chapter 25 covers tracking mileage.

Memorized Transaction List: This is a list of transactions that you frequently enter—for example, a monthly utility bill—and that you've asked QuickBooks to save as templates (called "memorizing") for future use.. You add to the list by creating an invoice, bill, check, purchase order, and more, and then choosing **Memorize** from the Edit menu. This is useful for recurring transactions.

The Least You Need to Know

- Lists help you enter data, keep accurate records, and generate detailed reports. You use lists throughout QuickBooks to help you quickly fill out forms.

- You don't have to set up all your lists at once. Throughout QuickBooks, you can add something on the fly by choosing **<Add New>** from menus where it appears.

- Classes let you classify your transactions by segment of your business (for example, by department, location, or service or product lines). Then you can track the segment's income and expenses.

- Using most lists is optional: if you don't use classes, you don't need a Class List; if you don't use price levels, you don't need a Price Level List.

Entering Balances and Historical Transactions

In This Chapter

- Entering beginning balances for assets and liabilities
- Entering outstanding invoices to get customer opening balances
- Entering outstanding bills to get vendor opening balances
- Re-creating historical transactions from your start date to today

You're almost there! Now that you have your customers, vendors, items, lists, and accounts set up, you can complete QuickBooks setup by entering beginning balances of your accounts and historical transactions. As daunting as this sounds, you need to do it so your QuickBooks accounts provide an accurate picture of your business finances. If you don't do it, your balances will be incorrect and incomplete, and the reports you generate will be useless. So stick around, grab an espresso, and find out how to enter the opening balances and historical transactions.

If your business is brand-new and your QuickBooks start date is today, lucky you! You don't need to enter historical transactions. But you do need to enter a few opening balances, like the money in your checking account and owner's equity account.

What This Chapter Is All About

This chapter aims to get you off to a good start with your QuickBooks data. You need to establish the opening balances for your assets, liabilities, and customer and vendor balances. These are the balances *before* your QuickBooks start date. So if your QuickBooks start date is the beginning of your fiscal year (for example, 1/1/2012), your opening balances should reflect the balances on 12/31/2011.

If today is your QuickBooks start date and you've established your opening balances, you're all set to start entering day-to-day transactions. You'll probably enter an opening balance in the checking account as a deposit and enter balances in other equity accounts (such as Owner's Equity).

If today is not your QuickBooks start date, you need to add historical transactions that took place between your start date and today.

This chapter is divided into two sections: entering your opening balances and entering historical transactions.

NUMBERS HAPPEN

If this all seems an insurmountable task, contact your accountant for help. Your accountant will likely be happy to keep you from getting into any messes you'll need to fix later!

About the Opening Trial Balance

An opening trial balance is a report that shows you the balances of all your accounts; those balances are either credits or debits. If you can, get the opening trial balance report from your accountant as of the start date of your QuickBooks file. This will help you enter opening balances. If you can't get an opening trial balance, you can try to come up with the amounts by digging through your paperwork or checking last year's tax return.

Entering Opening Balances

You need to enter opening balances for all your balance sheet accounts *except* Accounts Receivable, Accounts Payable, bank accounts, Inventory, and Sales Tax Payable. Balance sheet accounts that need opening balances include fixed assets, such as buildings, trucks, furniture (and their depreciation); and liabilities, such as mortgages and loans.

Before Entering Opening Balances

Gather this information for entering opening balances:

- Find the balances for all your assets, including fixed assets (the current value and the depreciation). You can get these balances through your accountant for the opening trial balance or from prior tax returns.

- Find the balances for all your liabilities, including mortgages and loans.

- Reconcile all your bank accounts as of the end of your prior fiscal year. You need the reconciled balance, not the balance currently shown in your check register.

- Make a list of all deposits and withdrawals that did not clear prior to the end of your fiscal year.

- Gather up and enter all the unpaid invoices/statement charges you have not collected from your customers. These invoices/statement charges must be dated *before* your start date. You'll enter these unpaid invoices to get your accounts receivable opening balance.

- Gather up any unpaid bills you owe to vendors dated *before* your start date. You'll enter these unpaid bills to get your accounts payable opening balance.

- If you track inventory, you need the inventory count from your previous year-end close.

- If you collect sales tax, you need the sales tax due amount from the opening trial balance report.

- If you do payroll, you need names of your employees and all their information, including deductions and salary.

After you enter your opening balances, you can enter any historical transactions from your QuickBooks start date to today.

Entering these balances assumes you've already created the relevant accounts (which you did if you diligently followed the instructions in Chapter 8). But if you didn't, you can just add the accounts on the fly. You enter the balance from the opening trial balance by creating a *journal entry* in what's called a *general journal*.

DEFINITION

A **general journal** lists transactions in chronological order. A **journal entry** represents either the credit side of a transaction or the debit side in the general journal. The credit and debit must balance out to zero.

Making Journal Entries for Opening Balances

You use journal entries to assign the opening balances for your fixed assets (furniture, equipment, vehicles), depreciation, and loans (mortgage or other loans). The date to use for these journal entries is the closing date of your prior fiscal year.

Now's a good time to explain what the *Opening Balance Equity account* is. QuickBooks creates this account for your use when making journal entries for opening balances. For every opening balance credit or debit you enter, you need to create an offsetting debit or credit. But which offsetting account should you use? That's where the Opening Balance Equity account comes in. It temporarily stores the credit (or debit) side of a transaction without your having to know which account should be the offsetting account. After entering your opening balances, you'll "zero out" this account by transferring the amounts to your Retained Earnings account.

DEFINITION

QuickBooks creates an **Opening Balance Equity account** for you to use when setting up opening balances so you can offset any debits and credits.

To make a journal entry, follow these steps:

1. Go to the **Company** menu and click **Make General Journal Entries**. Figure 11.1 shows the General Journal window.

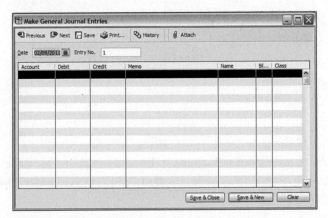

Figure 11.1: *The Make General Journal Entries window.*

2. Choose the closing date of your prior fiscal year.

3. Go through your trial balance report and enter the balances from the accounts to the lines in the general journal.

4. In the account column, choose the account (for example, Loan from Chuck).

5. In the Credit or Debit column, type the amount you find in the trial balance in either the credit or debit column (same as where the amount appears in the trial balance report). For example, if the trial balance shows a loan of $15,000 in the Credit column, enter the $15,000 in the credit column in the journal window.

6. In the Memo column, type something like "starting balance," to remind you and your accountant why you entered the amount.

7. To offset the amount of the entry, make another entry (remember, we're talking double-entry accounting here) to the Opening Balance Equity account (QuickBooks sets this up for you). Following the same example for the loan from Chuck, add a journal entry, choose the Opening Balance Equity account, and type $15,000 in the Debit column.

   When you click in the line below the first entry, QuickBooks assumes you're creating the offsetting entry, so it fills in the amount for you. Figure 11.2 shows how this entry would look.

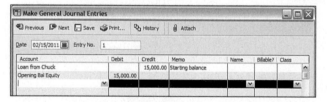

Figure 11.2: *Journal entry for a loan for both the credit side and the debit side.*

8. Repeat steps 3–7 for each entry in the opening trial balance report (except for Accounts Receivable, Accounts Payable, bank accounts, Inventory, Sales Tax Payable, and Retained Earnings). Examples of some of the entries you might need to add include fixed assets, depreciation, mortgages, and loans.

Entering Your Bank Account Opening Balance

Before entering any historical transactions, you need to enter a bank balance, using the bank register. If you haven't yet set up your bank account, follow these abbreviated steps. (Chapter 8 has more detail.)

To add a bank account, do this:

1. Go to the **Lists** menu and click **Chart of Accounts** (or press **Ctrl+A**).

2. Click the **Account** button and choose **New** (or press **Ctrl+N**).

3. From the Choose Account Type window, select **Bank** as the type of account you want to add, and click **Continue**.

4. Fill out the Add New Account window that appears. (Figure 8.7 shows the Add New Account window for a bank account.)

5. If you've turned on the Account Numbers feature, enter the number in the Number field. If you don't know what to enter, ask your accountant. (This is not the bank account number, but the number assigned to accounts in your Chart of Accounts.)

6. The only required field is the account name. Enter a name or click **Select from Examples** to choose from a list of suggested account names and descriptions.

7. (Optional) Type a description of the account.

8. Type the account number and routing number.

9. For now, ignore the Enter Opening Balance field. You'll be entering the opening balance soon.

10. Click **Save & Close**.

To enter the opening balance in the bank account you just created, first find your last bank statement as of your QuickBooks start date. Locate the ending balance as shown on the statement. This should be the reconciled balance, not the balance currently in your check register.

To enter the opening balance, follow these steps:

1. On the Home page, click **Check Register** (or go to the **Banking** menu and choose **Use Register**).

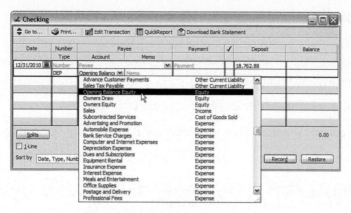

Figure 11.3: *Opening balance entry.*

2. For the date, choose the ending date of the statement.

3. Click in the deposit column and type the ending balance that appears on your statement.

4. Click in the **Account** field and choose where to post the offsetting balance (for example, the Opening Balance Equity Account). Figure 11.3 shows the opening transaction.

5. Click in the **Memo** field and type a reminder of where this amount came from, such as "Ending balance as of 12/31/2011 statement."

6. Click **Record** to save the entry.

7. Leave the register open. In the next section, you'll enter outstanding checks and deposits.

Entering Checks and Deposits from Before Your Start Date

In the bank account register, you'll start entering any outstanding checks and deposits that happened after reconciliation but *before* your QuickBooks start date. These transactions then will appear when you do the first account reconciliation in QuickBooks. These checks and deposits are not checks you've paid to your vendors or payments from your customers: you'll enter those transactions when you enter your historical transactions by creating invoices, receiving payments from the invoices, creating bills, and making payments on those bills.

Transactions to enter in the account register include these:

- Checks you wrote or deposits you made before your start date that haven't yet cleared. When entering the transactions, use the date of the original check or deposit, not today's date.

- Any bank fees or charges before your start date.

- Any interest paid before your start date.

Entering Outstanding Invoices or Statement Charges

To come up with the opening balance for your Accounts Receivable, you need to enter any outstanding invoices or statement charges from *before* your start date. You also need to enter any outstanding credit memos or refunds. When entering these transactions, use the date of the original transaction, not today's date.

Chapter 13 talks about how to create invoices and statement charges in more detail, but I'll give you a quick idea of what to do here.

For unpaid invoices, don't recreate the invoices exactly because that duplicates the sales information you'll enter later in your year-to-date income and expenses. Instead, for each sale, enter a lump sum for the total of the invoice without listing the individual items purchased. But before entering the invoices, you need to create an item to use on the invoice to enter the lump sum. Chapter 9 covers entering items, so I give you an abbreviated procedure here.

Open the Item List (see Chapter 9 for complete steps), click the **Item** button, and click **New**. Choose **Other Charge** as the item type. Type **Starting Balance** as the item name. Click to put a checkmark in the "This item is used in assemblies or is a reimbursable charge" check box, which basically tells QuickBooks to make this item available on both invoices and vendor bills. For both the Expense Account and Income Account, choose **Opening Balance Equity**. Choose **Non** as the Tax Code. Leave everything else blank.

Now you can enter the unpaid invoices. On the Home page, click **Create Invoices**. In the Create Invoices window, choose the customer and change the date and invoice number to match the date and number of the original invoice. Click in the **Item Code** field and choose the Starting Balance item you just created. Tab to or click in the **Amount** field, and type the total amount of the invoice, including any sales tax. Click **Save & New** to save the invoice and enter the next one.

For unpaid statement charges, on the Home page, click **Statement Charges**. (You'll need to have a customer set up before you can enter statement charges—Chapter 6 covered that, so you should be good to go here.) In the register, choose the customer and enter the details of the charges.

After you enter the unpaid invoices or statement charges, QuickBooks updates your customer opening balances.

Later in this chapter, you'll learn how to enter the invoices/statement charges that occurred between your start date and today. For now, you're just getting the *opening* accounts receivable balance.

Entering Outstanding Bills

To come up with the opening balance for your accounts payable, you'll need to enter any vendor bills you haven't yet paid from *before* your start date. You'll also need to enter any unapplied credits. When entering these transactions, use the date of the original transaction, not today's date.

Chapter 16 talks about how to enter bills in more detail, but I'll give you a quick idea of what to do here.

For unpaid bills, you follow the same steps you did with the invoices—enter the total of the bill, but not each individual expense. On the Home page, click **Enter Bills**. In the Enter Bills window, choose the vendor and change the date and reference number to match the date and number of the original bill. Click the **Items** tab, then click in the **Item Code** field and choose the **Starting Balance** item. Tab to or click in the **Amount** field, and type the total amount of the bill, including taxes. Click **Save & New** to save the bill and enter the next one.

After entering the unpaid bills, QuickBooks updates your vendor opening balances.

Later in this chapter, you'll learn how to enter the vendor bills that happened between your start date and today. For now, you're just getting the *opening* accounts payable balance.

Entering Opening Balances for Sales Tax Liability Accounts

If you collect sales tax, you may have a sales tax payable balance (what you owe as of your start date) to carry over into this year. Take the amount from the Sales Tax Payable line in your Opening Trial Balance report and make a journal entry as a credit. Create a debit and choose the Opening Balance Equity account.

After your start date, your sales tax is calculated on your invoices or sales receipts and adds the amounts into your Sales Tax Liability account.

Entering Year-to-Date Income and Expenses

At the beginning of a new fiscal year, your income and expense accounts have a zero balance. That's because any profits have been transferred to your Retained Earnings account. There are two ways to approach entering year-to-date income and expenses. The method you choose may depend on how far into your fiscal year you are. Talk with your accountant to see which is the best method for you.

If you've got only a few months of historical transactions to enter (this would be every invoice/statement charge, or every sales receipt and every bill, including the line items, that occurred between your QuickBooks start date and today), you can enter those transactions and have QuickBooks track your income and expenses as you create the transactions. If you want to do this, see the section "Entering Historical Transactions," later in this chapter.

The other method is to take the amounts from a fiscal year-to-date Trial Balance report and create a journal entry for each account. Have your accountant generate a Trial Balance report from the start of your fiscal year to your start date. This will give you the income and expense account balances you'll need to enter.

	Trial Balance		
Accrual Basis	As of May 31, 2012		
		Debit	Credit
Postage		35.00	
Repairs:Computer Repairs		0.00	
Repairs:Equipment Repairs		1,350.00	
Tools and Machinery		2,010.68	
Utilities:Gas and Electric		1,041.48	
Utilities:Telephone		841.15	
Utilities:Water		264.00	

Figure 11.4: *Opening Trial Balance report showing fiscal year-to-date expense account balances.*

To create a journal entry for income and expense balances, follow these steps:

1. Go to the **Company** menu and click **Make General Journal Entries**. Figure 11.1 shows the Make General Journal Entries window.

2. Choose the date shown in the Trial Balance report (today's date).

3. Go through the Trial Balance report and enter the balances from the accounts to the lines in the general journal.

4. In the account column, choose the account (for example, Repairs: Computer).

5. In the Credit (for income accounts) or Debit (for expense accounts) column, type the amount you find in the trial balance in either the credit or debit column. For example, if the trial balance shows a computer repair expense of $500 in the Debit column, enter the $500 in the debit column in the journal window.

6. In the Memo column, type something like "year-to-date total" to remind you and your accountant why you entered the amount.

7. To offset the amount of the entry, make another entry to the Opening Balance Equity account. So, to carry the same example for the computer repair, add a journal entry, choose the Opening Balance Equity account, and type $500 in the Credit column.

   When you click in the line below the first entry, QuickBooks assumes you're creating the offsetting entry and fills in the amount for you.

8. Repeat steps 3–7 for each income and expense account in the Trial Balance report.

Entering Inventory Opening Balances

If you track inventory and you have quantities on hand from the previous year, you need to enter the number of inventory items you have on hand as of your start date. Before you do so, make sure you've entered all your inventory part items and included a cost. Chapter 18 explains how to do this.

As part of your year-end closing last year, you probably took an inventory count. To get the inventory opening balances, you need to adjust your on-hand inventory quantities in QuickBooks to match the count you had at the end of last year.

To enter inventory opening balances, follow these steps:

1. Go to the **Vendors** menu, go to **Inventory Activities**, and click **Adjust Quantity/Value on Hand**. Figure 11.5 shows the Adjust Quantity/Value on Hand window.

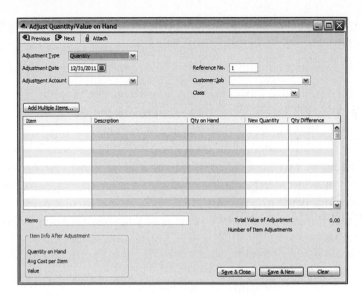

Figure 11.5: *Adjust Quantity/Value on Hand window.*

2. Make sure the Adjustment Type is Quantity, and choose the last day of your prior fiscal year.

3. For Adjustment Account, choose the Opening Balance Equity account, since you're establishing an opening balance for your inventory.

4. Click in the Item field and choose an inventory part item. QuickBooks enters the description and quantity on hand (if any).

5. In the New Quantity column, type the quantity you arrived at for this item during your inventory count. QuickBooks calculates the adjusted cost.

6. Continue adding items. Click **Save & Close** when done.

The Final Step for Opening Balances

As you entered the amounts from the Opening Trial Balance report and transactions prior to your start date, you selected the Opening Balance Equity account to offset the credits or debits. You'll need to "zero out" this account so that the account shows a zero balance for the start of your new fiscal year.

To zero out the Opening Balance Equity account, make a journal entry for the total amount in the account, using your QuickBooks start date, and make an offsetting entry in your Retained Earnings account.

Entering Historical Transactions

Does history repeat itself? Well, here you get to relive your sales and purchases.

If the start date you entered for your company is before today's date (for example, the beginning of your fiscal year, 1/1/2012), you need to enter your past (historical) transactions, beginning with that date (from 1/1/2012 to the current date). This ensures that your QuickBooks records will be completely up-to-date going forward from your start date and that your reports will reflect your business accurately.

Before Entering Historical Transactions

Gather the following before you enter historical transactions:

- Find all the invoices/statement charges made from your start date to today, and enter them into QuickBooks. You also need any credit memos you issued.

- Find all payments received from your customers on the invoices/statement charges from your start date to today, and enter them into QuickBooks. You also need to record those payments as a deposit.

- If you use sales receipts and receive payment at the time of the sale, you need the following between your start date and today: a record of what you sold and a record of the deposits made from those sales. You also need any refunds you issued.

- Find all the vendor bills from your start date to today and enter them into QuickBooks.

- Find all the payments you've made to vendor bills from your start date to today and enter them into QuickBooks.

- Enter any other checks you've written from your start date to today that aren't checks for vendor bills. When entering the checks, use the date of the original check, not today's date.

- Enter any other deposits you've made (other than payments you've received from customers) from your start date to today. When entering the deposits, use the date of the original deposit, not today's date.

QuickBooks has a preferred order for entering the transactions. If you work through the following sections in order, you'll be fine.

Entering Historical Invoices

Enter your existing invoices into QuickBooks in chronological order, starting with your QuickBooks start date.

For historical invoices (paid and unpaid), on the Home page, click **Create Invoices**. In the Create Invoices window, enter each invoice in chronological order from your start date using the date of the original transaction. Click **Save & New** to save the invoice and enter the next one.

Entering Historical Statement Charges

Enter your existing paid and unpaid statement charges into QuickBooks in chronological order, starting with your QuickBooks start date. On the Home page, click **Statement Charges**. In the register, choose the customer and enter the details of the charges using the date of the original transaction.

Entering Historical Sales Receipts

For historical sales receipts, on the Home page, click **Create Sales Receipts**. In the Create Sales Receipt window, enter what you sold and received payment for at the time of the sale. Enter each sale in chronological order from your start date using the date of the original transaction. Click **Save & New** to save the sales receipt and enter the next one.

BEHIND THE SCENES

After you enter the invoices, statement charges, or sales receipts, your customer balances will be up-to-date, you'll know which products and/or services you sold, and you'll know your current sales tax liabilities.

Entering Historical Credit Memos/Refunds

If you issued any credit memos or refunds on previous sales, on the Home page, click **Refunds & Credits**. In the Create Credit Memos/Refunds window, enter the customer, the items returned, and the quantities. Click **Save & New** to save the credit or refund and enter the next one.

Entering Historical Customer Payments

To record any payments received from customers from your start date to today, you must apply them to an outstanding invoice or statement (that's why you entered the invoices and statement charges first). On the Home page, click **Receive Payments**. In the Receive Payments window, record each payment received from a customer and select the invoice or statement charge to pay. The Date field should be the payment date.

Entering Historical Deposits from Customer Payments

You'll need to know which transactions make up a deposit total and the deposit date. On the Home page, click **Record Deposits**. In the Payments to Deposit window, click the customer payments that you deposited together on one date to select them. Click **OK**. In the Make Deposits window, be sure the Date field shows the deposit date. Click **Save & Close**. Repeat for each separate deposit you made on different days.

Entering Sales Tax Payments

If you made any sales tax payments from your start date to today, enter them in the Pay Sales Tax window (click **Manage Sales Tax** on the Home page and then click **Pay Sales Tax**). Choose the tax agency and the date you actually made the payment.

Entering Historical Vendor Bills

To enter vendor bills, click **Enter Bills** in the Vendor section of the Home page. In the Enter Bills window, enter each bill you've received since your start date, in the order you received them. If the bill included expenses, on the Expenses tab, assign the amounts to expense accounts. If the bill included items, click the **Items** tab, and enter the quantity and cost for items received. Click **Save & New** to save the bill and enter the next one.

To enter vendor credits, select **Credit** in the Enter Bills window. Enter the account to track the credit.

Entering Historical Vendor Payments

On the Home page, click **Pay Bills**. In the Pay Bills window, select the bills to pay and enter the amount for each payment made between your start date and today. Choose the date you made the payment and click **Pay Selected Bills**. Open the check register and change the check numbers to match.

> **QUICKTIP**
>
> Do not use the Write Checks window to pay vendor bills. Otherwise, the check will not be associated with a bill—the bill will remain outstanding and unpaid.

Entering Historical Checks and Deposits

If you wrote checks after your start date for items other than vendor bills (for example, to pay a credit card charge), enter those checks in the Write Checks window. On the Home page, click **Write Checks**. In the Write Checks window, enter any checks you wrote that were not for bills or payroll. You don't want to record duplicate transactions. Type the check number and click the To Be Printed checkbox to remove the check mark. Choose any relevant accounts (for example, for a loan payment or expense). Click **Save & New** to enter the next check.

To record deposits made between your start date and today, click **Record Deposits** on the Home page. If you see the Select Payments to Deposit window, click **Cancel**. In the Make Deposit window, record any deposits you made that were not from customer payments. Click **Save & New** or **Save & Close**.

To record bank fees or charges from your bank statements, open the check register (click **Check Register** on the Home page). Enter any fees and other charges using the date of the actual fee or charge.

Entering Historical Credit Card Charges and Payments

As with your bank accounts, you'll need to enter any credit card charges and payments made between your start date and today.

On the Home page, click **Enter Credit Card Charges**. Enter the charges and choose the appropriate expense accounts. In the Write Checks window, enter the check you used to pay the account. Be sure to choose the credit card account in the Account field of the check, not an expense account.

Enter any interest and other fees in the credit card account register.

Entering Historical Payroll

If you use payroll, you'll need to enter a summary for payroll amounts for this year to date. See Chapter 24 for details on setting up and using payroll, including using the Payroll Setup Wizard to enter payroll history.

Entering Purchase Orders and Estimates

If you use purchase orders and/or estimates, you can enter those even though they don't affect any balances. These are called *nonposting accounts*, but you might want to enter them as of today's date so you'll have a record of them.

DEFINITION

Nonposting accounts are accounts that don't affect income, expense, or balance sheet accounts. Estimates and purchase orders are nonposting accounts.

After Entering Historical Transactions

To make sure everything checks out correctly, reconcile your bank statements with the transactions entered into QuickBooks. You may also want to run a Trial Balance report as of your start date.

After entering your invoices and bills, check to make sure your Accounts Receivable and Accounts Payable balances in QuickBooks match the totals you had in your previous system. In QuickBooks, run the Open Invoices and Unpaid Bills reports to double-check you've entered everything correctly.

The Least You Need to Know

- Enter opening balances before your start date so your records are complete.
- Enter outstanding invoices or statements, to come up with customer opening balances.
- Enter outstanding bills to come up with vendor opening balances.
- Enter historical transactions to ensure that your accounts accurately reflect your profit and loss.

Money Coming In

This is where the fun begins. You're ready to start tracking sales and handling transactions. The chapters in this part show you how to create estimates, invoices, statements, and sales receipts. You also learn to record customer payments and handle overdue payments from customers.

Chapter 12 prepares you for your first sale by helping you determine which sales forms work best for your business and walking you through the process of generating those forms. Many businesses use estimates, and this chapter also explains how to use QuickBooks to create estimates.

Chapter 13 tells you what you need to know about invoicing customers, creating statements, and generating invoices based on an existing QuickBooks estimate.

Chapter 14 is all about the money; this chapter covers all the ways you receive payments from customers: invoice/statement payments, down payments, credit card sales, and cash sales.

Finally, Chapter 15 helps you deal with overdue payments and set up and apply finance charges.

Before Making Sales to Customers

In This Chapter

- Understanding sales forms and when to use them
- Preparing for your first sale
- Using estimates to bid on projects
- Making estimates active or inactive

Making sales to your customers should be your primary goal if you want to stay in business. To help you keep track of sales, QuickBooks uses a few different types of sales forms. This chapter covers how to choose the right form, as well as some preparations to make before you log your first sale. This chapter also describes how to create estimates, another useful sales tool.

Chapter 13 delves into how to bill a customer after you've made a sale. It also explains how to generate an invoice from an estimate. Chapter 14 discusses how to use a sales receipt.

Choosing a Sales Form

QuickBooks offers three types of forms you can use when making sales; the one you choose depends on how you run your business. The following sections describe each form and when to use it.

Sales Receipts

Use sales receipts when your customers pay you the full amount at the time of sale. Some business that use sales receipts include retail stores, espresso stands, spa service salons, and more. Basically, any business that doesn't need to track whether customers owe money uses sales receipts: the customers pay for the products or services at the time they receive them. See Chapter 14 for more information.

Statements

Use statements instead of invoices if you perform services for customers, say, in small time increments over a period of time, and you want to send one statement with the total they owe you instead of lots of separate invoices. For instance, a graphic designer who creates icon images for a software package—sometimes spending 10 minutes to tweak one image or several hours designing 10 images—would use statements. Another good use of statements is for dental and medical practices or club member-ships that charge monthly or quarterly, like a health club or a wine club. Keep in mind, though, that statements don't handle sales tax, percentage discounts, or subtotals. (Chapter 13 describes how to use statements.) You can also use reminder statements to periodically remind customers that they owe you money, along with any added finance charges. See Chapter 15 for more on reminder statements.

Invoices

Use invoices to track products and services you sell to customers. Invoices list the products or services you sold, the quantity, and price. Invoices can also record sales tax, discounts, markups, subtotals, and billable time and expenses. In addition, if you plan to use estimates, you can easily turn the estimates into invoices. As noted previously, Chapter 13 describes how to create and use invoices.

Before Your First Sale

Although they're not required, you should take a couple of actions in QuickBooks before you make your first sale. Make sure you've tweaked your chart of accounts; set up items for what you sell; set up your customer list, price level list, and other lists; and entered your starting trial balance. Also check the Jobs & Estimates, Sales Tax, and Sales & Customers preferences. In other words, take care of all the recommenda-tions we discussed in the previous chapters.

The next part of this chapter discusses using estimates. You can skip this material if your business doesn't use estimates.

About Estimates

Some businesses use estimates to give customers an idea of the costs prior to an actual sale. Estimates are sometimes referred to as bids, quotes, or proposals. The amounts you enter on an estimate don't post an entry into any of your accounts, but if your bid is accepted, you can easily turn the estimate into an invoice. If you need to invoice in stages instead of with the full estimate, you can use progress invoicing (see Chapter 13).

Setting Up Preferences for Estimates and Jobs

In Chapter 6, you learned about jobs and how to create them. Generally, estimates and jobs go hand-in-hand; often you give a customer a bid or estimate for a particular job. To use jobs and estimates, you need to tell QuickBooks in Preferences.

To turn on and activate estimates, follow these steps:

1. Go to the **Edit** menu and click **Preferences**.

2. In Preferences, click **Jobs & Estimates** in the left panel of the window and click the **Company Preferences** tab (see Figure 12.1).

Figure 12.1: *Jobs & Estimates preferences.*

3. In the five job status fields, change the text QuickBooks provides if you want to use different wording.

4. Click **Yes** for "Do You Create Estimates?" (unless QuickBooks has already turned on the estimates feature based on your answers when you set up your company file).

5. If you want to use progress invoicing against an estimate, click **Yes** for "Do You Do Progress Invoicing?"

6. Click **OK**.

Estimating Jobs

When bidding on a job for a customer, you can create an estimate to itemize the services and products involved in completing the job. QuickBooks reports on estimates can help you track the actual income and costs compared with your estimated income and costs. You can use this information to improve your accuracy on future estimates.

Writing Up an Estimate

Writing estimates doesn't affect your financial information. When you turn on the estimates feature, QuickBooks creates a *nonposting* account called Estimates to store the amounts in the estimate.

DEFINITION

Transactions posted to a **nonposting account** don't affect income, expense, or balance sheet accounts.

To write an estimate, follow these steps:

1. Go to the **Customers** menu and click **Create Estimates** (see Figure 12.2). (You can also click the **Estimates** icon in the Customer section of the Home page.)

2. Choose the customer and job from the **Customer:Job** menu.

3. In the line item area, start by adding items. From the Item menu, choose the first item and type a quantity into the Qty field. QuickBooks calculates the amount and total, as well as the markup. (QuickBooks calculates the markup based on what you pay for the item and how much you sell it for.)

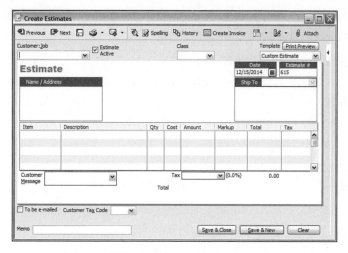

Figure 12.2: *The Create Estimates window.*

4. To change the markup, enter either a dollar amount or a percentage (including the % sign) in the Markup column. (The markup column doesn't appear on the estimate you give the customer. To see what the estimate would look like, click the arrow next to the Printer icon at the top of the window and click **Preview.**)

5. If you use class tracking, choose the class. When you create an invoice based on this estimate, the class also appears on the invoice.

6. Continue adding items as needed and type in an optional customer message. You might want to add a message that gives the terms of the estimate, like "Pricing good for 30 days from the date of the estimate."

7. Click the **To Be E-mailed** check box to e-mail it to the customer at a later time. To print the estimate, click the **Printer** icon at the top of the window.

8. Click **Save & Close** or **Save & New**.

Writing More Than One Estimate for a Job

You may need to write more than one estimate for a job. This can be useful for estimating each phase of a job or for creating a second estimate for a customer if the first estimate was rejected as too high.

You can create multiple estimates in a couple of ways:

- Simply follow the preceding steps to create a new estimate and assign it to the same Customer and Job.

- With the estimate you want to copy opened, go to the **Edit** menu and click **Duplicate Estimate**. QuickBooks gives the estimate a different number. Make your changes and click **Save & Close**.

Memorizing Estimates in QuickBooks

If you find that you create similar estimates for different customers, you can create a boilerplate estimate. Creating a boilerplate lets you create a new estimate quickly and helps ensure that you don't leave out any items.

To create an estimate to memorize, follow these steps:

1. Go to the **Customers** menu and click **Create Estimates**. (You can also click the **Estimates** icon in the Customer section of the Home page.)

2. Enter the fields and line items that you want to memorize, leaving the Qty field empty.

3. Go to the **Edit** menu and click **Memorize Estimate**. QuickBooks tells you that it doesn't memorize the customer or job information, so you can change it when you recall the estimate.

4. Click **OK** to confirm that you want to memorize the estimate.

5. Type a name for the estimate that describes what the bid is for and click the **Don't Remind Me** button. (Since you will recall the memorized estimate only when you need it for a similar bid, you don't need QuickBooks to remind you.)

6. Click **OK**.

To open a memorized estimate, follow these steps:

1. Go to the **Lists** menu and click **Memorized Transaction List** (see Figure 12.3).

2. In the list, double-click the memorized estimate you want to open.

3. Choose the customer.

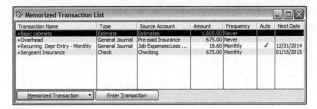

Figure 12.3: *The Memorized Transaction List window.*

4. Enter the quantities and any other changes.

5. Click Save & Close.

6. Click **Yes** to record the changes.

QuickBooks saves the new estimate you created from the memorized estimate but doesn't change the memorized estimate.

For information on generating invoices from estimates and to do progress invoicing based on estimates, see Chapter 13.

Making an Estimate Inactive

If you've created several bids on a job for a customer, you may end up with several rejected estimates. You probably don't want those rejected estimates cluttering up the list of estimates (Figure 12.4 shows the list of estimates). Instead of deleting them, you can make them inactive. This removes them from the list but keeps them around, in case you want to refer to them later. QuickBooks doesn't use any inactive estimates in reports.

To make an estimate inactive, follow these steps:

1. Click **Customer Center** in the navigation bar to open the Customer Center.

2. Click the **Transactions** tab.

3. Click **Estimates**.

4. Double-click the estimate you want to make inactive.

5. On the estimate form, click the **Estimate Active** check box to remove the check mark. (Alternatively, if you don't care about keeping the estimate, you can choose **Delete Estimate** from the Edit menu.)

6. Click **Save & Close**.

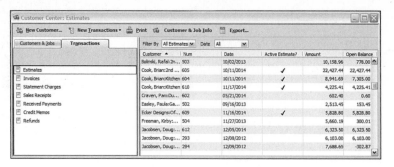

Figure 12.4: *The List of Estimate Transactions.*

The Least You Need to Know

- QuickBooks offers three types of forms you can use when making sales; the one you choose depends on how you run your business.

- Use sales receipts when your customers pay you the full amount at the time of sale.

- Use invoices to track products and services you sell to customers. Invoices list the products or services you sold, the quantity, and the price.

- Use statements instead of invoices if you perform services for customers and you want to send one statement with the total they owe you instead of lots of separate invoices.

- Use estimates to give customers an idea of the costs before they hire you or buy products. Sometimes estimates are referred to as bids, quotes, or proposals. Not all businesses use estimates.

Invoicing Customers

In This Chapter

- Creating invoices
- Applying price levels to line items
- Adding subtotals, discounts, and payments to invoices
- Generating an invoice from an estimate
- Creating credit memos and issuing refunds
- Generating statements

Do you want to get paid? Do you want to be able to track what your customers owe you? I suspect you do, although one business I deal with is rather lackadaisical. I live in the boonies and I'm on a propane tank. The guy comes to fill the tank on an irregular basis, so I never know when he stops by. He fills the tank if needed and leaves a tiny yellow receipt smashed between two slats in the gate leading to the tank. Now, if I don't see it for a few days, it gets damp and soggy and unreadable. At first, I waited for an invoice or billing statement from them. Never got one. I have to call them periodically to see how much I owe and I write them a check. How many of their customers fail to call them? Do they ever have to pay? Am I being stupid? Obviously, they could use some help in this area.

About Invoices and Statement Charges

Invoices list the products or services you sell to a customer, the quantity, and the price. Not all businesses use invoices. Consultants, gardening and landscaping services, online shop owners, mail order companies, and cabinet makers are among many of the businesses that do use them. Generally, these businesses need to track how much their customers owe.

Other businesses, such as accountants and lawyers, who provide hourly services, use statement charges instead of invoices. You enter charges as you perform the service for a customer. For example, if you work an hour one day and 15 minutes another day, each of those would be a statement charge. When you're ready to receive a payment, you send the customer a statement of the accumulated charges. Businesses that charge a monthly fee, such as health clubs or memberships, also use statement charges.

Retail businesses, manicure salons, and restaurants, on the other hand, don't usually use invoices or statement charges because they receive payments at the time of the sale. These types of businesses generally use sales receipts, which are covered in Chapter 14.

Choose the form that works best for your business. Can't decide? If you need to collect sales tax, record advance payments, give discounts, apply markups, provide subtotals, or include a customer message, use invoices instead of statement charges. Also, if you plan to use estimates, you can easily turn the estimates into invoices.

This chapter covers both invoices and statement charges.

Choosing an Invoice Type

QuickBooks offers several types of invoice templates you can use to record sales. Which one you choose depends on how you run your business. Figure 13.1 shows the list of templates that QuickBooks supplies (the templates you see in the menu may vary, depending on Preferences you've set).

Figure 13.1: *Invoice Template menu.*

The following table describes the standard invoice forms. All types of invoices provide fields for date, invoice number, customer name, item name, description, quantity, rate or price, amount, and tax. Other differences are noted in the table.

It might help you to see the actual invoice types on the screen and then view the descriptions in the table.

To view the invoice forms on the screen, in QuickBooks, click **Create Invoices** on the Home page. In the menu that appears below Template in the upper-right corner, choose the invoice type you want to view. Depending on how you answered some questions when you set up your company file, the invoice types you see in the menu may vary.

Invoice Template Type	Description
Product	Designed for selling products. Includes fields for your products and their descriptions, and provides address and shipping information. Also includes fields for a purchase order number, payment terms, sales rep, shipping date, shipping method, and F.O.B. (F.O.B. is defined later in this chapter.)
Professional	Designed for businesses that sell professional services, such as public relations firms. Includes lots of room for service descriptions and a payment terms field.
Service	Designed for businesses that sell primarily services but also some products, such as an interior design company. Includes fields for a purchase order number and payment terms.
Packing Slip	Include in the shipment to a customer when a product is being shipped. Includes a list of items purchased, as well as fields labeled P.O. Number, Ship Date, Ship Via, and F.O.B.
Progress Invoice	Appears if you indicated in Jobs & Estimates preferences that you do progress invoicing. Includes fields labeled Estimate Amount, Prior Amount, and Total %.
Finance Charge	Appears if you entered a finance charge option in Finance Charge, Company preferences. Includes a field labeled Payment Terms.

Anatomy of an Invoice

The product invoice has the most fields; other invoices are subsets of this. In the examples that follow, I use the product invoice. All invoices in QuickBooks have the same basic anatomy: the invoice header section at the top, the line item area in the middle, and the footer section at the bottom. Figure 13.2 shows the parts of an invoice.

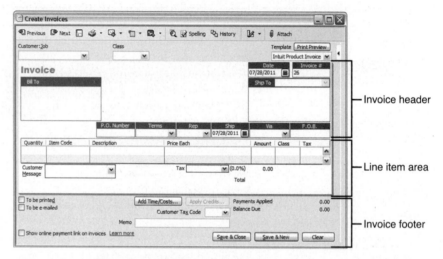

Figure 13.2: *Product invoice parts.*

The invoice header holds customer information; the date and number of the invoice; and fields such as purchase order number, terms, and shipping information.

In the line item area, you list the products or services you're selling to the customer. This is also where you apply discounts, subtotals, markups, and taxes. You can add a message to the customer here, too.

In the invoice footer area, you can indicate whether to print or e-mail the invoice, write a memo for yourself, and see information from QuickBooks on any payments that have been applied and the amount due.

QUICKTIP

QuickBooks invoices also have a History panel that shows transactions with the selected customer and includes the balance due (see Figure 13.3).

Creating an Invoice

Because filling out an invoice involves many steps, I've broken down the steps into smaller chunks. You'll start by opening the invoice form. Then you'll fill out the invoice header, line item area, and invoice footer.

To open the invoice form, follow these steps:

1. Open the invoice form using one of these methods: go to the Customers menu and click **Create Invoices**, click the **Create Invoices** icon on the Home page, or press **Ctrl-I**.

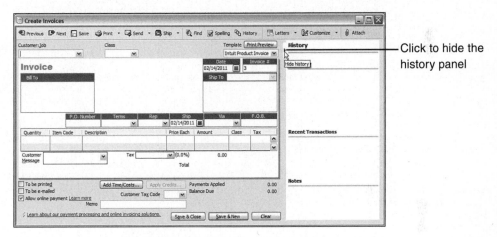

Click to hide the history panel

Figure 13.3: *The Create Invoices window.*

2. Follow the steps in the next section to fill out the invoice.

Filling Out the Invoice Header

If you've done the work of setting up your customers, QuickBooks makes filling out the invoice header a very quick and easy task. Some of the fields described here may not appear on your invoice form. The fields that do appear depend on some of the preferences you've set up, as well as the invoice template you're using. For example, if you indicated in preferences that you don't use purchase orders, the P.O. Number field doesn't appear.

To fill out the invoice header, follow these steps:

1. Choose the **invoice template** from the Template menu. The product template contains the most fields, so I'm showing the product invoice in these steps.

2. Click the arrow to the right of the Customer:Job field and choose the customer (or customer and job, if you've set up jobs) for the invoice you're creating. Or click **<Add New>** at the top of the menu to add a new customer or job. See Chapter 6 for how to add customers and jobs.

   After you choose a customer, QuickBooks shows you a summary of the transactions, including the current balance, associated with this customer in the History panel (see Figure 13.4).

Figure 13.4: *The History panel shows prior transactions and balance due.*

3. If you turned on class tracking in Accounting preferences, choose the class from the Class menu.

4. Check the date in the Date field (which is set to the current date), and change it if you need to.

5. If this is the first invoice you've created, type the invoice number you want to use in the Invoice # field. QuickBooks automatically increases the number by 1 in subsequent invoices. (By the way, you can set a preference in Sales & Customers Preferences to warn you if you enter a duplicate invoice number.)

6. QuickBooks takes the address information from the customer record to fill out the Bill To and Ship To addresses. To change the Ship To address, choose another one from the Ship To menu or click **<Add New>**.

7. If you have a purchase order number for this transaction, enter the number in the P.O. Number field.

8. To change the payment terms (taken from the customer's record), choose the terms. If you didn't assign payment terms when you added the customer, you can choose terms here. Or choose **<Add New>** to add a new term.

9. From the Rep field, choose the salesperson associated with this customer, if any. Or choose **<Add New>** to add one.

10. Check the date that appears in the Ship field and, if necessary, change it to the date you will actually ship the item.

11. From the Via menu, choose the shipping method or choose **<Add New>**.

12. In the *F.O.B.* field, type the location information (using up to 13 characters) in this field.

DEFINITION

F.O.B. is the location the order is shipped from and the point at which the package becomes the customer's responsibility. It stands for *Free on Board* but is also commonly referred to as *Freight on Board*.

Entering Line Items

The line item area is where you enter a description of what the customer is purchasing. I describe the fields as they appear on the product invoice template. If you're using a different template, the order and names of the fields may differ. The line item area is also where you apply discounts and payments, adjust price levels (if you use them), and enter a subtotal. Each of these is described in the following sections.

To enter line items, follow these steps:

1. In the Quantity field, type the number of the item the customer is buying (if you're selling your services, type the number of units of time, such as hours or days). (For subtotals, discounts, and sales tax, you do not type in a quantity.)

2. Click in the **Item Code** field, and then click the down arrow that appears to choose the item from your list. Or you can start typing in the item field, and QuickBooks suggests the item code based on the characters. Press **Tab** and QuickBooks fills in the description and price (or rate). You can edit these field, if you want.

   QuickBooks also calculates the total and tax (if the item and customer are taxable).

3. Continue adding line items. The following sections describe how to apply price levels, discounts, and payments, and how to add a subtotal item.

Applying Price Levels

My friend Chuck is a financial planner. He complained to me that friends and family members expect him to provide free financial advice. Sadly, I was hoping for a bit of free advice myself, but instead I told him about price levels. Now he can avoid looking like a jerk when he declines their requests. By saying, "Well, I can offer you my 'friends and family' discount," he can be a hero and still get paid.

With price levels, QuickBooks lets you charge different prices for different customers. Each time you create an invoice, sales receipt, or credit memo for a particular customer, QuickBooks uses the price level associated with that customer to calculate the price for services, inventory, and noninventory items.

Chuck can set up discounts and markups as price levels and then assign them to customers. Price levels adjust the amounts on an invoice up or down, based on a percentage. He can assign his best friends to the deeply discounted "BFF" price level and give his barely tolerable cousin a smaller discount. As for his cranky, high-maintenance aunt, he can assign her a price level that marks up the price, to make up for her crotchety ways.

On a sales receipt, invoice, or credit memo, you can apply price levels to service, inventory, and noninventory part items. If you've already assigned a price level to a customer (see Chapter 10), QuickBooks applies the price level automatically.

But you can also change the price level for each item on the invoice. After entering the item, click the arrow to the right of the Price Each (or Rate) field and choose the price level to use. Figure 13.5 shows the Price Level menu.

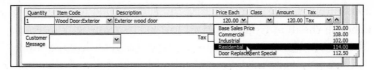

Figure 13.5: *Applying a price level to an item.*

Adding a Subtotal

A subtotal item adds all the line items above it, up to a previously entered subtotal, if any. Subtotals are useful for applying a discount to one or more items. For example, an interior designer provides both services and products. He could enter the services first and then add a subtotal. He then could enter the products sold and add a subtotal after those items. This way, he can give a discount to the products only, not the services.

To add a subtotal, enter all the items you want to include in the subtotal and then add the subtotal item.

See the next section for how to apply a discount.

Applying Discounts

You can change the total amount due on an invoice by giving a discount to the customer and applying a payment the customer has already made.

Before you can add a discount line item, you must set it up in your item list (see Chapter 9). In the line item area, you add a discount item, just like when adding a product or service item.

 QUICKTIP

Price level or discount? Use a price level to adjust the price for a group of customers automatically; use a discount to adjust the price one time. If you want your customer to see how generous you are, show the price break as a discount.

To add a discount item, first enter the item you want to discount and then enter the discount item. If you want to discount more than one item, enter all the items, then enter a subtotal before applying the discount. QuickBooks applies the discount to the item or items above it in the line item area, up to a previous subtotal.

You can create more than one discount item, such as one for 10 percent and another for 15 percent. You can apply both on an invoice by using subtotals. Subtotal the items for the 10 percent discount and use the 10 percent discount item. Add the items you want to give a 15 percent discount to, add a subtotal, and then add the 15 percent discount item. For any items you don't want to discount, enter those below the last discount item.

Applying Payments

Sometimes a customer may make a down payment or partial payment for a purchase. On the invoice, you need to account for that payment. To do this, you first create a payment item (see Chapter 9). A payment item reduces the amount due on the invoice.

To enter a payment item on an invoice, click in the item field and choose **Payment** (or whatever you called the payment item you set up). In the Amount field, type how much the payment was. QuickBooks subtracts the payment from the invoice total. When you add a payment on the invoice, the payment is automatically recorded and put in the Make Deposits window, so you don't have to receive the payment again.

QUICKTIP

If a customer pays you the full amount at the time of sale, use a sales receipt instead of a payment item on an invoice.

Inserting and Deleting Line Items

You can easily insert a line item between two other items. You might do this if you want to create a subtotal for the services you provided, but you forgot to add it before adding the products the customer purchased.

To insert a line item, right-click in the line below where you want to add a new line. Choose **Insert Line** from the menu. QuickBooks inserts the new line above the line you clicked in.

To delete a line item, right-click in the line you want to delete. Choose **Delete Line** from the menu.

Filling Out the Invoice Footer

QuickBooks keeps a running total, along with taxes, in the footer area. You can also add a message to the customer. QuickBooks supplies a few "canned" messages, such as "We appreciate your business," in the Customer Message List (see Chapter 10).

Figure 13.6: *Adding a customer message.*

Click the arrow to the right of the Customer Message text box and choose a canned message, or choose **<Add New>** to add a new message (see Figure 13.6). You can also just start typing in the text box; QuickBooks will ask you if you want to add it to the Customer Message List.

Also in the invoice footer, you indicate whether the invoice should be e-mailed or printed. Click the appropriate check box to put a check mark in it. (There's also a check box for online payments, but this requires an extra fee.)

The Memo field at the bottom of the invoice is for your use; however, keep in mind that if you send statements, your customer will see this memo (it doesn't appear on the invoice, though).

Saving the Invoice

To save the invoice and start a new one, click **Save & New**; otherwise, click **Save & Close**.

NUMBERS HAPPEN

In General preferences, you'll see a preference called Save Transactions Before Printing. Leave it checked, to avoid potential fraud.

When you save an invoice, the following things happen: your accounts receivable amount increases to reflect the amount on the invoice; the customer balance increases; the Sales by Item reports track the items sold; the Profit and Loss reports show the income from the sale; and, if you track inventory, the item counts are reduced.

Sending an Invoice

You can send an invoice by printing and mailing it or by e-mailing it. You can e-mail an invoice one at a time or in a batch. Same with printing. Chapter 5 covers printing and e-mailing.

Generating Invoices from Estimates

In Chapter 12, you learned about creating estimates. You can base an invoice on an estimate you created for a customer. If your business uses progress invoicing (by turning on the Progress Invoicing option in preferences), you can create several invoices from one estimate as the job progresses.

QuickBooks offers two main ways to create an invoice based on an estimate: from the Customer Center or from a blank invoice form. These steps assume you're not using progress invoices (see the next section if you use progress invoicing).

To create an invoice from an estimate in the Customer Center, follow these steps:

1. Open the Customer Center and do one of the following:

    • On the Customers & Jobs tab, select the customer whose estimate you want to use. In the list of transactions in the lower panel, choose **Estimates** from the Show drop-down menu. Double-click the estimate you want to use.

    • On the Transactions tab (see Figure 13.7), click **Estimates** and then locate the estimate you want to use. Double-click it.

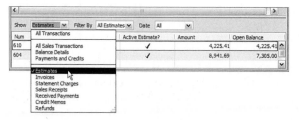

Figure 13.7: *Show only the estimates for a customer.*

2. At the top of the estimate, click **Create Invoice**.

3. Click **OK** at the message that QuickBooks has copied the estimate. (If you see a message about progress invoicing, you have the progress invoicing feature turned on. See the next section for how to work with progress invoices.)

4. Make changes to the invoice as needed.

5. Click **Print** to print the invoice now, or click the **To Be Printed** check box to print it later. You can also click the **To Be E-mailed** check box.

6. Click **Save & Close**.

To create an invoice from an estimate from a blank invoice form, follow these steps:

1. On a blank invoice, choose the customer whose estimate you want to use.

2. In the Available Estimates window, click the estimate you want to use and click **OK**.

3. Make changes to the invoice as needed.

4. Click **Print** to print the invoice now, or click the **To Be Printed** check box to print it later. You can also click the **To Be E-mailed** check box.

5. Click **Save & Close**.

Using Progress Invoicing

In progress invoicing, you invoice a project or job in stages. This is useful if a project will last several weeks and you want to invoice based on project milestones.

Before you can use progress invoicing, you need to turn it on in preferences. Go to the **Edit** menu and click **Preferences**. Click **Jobs & Estimates** and select **Yes** for the question Do You Do Progress Invoicing?

To create a progress invoice from an estimate, follow these steps:

1. Open the Customer Center and do one of the following:

    •   On the Customers & Jobs tab, select the customer whose estimate you want to use. In the list of transactions in the lower panel, choose **Estimates** from the Show drop-down menu. Double-click the estimate you want to use.

    •   On the Transactions tab, click **Estimates** and then locate the estimate you want to use. Double-click it.

2. At the top of the estimate, click **Create Invoice**.

3. Choose what you want to include on the invoice (see Figure 13.8):

Figure 13.8: *Choose what to include on the invoice.*

- **Create Invoice for the Entire Estimate (100%):** Select this option if the job is finished and you want to bill the entire amount. Note that this option changes the next time if you didn't bill the entire amount—it changes to Create an Invoice for the Remaining Amounts of the Estimate. Use this option for the final invoice so you don't have to figure out the final balance.

- **Create Invoice for a Percentage of the Entire Estimate:** Select this option to bill in installments at a certain percentage. For example, if you agreed with the customer to bill in five equal installments, you can enter 20 in the % of Estimate field.

- **Create Invoice for Selected Items or for Different Percentages of Each Item:** Select this option if you bill your customer when a certain part of the job is completed. For example, if an estimate for a landscaping project was based on items for the initial design, excavation, sprinklers and drainage, and planting, you can select only the completed items to bill the customer. You can specify the items by amount or percentage.

4. After selecting one of the preceding options, click **OK**.

5. (Optional) Change any line items, amounts, or quantities, if needed. To keep a history of the changes you make on a progress invoice based on an estimate, click the **Progress** button at the top of the invoice.

6. In the Specify Invoice Amounts for Items on Estimate window (see Figure 13.9), choose Show Quantity and Rate or Show Percentage, depending on how you want to change the items.

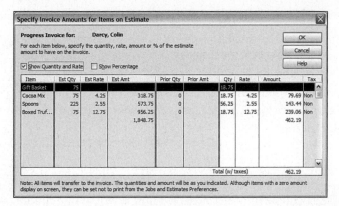

Figure 13.9: *Change the items on the progress invoice and keep a history of the changes.*

7. Change the quantity or rate, or change the percentages.

8. Click **OK**.

9. Click **Save & Close** to save the invoice.

NUMBERS HAPPEN

Your accountant would probably tell you to not make changes directly to the line items on a progress invoice. Use the Progress button to keep a history of the changes, for a better audit trail.

Invoicing for Reimbursable Expenses

Some businesses work on a time and materials basis. Usually, they pass on these costs to the customer as *reimbursable expenses*. These are expenses you incur during the course of a job that you can charge back to the customer. They can include time, mileage, material costs, and products and services you buy on behalf of the customer. When you enter time or mileage (explained in Chapter 25), you can associate those expenses with a particular customer. Similarly, when you enter a transaction (bill, check, or credit card charge) for a vendor, you can associate that expense with a customer so you can track those reimbursable expenses, also known as time and materials billing. (Entering bills is explained in Chapter 16.)

> **DEFINITION**
>
> **Reimbursable expenses** are expenses incurred during the course of a job that you can charge back to the customer.

How you handle reimbursable expenses depends on the type of expense. But first, you have to turn on Time & Expenses preferences to set up how you want to track reimbursable expenses.

Setting Up

You need to set a couple of preferences for how you handle reimbursable expenses. To open the Time & Expenses preference, go to the **Edit** menu and click **Preferences**. At the bottom of the left panel, click **Time & Expenses**, then click the **Company Preferences** tab, shown in Figure 13.10.

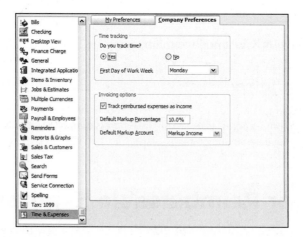

Figure 13.10: *Choose invoicing options for reimbursable expenses.*

For the Track Reimbursable Expenses As Income check box, click it to put a check mark in it to track your expenses and your reimbursements for expenses in separate accounts. Reimbursable expenses can be assigned to an income account, and then costs can be deducted as an expense. Check this check box if you charge sales tax on the expenses. If you don't check the check box, the income you receive for reimbursable expenses posts to the expense account as a positive amount, which ends up canceling the original expense.

For Default Markup Percentage, enter a percentage if you want to mark up your costs for expenses by a certain percentage. When you create an item and enter the item's cost, QuickBooks calculates the sales price and enters it in the Sales Price field.

If you use a default markup percentage, you'll also need an income account to post to—for example, by creating a Markup Income account.

You can also set some personal preferences on whether you see messages when invoicing customers who have reimbursable expenses associated with them. To open the Sales & Customers preference, go to the **Edit** menu and click **Preferences**. In the left panel, click **Sales & Customers**; then click the **My Preferences** tab.

In the Add Available Time/Costs to Invoices for the Selected Job section, choose from the following prompt options:

- Select **Prompt for Time/Costs to Add** if you want to be alerted when you create an invoice or sales receipt that a customer has some outstanding reimbursable expenses. You can choose which expenses to add to the invoice or sales receipt.

- Select **Don't Add Any** if you don't want to be alerted. Choose this option if you charge for reimbursable expenses on a separate invoice. When you're ready to invoice for reimbursable expenses, click **Add/Time Costs** on the invoice itself.

- Select **Ask What to Do** if you want to choose how to proceed at the time of creating the invoice or sales receipt.

Adding Billable Time and Expenses

Chapter 25 talks about how to set up time tracking and how to track your time. (In a nutshell, you enter the hours you worked on a customer's job on either a weekly timesheet or a single activity entry window. Then you associate the hours with the customer or job.) This section shows you how to add billable time to invoices.

To add billable time and expenses to an invoice, follow these steps:

1. Open the invoice form using one of these methods: go to the Customers menu and click **Create Invoices**, click the **Create Invoices** icon on the Home page, or press **Ctrl+I**.

2. Choose the customer from the Customer:Job menu.

3. Depending on the preferences you set for billable time, you may see an alert message (see Figure 13.11) if the customer has any outstanding billable time and expenses.

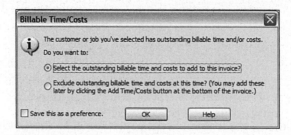

Figure 13.11: *Choose how you want to handle billable time and costs for the invoice.*

4. Select the option that adds the time/costs to the invoice.

5. Alternatively, if you didn't set a preference, click the **Add Time/Cost** button in the footer area of the invoice.

6. In the Choose Billable Time and Costs window (see Figure 13.12), click the tab for the type of cost you're adding (Time, Expenses, Mileage, and Items):

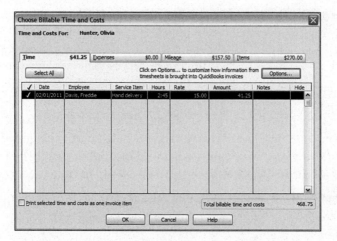

Figure 13.12: *Choose which costs to add to the invoice.*

7. Click in the checkmark column to add the costs to the invoice. As you select the costs, the amount is shown on the tab.

8. Repeat for each tab, if needed.

9. (Optional) On the Expenses tab, choose a markup percentage and the markup income account. If you charge sales tax for this customer and the expense is taxable, click the **Selected Expenses Are Taxable** check box. If some expenses are taxable and others are not, you'll need to select the taxable ones together and add them to the invoice, and go back to the Expense tab to add the nontaxable ones.

10. (Optional) On the Time and Mileage tabs, click the **Options** button to choose how you want the time and mileage costs to appear on the invoice.

11. Click the **Print Selected Time and Costs As One Invoice Item** check box if you want to combine all the time and costs and show the total amount (the customer won't see the breakdown of the costs and won't see any markup amounts). QuickBooks shows the total costs and labels the description as Total Reimbursable Expenses.

12. Click **OK**.

Memorizing a Recurring Invoice

A recurring invoice is an invoice that you issue frequently, such as a monthly retainer or rent; that invoice is usually the same amount each month. Instead of re-creating the invoice each time, you can have QuickBooks memorize the invoice.

To have QuickBooks memorize an invoice, follow these steps:

1. Create the first one by filling in the fields that will be the same each time. For fields that will change, leave them blank. You'll fill them in later when you create a new invoice.

2. When you're ready to have QuickBooks memorize the invoice, go to the Edit menu and click **Memorize Invoice,** or press **Ctrl+M**. Figure 13.13 shows the Memorize Transaction window.

Figure 13.13: *The Memorize Transaction window.*

3. Give the memorized invoice a name, such as Monthly Retainer.

4. If you want to add the memorized transaction to your Reminders List, click **Remind Me** and then, from the How Often menu, choose how often you want to be reminded; then choose the **Next Date**.

5. If you don't want to add the memorized transaction to your Reminders List, click **Don't Remind Me** and then click **OK**.

6. To have QuickBooks create the invoice automatically, click **Automatically Enter**. Choose the schedule for QuickBooks to enter it.

7. Click **OK**.

8. Click **Save & Close**.

To later use the memorized invoice, go to the Lists menu and click **Memorized Transaction List**. Double-click the memorized invoice and fill in the empty fields. Click **Save & Close**.

QUICKTIP

You can also duplicate an invoice, which could be handy if you invoice a customer multiple times for the same items. When duplicating, the information on the invoice is identical except the invoice number. After creating the invoice, go to the **Edit** menu and click **Duplicate Invoice**.

Handling Credits and Refunds

At some point in your business, a customer will want to return something or will want a reduction on the price you charged for a service, for example. You handle this by issuing a *credit memo*. The customer may want to use the credit to make a payment on a current balance or to go toward a future purchase, or the customer may want a refund by check.

DEFINITION

A **credit memo** is similar to an invoice, but it reduces the customer's balance.

Creating Credit Memos

You start the credit/refund process by creating a credit memo. A credit memo is the starting point for reducing a customer's balance or for writing a refund check.

To create a credit memo, follow these steps:

1. Go to the Customers menu and click **Create Credit Memos/Refunds**, or, on the Home page, click **Refunds & Credits**. (You can also create a credit memo directly from a customer's invoice by displaying the invoice and choosing **Credit Memo for this Invoice** from the **Create** menu button.)

2. Choose the customer from the Customer:Job menu.

3. Choose the item and then enter the quantity the customer is returning. Do not enter the quantity as a negative number; QuickBooks decreases the income accounts by the amount of the items returned.

4. Add all the items associated with the return, such as shipping costs or handling charges.

5. (Optional) Add a memo to remind yourself of the return or to write down the related invoice number. (This memo will appear on billing statements, so the customer will see it if you issue billing statements.)

6. Click **Save & Close**.

Read the following sections to find how to apply credits or write a refund check.

Applying Credits

After you save the credit memo, you'll see the Available Credit window (see Figure 13.14). You have three options: keep the credit on file for a future invoice, issue a refund, or apply the credit to an open invoice. This section talks about applying the credits; the following section explains how to write a refund check.

Figure 13.14: *Choose what you want to do with the credit.*

If you choose **Retain As an Available Credit**, QuickBooks enters the amount of the credit as a negative number in your Accounts Receivable register. Later, when you receive a payment from the customer, you can apply the credit. See Chapter 14 for how to apply the credit when receiving a payment.

If you choose **Apply to an Invoice**, you'll see the Apply Credit to Invoices window. Select the open invoice to apply the credit to.

You can also apply the credit directly from the credit memo form: click **Use Credit To** and then choose **Apply to Invoice**.

Writing a Refund Check

Right after creating a credit memo, you can choose **Give a Refund** if the customer wants a check for the refund. You can also open an existing credit memo and click the **Use Credit To** icon at the top of the credit memo. Then choose **Give Refund**.

Figure 13.15 shows the Issue a Refund window.

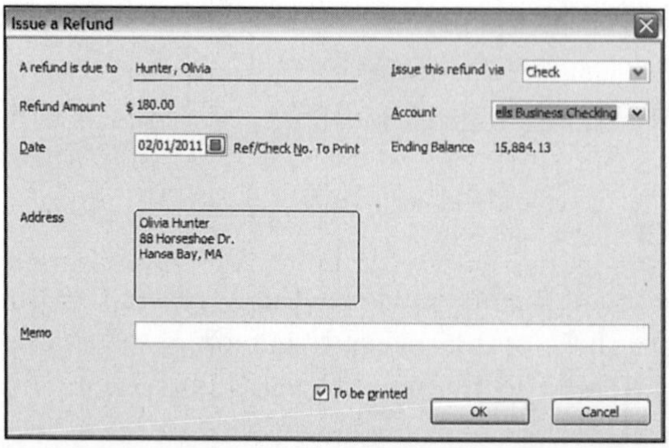

Figure 13.15: *QuickBooks assumes that the refund is by check and selects your checking account.*

QuickBooks also checks the To Be Printed check box to put the check in the queue for your next batch printing.

If you need to refund the credit on the spot in your store, you can choose Cash instead of Check.

If everything looks okay to you in the window, click **OK**.

QuickBooks stamps the word REFUNDED on the credit memo and records the check in your register.

Deleting and Voiding Invoices

Although QuickBooks lets you delete an invoice, it's better to keep the invoice for your records, especially so that you can track invoice numbers. If you delete the invoice, that invoice number doesn't exist. If you've printed or e-mailed the invoice, don't delete it—void it. Voiding an invoice keeps the invoice for your records but doesn't affect the quantities, amounts, and customer balances.

To void an invoice, open the invoice and choose **Void Invoice** from the Edit menu.

If you just created an invoice and you haven't saved it, it's okay to delete it. To delete an invoice, choose **Delete Invoice** from the Edit menu.

QUICKTIP

Two reports may come in handy for tracking voided and deleted transactions: the Voided/Deleted Transaction Summary report and the Voided/Deleted Transaction Detail report (found in the Accountant & Taxes reports).

Batch Invoicing

Batch invoicing lets you send the same invoice to multiple customers instead of creating a separate invoice for each customer. For example, a cleaning service might perform the same weekly cleaning for several customers. Batch invoicing makes it easier to invoice the customers as a group.

Before you begin, make sure you've set up the terms, sales tax rate, and send method for each customer you want to include in the batch. (See Chapter 6 for details on setting up customers.)

To create a batch invoice, follow these steps:

1. Go to the Customers menu and click **Create Batch Invoices** (see Figure 13.16).

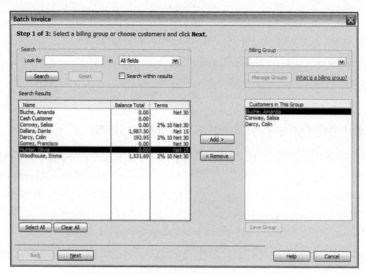

Figure 13.16: *Creating a batch invoice.*

2. Do one of the following:

   • Select each customer in the list on the left and click **Add**.

   • Alternatively, create a billing group: Click **<Add New>** from the Billing Group menu. Give the group a name and click **Save**. Select each customer in the list and click **Add**. Click **Save Group**.

3. Click **Next**.

4. Choose the items to include in the batch invoice and click **Next**.

5. Review the list of invoices. To remove a customer from the batch, click the checkmark for that customer to remove it. Write an optional customer message. When finished, click **Create Invoices**.

6. In the Batch Invoice Summary window, click **Print** to print the invoices that need to be printed, or click **E-mail** to e-mail the invoices to be emailed. (These options are determined by the customer's preferred send method.)

7. Click **Close**.

Creating a Statement Charge

As I mentioned earlier, some businesses will want to use statement charges instead of invoices. But even if you use invoices, you might want to send periodic billing statements to remind customers of their outstanding invoices. Statement charges are the amounts you charge a customer for any services performed.

When you add charges to a customer's register, those charges will appear on the next billing statement you send to the customer. The customer's register also shows any invoices or other transactions, if any. Figure 13.17 shows a customer register.

To add a statement charge for services performed, follow these steps:

1. Go to the Customers menu and click **Enter Statement Charges**. Or if you see the **Enter Statement Charges** icon on your Home page, click it.

2. In the register that appears, choose the customer.

3. In the first empty row, choose the date that you performed the services.

4. Click in the Item field and choose a service item. QuickBooks adds STMTCHG as the type of transaction.

5. Do one of the following:

    -   Click in the QTY field and enter the quantity (for example, hours, depending on how you set up the service item). Press **Tab**. QuickBooks updates the amount charged based on the rate.

    -   Alternatively, do not enter a quantity—just enter the amount of the charge in the Amt Chrg field.

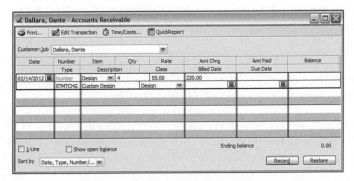

Figure 13.17: *Adding a statement charge.*

6. Skip the Amt Paid and Balance fields (pressing **Tab** skips those fields). QuickBooks fills in those fields later.

7. Choose a class, if you track classes.

8. Leave the Billed Date and Due Date blank, to have QuickBooks fill in those dates when you send the statement. Alternatively, you can postdate the Billed Date so that the charge doesn't appear on a statement until after that date.

9. Click **Record** to save the transaction.

Generating Billing or Reminder Statements

Billing statements and reminder statements are actually the same thing: if you use statement charges, you bill your customers regularly using billing statements; if you use invoices, you can periodically send reminder statements to remind customers of amounts due or past due. You can add finance charges to both billing statements and reminder statements. Chapter 15 explains how to add finance charges.

Before you can generate billing statements, you have to enter the charges, as described in the previous section. After entering statement charges, you can create billing statements for your customers. A billing statement lists all the charges a customer owes for the time period you select.

You should also make sure you've entered all the customer transactions, such as payments, credits, invoices, and refunds, before you generate the statements.

The steps for printing billing statements and reminder statements are the same, but they show different transactions. Reminder statements show the invoices, credits, and payments for the time period you select. Billing statements show the charges a customer has incurred during the time period you select.

To generate statements, follow these steps:

1. Go to the Customers menu and click **Create Statements**. Or if you see the **Statements** icon on your Home page, click it.

2. In the Create Statements window (see Figure 13.18), choose the date you want to appear on the statement.

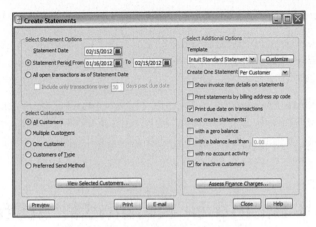

Figure 13.18: *Generating statements.*

3. Choose the date range you want to show:

- Select **Statement Period From ... To** to choose a specific time period, such as from the first day to the last day of a month.

- Select **All Open Transactions As Of** to show only the unpaid transactions and unapplied credits as of the date you specify. To further filter the list, click the **Include Only Transactions <#> of Days Past Due** check box and enter the number of days.

4. Choose the customers to send the statements to, from among these options:

- **All:** Sends statements to all your customers.

- **Multiple:** Sends statements to the customers you choose.

- **One:** Sends statements to just the one customer you choose.

- **Customers of Type:** Sends statements to a group of customers of the same type (if you categorize your customers by type).

- **Preferred Send Method:** Groups the statements by send method, so you can do all printed ones together (choose **None**) or all e-mailed ones together (choose **E-mail**). Note that the Mail choice works only if you have subscribed to QuickBooks Billing Solutions, at an extra fee.

5. Select the optional Additional Options (see Figure 13.18):

- **Create One Statement:** Choose **Per Customer** to list all the jobs for that one customer; choose **Per Job** to produce a new statement for each job.

- **Show Invoice Item Details on Statements:** Click this check box if you want to show a list of the items on each invoice. This makes the statement longer, but it could also remind customers of what each invoice was for.

- **Print Statements by Billing Address Zip Code:** Click this check box if you have a bulk mail permit that allows you to send mail by zip code.

- **Print Due Date on Transactions:** Keep this option checked to show the due date for each transaction in the statement.

- **Do Not Create Statements:** Choose the options if you want to skip printing statements for some customers. For example, you may not want to print and mail a statement to a customer with a zero balance. On the other hand, you may want to print the zero balance statement to let the customer know everything has been paid. You could also choose to omit statements for customers whose balance is less than the amount you enter.

6. To assess finance charges, click the **Assess Finance Charges** button. Chapter 15 explains how to assess finance charges.

7. To preview the statements, click **Preview**. This is useful as a final check before printing. On the Preview page, click **Prev** and **Next** to cycle through the statements.

8. To print the statements, you have two choices. Click **Print** in the preview window to print the statements without setting printer options. Or close the preview window and click **Print** on the Create Statements window. Choose the printer options and click **Print**.

   To e-mail the statements, click **E-mail** instead of Print in the Create Statements window.

The Least You Need to Know

- Use invoices to bill customers if you need to charge sales tax, want to apply discounts or markups, need to add a message to the customer, or keep a detailed record of each product and service you sell.

- Use statement charges to bill customers if you enter several charges over time before requesting payment, or if you assess a regular monthly charge.

- If you use estimates, you can easily generate an invoice from an estimate, as well as use progress invoicing against an estimate.

- If a customer returns something, issue a credit memo and either apply the credit to another invoice or write a refund check.

Receiving Customer Payments

In This Chapter

- Understanding accounts receivable
- Setting A/R options
- Recording a customer invoice payment
- Handling down payments
- Recording credit card sales
- Recording cash sales

You've sent out invoices and customers have started sending in payments. You need to record those payments and apply them against invoices. The customer balance goes down when you receive the payment, and that payment goes to the Undeposited Funds account until you're ready to make a deposit.

About Accounts Receivable

Accounts Receivable is the account in the chart of accounts that tracks money owed to you from sales you've made that haven't yet been paid for. Accounts receivables are also known by the abbreviation A/R. When you create an invoice for products a customer purchased or when you receive a payment from a customer, QuickBooks records the transactions in the A/R account.

Setting Up Accounts Receivable Options

Most of the options on the Payments: Company Preferences panel refer to optional, fee-based "solutions," which I don't cover here. (Also, the first time you open the Receive Payments window, QuickBooks asks you to take a Payments Interview to see if you might benefit from these solutions. You don't have to take the interview; just click **No** or close the window.)

You can set three free options in Payments preferences to affect receiving payments as shown in Figure 14.1. Each one is described in the following sections.

To open the Preferences panel, follow these steps:

1. Go to the **Edit** menu and click **Preferences**.

2. Click **Payments** and then click the **Company Preferences** tab.

Figure 14.1: *Receive Payments Options.*

Automatically Apply Payments

If you turn on this preference (meaning a check mark appears in the check box), QuickBooks automatically applies a customer's payment to the customer's open invoices. If QuickBooks finds an invoice that exactly matches the payment amount, QuickBooks applies the amount to that invoice. If the amount received is less than the customer's outstanding balance, QuickBooks applies the payment to the oldest invoice first. If the amount received is more, QuickBooks applies the payment to the oldest invoices first, until the payment amount is used up.

If you prefer to apply payments manually, uncheck the check box.

Automatically Calculate Payments

If you turn on this preference, you can select an invoice in the Receive Payments window before entering an Amount Received. QuickBooks then enters the amount of that selected invoice for you. As you select or deselect invoices, QuickBooks automatically calculates the Amount Received. The amount received should match the amount of the customer's payment.

If you turn off this preference, QuickBooks doesn't automatically calculate payments and you must enter the amounts manually.

Use Undeposited Funds as a Default Deposit to Account

Select this option to have QuickBooks use Undeposited Funds as the default account for depositing payments. When you're ready to deposit the money, the payments then are all located in the same account. Using this account is convenient for collecting several payments and depositing them later.

If you don't check this option, you can choose the Deposit To account on the Receive Payments and Enter Sales Receipt windows.

Receiving Customer Payments

After you send an invoice or statement to a customer, the customer will presumably pay you—eventually. How you record a customer payment depends on which of the following payment methods you use:

- You can use the Receive Payments window to record a partial or full payment received against a customer's invoice or statement.

- You can apply credits or early payment discounts on an invoice or statements.

- You can receive down payments or prepayments on invoices.

- You can use a sales receipt to record full payment at the time of a sale.

Recording a Payment on an Invoice or Statement

Before you can record a payment from a customer, you must have created an invoice (or statement); you receive payments against customer invoices (or statements). Of course, if you are a retail store and you use sales receipts, you get paid at the time of the sale; you don't receive a payment against the sales receipt. You record a payment in the Receive Payments window.

When a customer makes a payment, you may run into one of these situations:

- The customer has one open invoice and has made a payment in full.

- The customer has one or more open invoices, and the payment does not cover any invoice amount (a partial payment).

- The customer has more than one open invoice, and the payment covers one of those invoices.

- The customer has more than one open invoice, and the payment covers all the invoices.

- The customer has more than one open invoice, and the payment is more than all the invoices (overpayment).

- The customer has one or more open invoices, and the payment does not cover any invoice amount, but the customer has a credit that can be applied.

To record a payment in full, follow these steps:

1. On the Home page, click **Receive Payments** or choose **Receive Payments** from the **Customer** menu. (You can also go to the Customer Center, select the customer, click **New Transactions**, and choose **Receive Payments**. Or, on an invoice, click the **Create** button and choose **Payment for this Invoice**.) Figure 14.2 shows the Receive Payments window.

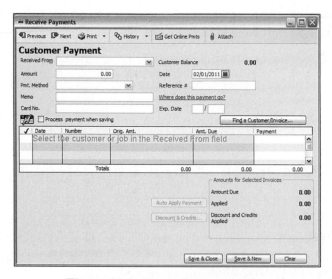

Figure 14.2: *Receive Payments window.*

2. Choose the customer from the Received From menu. QuickBooks lists the customer's open or unpaid invoices, as well as the customer's balance.

3. In the Amount field, type the payment amount. (Or, if you turned on the preference to have QuickBooks automatically apply invoice amounts, you can leave the Amount field blank.)

4. Enter the payment date.

5. (Optional) Choose the payment method.

6. Enter the reference number (or check number, if payment is by check). This is optional, but it could come in handy later if a customer questions which check paid for which invoices.

7. (Optional) Type a memo description.

8. In the list of open invoices, click in the check mark column to put a check mark next to the invoices you want to apply the payment to.

9. Click **Save & Close.**

Recording a Partial Payment

If when you're recording a customer payment the amount doesn't cover the full amount of the invoice, QuickBooks asks you how you want to handle the underpayment, as shown in Figure 14.3.

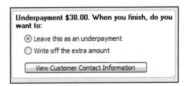

Figure 14.3: *Handling an underpayment.*

Select how you want to handle the underpayment: **Leave This As an Underpayment** or **Write Off the Extra Amount**. You may have to use the Write Off the Extra Amount option when customers don't pay the finance charges, or when you know you won't be able to collect the rest of the money.

You can quickly view the customer record if you want to contact the customer to ask about the partial payment: click the **View Customer Contact Information** button.

When you choose **Leave This As an Underpayment**, QuickBooks applies the partial payment to the selected invoice and keeps the remaining balance for the invoice in your receivables.

When you choose **Write Off the Extra Amount**, QuickBooks displays a window where you can choose the account you use to track write-offs. It's probably a good idea to check with your accountant to choose which type of account to use for this purpose.

Handling an Overpayment

When you record a customer payment that's more than the full amount of the invoice, QuickBooks asks you how you want to handle the overpayment.

You can choose to leave the credit to be used later or refund the money. If you choose to leave it as a credit, you can print it and send a Credit Memo to the customer. If you choose to refund the overpayment amount, the Issue a Refund window appears so you can record the refund.

Applying Credits

If a customer has a credit (the customer returned an item or made an overpayment and you've issued a credit memo), that credit can be applied to an invoice or statement. This credit reduces the amount the customer owes you.

On the Receive Payments window, if a customer has a credit available, QuickBooks displays a message (see Figure 14.4). You can either apply the credit to the customer payment or issue a check to the customer.

To apply a credit when you receive a customer payment, follow these steps:

1. Go to the **Customers** menu and click **Receive Payments**, or click **Receive Payments** on the Home page.

2. In the Receive Payments window, choose the customer with the credit. QuickBooks alerts you that the customer has a credit, as shown in Figure 14.4.

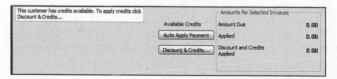

Figure 14.4: *Choose the Discounts & Credits button to apply a credit.*

3. In the list of customer invoices, click the invoice you want to apply the credit to (but don't click in the check mark column—that's for receiving an actual payment).

4. Click **Auto Apply Payment** to have QuickBooks apply the payment to the oldest invoices first. Or click **Discounts & Credits** to choose the invoice(s) to apply it to. Figure 14.5 shows the Credit tab of the Discounts and Credits window.

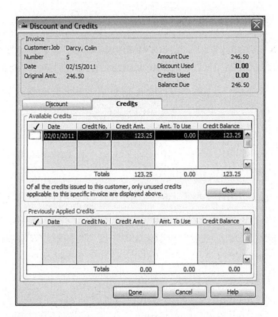

Figure 14.5: *Choose the invoices to apply the credit to.*

5. Click in the check mark column to choose the credit you want to apply.

6. Click **Done**. You'll notice that the Amount Due does not change. The credit is not applied when you save the credit.

7. Click **Save & Close**.

To see the credit applied, open the Customer Center and choose the customer. Open the invoice you applied the credit to; you'll see the credit in the Payments Applied and the Balance Due reduced by the amount of the credit.

Applying Discounts for Early Payments

If you offer discounts for early payment, QuickBooks keeps track of those discounts, and you must apply the discounts when available. For example, if your payment terms are something like "1% 10 Net 30" or "2% 10 Net 30," that means you give a 1 percent or 2 percent discount if you receive the payment within 10 days. Figure 14.6 shows the message QuickBooks displays when a customer has discounts available.

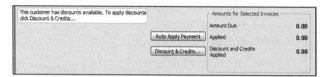

Figure 14.6: *A customer with discounts available.*

To apply a discount, follow these steps:

1. In the Receive Payments window, select the invoice, to see if any discounts are available for this invoice.

2. Click the **Discounts & Credits** button (see Figure 14.7).

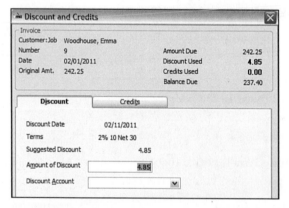

Figure 14.7: *Applying a customer discount.*

3. Click the **Discounts** tab, if it is not already displayed. QuickBooks shows you the amount of the discount based on your payment terms with the customer and the payment date, but you can change that amount (for example, when a customer pays early but does not pay the full amount).

4. Choose the expense account you use to track discounts. Some businesses create a Discounts Given expense account to track discounts; others use an Interest Expense account.

5. Click **Done**. QuickBooks adds a discount column and applies the discount amount.

6. Click **Save & Close**.

Handling Down Payments

Sometimes a customer will give you a down payment on a project. You'll need to track that down payment and apply it to the customer's balance.

Recording a Down Payment

To record a down payment or prepayment, you must use an invoice or statement. You can't record a down payment or prepayment on a sales receipt. To avoid messing up the accounting, record down payments in the Receive Payments window (see Figure 14.8), not the Make Deposits window

To enter a down payment, follow these steps:

1. On the Home page, click **Receive Payments** or choose **Receive Payments** from the **Customer**s menu. (You can also go to the customer center, select the customer, click **New Transactions**, and choose **Receive Payments**.)

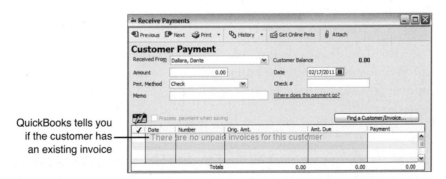

QuickBooks tells you if the customer has an existing invoice

Figure 14.8: *The Receive Payments window for a customer with no invoices to apply the payment to.*

2. Choose the customer's name from the Received From menu.

3. Enter the amount of the down payment or prepayment.

4. Click the Payment Method arrow and choose the method of payment.

5. (Optional, but recommended) In the Memo field, type what the down payment is for.

6. If the customer does not yet have an invoice, choose to leave the payment as a credit to use later (see Figure 14.9) when you have an invoice for this customer. When you create the invoice for the customer, QuickBooks reminds you of the down payment so you can apply it to the invoice.

Figure 14.9: *QuickBooks asks how to handle the overpayment because there is no invoice.*

7. Click **Save & Close.**

8. (Optional) If your customer wants a receipt of the down payment, click **Print Credit Memo**; otherwise, click **OK**.

Refunding a Down Payment

Alas, customers can change their minds. That multilevel Victorian chicken coop was deemed "too over-the-top" by the building code department. If, after giving you a down payment, a customer decides to cancel the project or order, you can write a check for the refund.

To refund a down payment, follow these steps:

1. On the Home page, click **Write Checks** (or choose **Write Checks** from the **Banking** menu).

2. In the Pay to the Order of field, choose or start typing the customer's name.

3. In the amount field, type the down payment refund amount.

4. (Optional) Type a memo to remind you that this check was a down payment refund.

5. On the Expenses tab, click in the **Account** field, click the arrow, and choose **Accounts Receivable**.

6. Click **Save & Close**.

To account for the check correctly, you need to open the Receive Payments window and apply the check as a credit against the down payment you created for the customer.

To apply the credit, follow these steps:

1. Open the Receive Payments window and choose the customer name from the Received From menu.

2. Don't type any amount in the Amount field; leave it at 0.00.

3. Click the **Discounts & Credits** button.

4. On the Credits tab, make sure the payment received from the customer is selected (has a check mark in the check mark column).

5. Click **Done**.

6. Click **Save & Close**. Figure 14.10 shows the transaction for the refund in the A/R register.

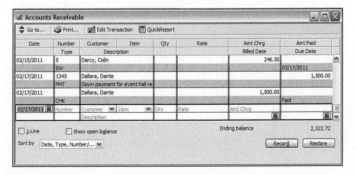

Figure 14.10: *The A/R register showing the correct accounting for the refund.*

Handling Credit Card Sales

To accept credit card payments, you must first get a merchant account. You can do this in two ways, and fees apply to both: you can use the QuickBooks Merchant Service or use a non-QuickBooks merchant account.

With the QuickBooks Merchant Service, you apply online within QuickBooks and set up your account. Then you can process a customer's payment by credit card (for example, on the Receive Payments window, you would choose Credit Card from the Payment Method menu).

With a non-QuickBooks merchant account, such as through your bank, you need a credit card swipe terminal to process payments. You enter the payment manually in QuickBooks.

Explaining how to get set up to accept credit cards is beyond the scope of this book, but you can go to QuickBooks Help and search for "credit card payments from customers."

To receive and process a credit card payment on an invoice or statement, follow these steps:

1. Go to the **Customers** menu and click **Receive Payments**.

2. Choose the customer or job.

3. Choose the credit card from the Payment Method menu.

Figure 14.11: *Fill in the credit card information.*

4. Fill in the customer's credit card information (see Figure 14.11).

5. If you use a QuickBooks Merchant Service, click the **Process <Credit Card Name> Payment When Saving** check box.

6. QuickBooks is set to apply the payment to the oldest invoice first, then to the next oldest, and so on. To apply the payment differently, in the list of open invoices, click in the check mark column to put a check mark next to the invoice(s) you want to apply the payment to.

7. Click **Auto Apply Payment** (or **Unapply Payment**, if you made a mistake).

   When you select an invoice, QuickBooks puts the amount to be applied in the Payment column. If the customer paid less than the amount due, QuickBooks leaves a balance due on the invoice.

8. If your preferences aren't set to use the Undeposited Funds account by default, choose where to deposit the payment from the Deposit To drop-down list.

9. Click **Save & Close**.

10. In the Process Credit Card Payment window, enter the name and address associated with the credit card. This is used for verification.

11. Click **Submit** to process the credit card payment.

12. When you receive notification that the payment has been approved, click **Print** to print a receipt for the customer.

Handling Cash Sales

The local bakery in my small town is quite famous—people come from miles, sometimes from other states, to line up gleefully outside the doors to buy their bread—especially after a mention in *Sunset Magazine*. Their business is totally cash only—no debit cards, no checks, no credit cards (except for the occasional I.O.U. from us locals). The cash drawer is never closed, and bills are stacked in precarious piles until the behind-the-counter people have a lull to clear it out. But I'm going to assume you want to be more organized about your cash sales than the baker. That's where sales receipts come in.

Use sales receipts when your customers pay you the full amount at the time of sale. QuickBooks gives you two ways to handle cash sales: you can create a sales receipt for every sale, or you can create one sales receipt in QuickBooks at the end of the day to summarize your cash sales.

QUICKTIP

If you don't need to track every sale, save time by creating a summary sales receipt at the end of the day or week.

Any business that doesn't need to track whether customers owe money would use sales receipts. Some businesses that use sales receipts include retail stores, spa service salons, and tea parlors. The customers pay for the products or services at the time they receive them. If, on the other hand, you sell espresso and pastries from your portable espresso cart, making a sales receipt for each sale in your busy, cash-only cart would be quite tedious and time-consuming. Here, a summary sales receipt would come in handy.

Creating a New Sales Receipt

A sales receipt (see Figure 14.12) probably gives you a sense of déjà vu if you've read the chapter on invoices. In fact, the two have many similarities.

To open a sales receipt form, follow these steps:

1. Open the sales receipt form using one of these methods: Go to the **Customers** menu and click **Enter Sales Receipts**; click the **Create Sales Receipts** icon on the Home page; or in the Customer Center, select the customer, click **New Transaction**, and choose **Sales Receipts**.

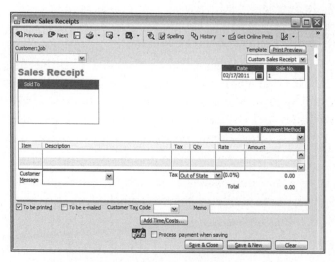

Figure 14.12: *The Create Sales Receipt window.*

2. Follow the steps in the next sections to fill out the sales receipt.

Filling Out the Sales Receipt Header

Filling out a sales receipt is similar to filling out an invoice. But QuickBooks handles the payment amounts differently. For an invoice, QuickBooks adds an entry of the transaction to your Accounts Receivable account; for a sales receipt, QuickBooks adds the sale to your Undeposited Funds account because you don't need to track the customer's balance; the transaction is considered as cash.

See "Anatomy of an Invoice" in Chapter 13 to learn about the header, line item area, and footer.

QUICKTIP

On a sales receipt, choosing a customer is optional if you don't want to track individual customers. Instead, you can create a "generic" customer, called Cash Customer. This way, you can still create customer reports.

To fill out the sales receipt header, follow these steps:

1. Click the arrow to the right of the Customer:Job field and choose the customer for the sales receipt you're creating. Or click **<Add New>** at the top of the menu to add a new customer or job. See Chapter 6 for how to add customers and jobs.

2. If you turned on class tracking in Accounting preferences, choose the class from the Class menu.

3. Check the date in the Date field (which is set to the current date), and change it if you need to.

4. If this is the first sales receipt you've created, type the sales number you want to use in the Sale No. field. QuickBooks automatically increases the number by 1 in subsequent sales receipts.

5. QuickBooks uses the address information from the customer record to fill out the Sold To address.

6. If the customer is paying by check, enter the check number. If the customer is paying in cash, leave the Check No. field blank.

7. From the Payment Method menu, choose how the customer is paying you: check, credit card, or cash, among others.

Entering Line Items

The line item area is where you enter the items the customer is purchasing. The line item area is also where you apply discounts and enter subtotals. Each of these is described in the following sections.

QUICKTIP

If the customer wants to pay for an item or service over time, don't use a sales receipt, since that's for full payment only; use an invoice instead.

To enter line items, follow these steps:

1. Click in the first Item field and click the down arrow to open the item menu.

2. Click the item in the list. QuickBooks fills out the description and rate fields.

3. In the Qty field, type the number of the item the customer is buying (if you're selling your services, type the number of units of time, such as hours or days). (For subtotals and discounts, you don't type in a quantity.)

   QuickBooks calculates the total and tax (if the item is taxable), as well as the customer.

4. Continue adding line items. The following sections describe how to add a subtotal item and how to apply discounts.

5. (Optional) Add a message to the customer by choosing a "canned" message, or just start typing the message. QuickBooks asks if you want to add it to the Customer Message List.

6. Change the Customer Tax Code if QuickBooks has entered the incorrect tax.

Adding a Subtotal

A subtotal item adds all the line items above it, up to a previously entered subtotal, if any. Subtotals are useful for applying a discount to one or more items. For example, a retail art store may be offering a 10 percent discount on canvases, but not on brushes or paints. The clerk could list the canvases first, then add a subtotal, and then apply a discount item to that subtotal before adding other items, such as the brushes or paints. (See the next section for how to apply a discount.)

To add a subtotal, enter all the items you want to include in the subtotal, and then add the subtotal item below those items.

Applying Discounts

You can change the total amount due on a sales receipt by giving a discount to the customer. In a retail setting, you might have created a discount item for your sales events, such as a 25 percent off sale.

Before you can add a discount line item, you must set it up in your item list (see Chapter 9). In the line item area, you add a discount item, just like adding a product or service item.

To add a discount item, enter all the items you want to discount and then add a subtotal. Then add the discount item just below the subtotal. Or, to give a discount on just one item, add the discount item right below that one item. QuickBooks applies the discount to the item above it in the line item area.

Inserting and Deleting Line Items

You can easily insert a line item between two other items. To insert a line item, right-click in the line below where you want to add a new line. Choose **Insert Line** from the menu. QuickBooks inserts the new line above the line you clicked in.

To delete a line item, right-click in the line you want to delete. Choose **Delete Line** from the menu.

Filling Out the Sales Receipt Footer

In the sales receipt footer, you indicate whether the sales receipt should be e-mailed or printed. Although it might not make sense to print the sales receipt later, the customer might prefer an e-mailed receipt instead of a printed one (assuming that you have the customer's e-mail address on file). Click the **To Be E-mailed** check box to put a check mark in it for later e-mailing. See the next section for printing the sales receipt at the time of the sale.

The Memo field at the bottom of the sales receipt is for your use; it doesn't appear on the printed sales receipt.

Printing and Saving Sales Receipts

Before saving the sales receipt, you can print it to give to your customer.

To print the sales receipt now, click the **Print** icon.

To print a batch of sales receipts later, make sure the To Be Printed box is checked.

> **NUMBERS HAPPEN**
>
> In General Preferences, you'll find a Save Transactions Before Printing preference on the Company Preferences tab. This is turned on by default, and it's recommended that you leave the check box checked. Printing without saving could lead to potential fraud.

To save the sales receipt and start a new one, click **Save & New**; otherwise, click **Save & Close**.

When you save a sales receipt, QuickBooks does the following:

- Increases the income accounts associated with the items sold. You can open the income account register by double-clicking it in your chart of accounts. You can also see the amounts by generating profit and loss reports.

- Increases the number of the items you've sold. You can generate a Sales by Item Summary report to subtotal sales by the types of items.

- Applies the payment to the receipt and adds the payment to the Undeposited Funds account so you can later make a deposit and deposit the payment alone or with other payments.

Creating a Summary Sales Receipt

If you're making cash sales out of your mobile, gluten-free cupcake truck, you probably don't care about tracking your customers, and they probably don't need printed receipts. In these types of businesses, you can summarize your sales at the end of the day. Even if you are a retail store, you may think creating a sales receipt in QuickBooks for every single sale is just crazy. But you could, at the end of the day, create one or more sales receipts to record your daily sales.

To do this, you need to add a "generic" customer, explained in step 2 in the following instructions.

You'll want to create an invoice for the full sales for the day and then apply the payments for each payment type to the one invoice.

To create a summary sales receipt, follow these steps:

1. Open the sales receipt form using one of these methods: go to the **Customers** menu and click **Enter Sales Receipt**; click the **Create Sales Receipts** icon on the Home page; or, in the Customer Center, select the customer, click **New Transaction**, and choose **Sales Receipts**.

2. If you haven't created a generic customer, click **<Add New>** in the Customer:Job field. In the Customer Name field, type something like "Cash Customer" and click **OK**.

3. Leave the Check Num field blank.

4. Choose the payment method (since you want to group by payment method), such as Visa or MasterCard.

5. In the line item area, choose an item that you sold during the day and enter the total quantity sold that day. Let's say you sold 42 bars of lavender soap and 18 jars of lemon-thyme lotion to customers who used their Visa cards. You would enter the soap as one item with a quantity of 42 and the lotion as another line item with a quantity of 18. Figure 14.13 shows a summary sales receipt.

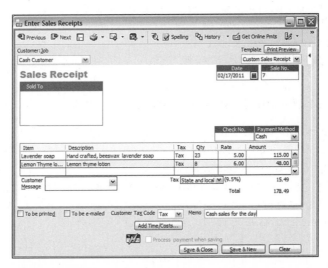

Figure 14.13: *Summary sales receipt for payments by cash.*

6. Make sure the tax is recorded, if any.

7. Click **Save & New** to save the receipt and create the next one.

If you look at the payments to be deposited (go to **Banking** and click **Make Deposits**), you'll see the deposit grouped by payment method, as shown in Figure 14.14. Chapter 21 talks about how to make deposits.

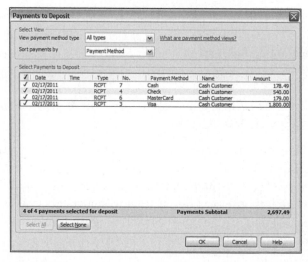

Figure 14.14: *The payments to deposit, grouped by payment method.*

QUICKTIP

If the QuickBooks sales receipt doesn't meet your needs (for instance, you want to track the salesperson who made the sale or you want to add a shipping address), you can customize the sales receipt form. In QuickBooks Help, search for "customize sales receipts."

The Least You Need to Know

- Accounts Receivable is the account on the chart of accounts that tracks the sales to customers and customer payments. Accounts receivable is also known by the abbreviation A/R.

- QuickBooks makes it easy to track customer payments, overpayments, under-payments, and down payments, and it reminds you when they're available to use.

- Use a sales receipt to handle sales in which you're paid in full at the time of the sale.

- Create a summary sales receipt at the end of the day if you don't want to track every sale to every customer.

Reminding Customers of Overdue Payments

In This Chapter

- Using the Collections Center to keep on top of customer accounts
- Viewing aging reports and customer snapshots to track balances
- Setting up and assessing finance charges on overdue balances
- Sending out monthly reminder statements
- Preparing collection letters

If you're like me, nagging customers for payments isn't your favorite part of running a business. I know one guy who hadn't been paid after a couple months for a graphic design project even though the terms were net 15. It got so bad that he went to the company's lobby and sat there until they issued him a check. A little extreme, but hopefully QuickBooks can help you avoid that fate.

Using the Collections Center

The Collections Center (inside the Customer Center) can make this dreaded task a little easier. In one place, you can see at a glance who has past-due invoices and who has almost-due invoices. From the Collections Center, you can send one or more e-mail reminders and keep notes to record your collection efforts.

To open the Collections Center, follow these steps:

1. First, open the Customer Center.
2. Click the **Collections Center** button at the top of the Customer Center. If you see a red exclamation mark (see Figure 15.1), one or more customers have an overdue invoice.

Figure 15.1: *Collections Center button.*

3. To see a list of overdue invoices, click the **Overdue** tab. Double-click the invoice number or **Days Overdue** to open the invoice. Click the customer name to open the customer record. Figure 15.2 shows the Collections Center Overdue tab.

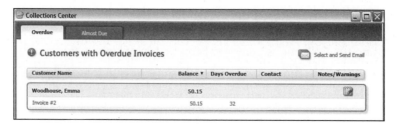

Figure 15.2: *Collections Center Overdue tab.*

4. If you have an e-mail address on file for the customer, you can send an e-mail by clicking **Select and Send E-mail**.

5. Click the check box to select the invoices you want to send an e-mail about. QuickBooks has already provided the text for the e-mail, but you can change it. Click **Send** to send the e-mail to the selected customers.

6. To see a list of almost-due invoices, click the **Almost Due** tab. Double-click the invoice to open it. Click the customer name to open the customer record.

7. To add notes to track your collection efforts, click the **Notes** icon. If you don't have an e-mail address on file for a customer, you'll see an envelope icon, which you can click to add the e-mail address.

BEHIND THE SCENES

QuickBooks uses the date the invoice is due to determine the invoice status. It is "overdue" if it is still unpaid five days after the due date. It is "almost due" if it is unpaid 15 days before the due date. You can change the number of days in Reminders preferences.

Tracking Customer Balances and History

In addition to the Collections Center, the Customer Center provides several tools to help you keep an eye on customers and the balances they owe you. You can run reports by selecting the customer and clicking the following report types:

- **Quick Report** shows all transactions for the selected customer, by date range.

- **Open Balance** shows the outstanding invoices so you can see how much the customer still owes for each invoice or statement.

- **Show Estimates** (appears only if the customer has estimates) lists all the estimates you've created for the customer, by date range.

- **Customer Snapshot** shows you the big picture on the customer, such as recent invoices and payments, graphs of their sales history and items they buy most often, and summary information on their sales and history doing business with you (see Figure 15.3).

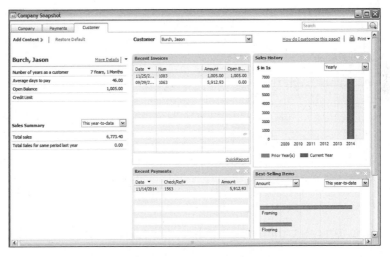

Figure 15.3: *Customer Snapshot.*

About Aging Reports

Several A/R *aging reports* also are available from the Reports Center. Aging reports show you the amount owed to you by all your customers.

> **DEFINITION**
>
> **Aging reports** show how much is due across all open invoices, how much is overdue, and how many days they are overdue.

To generate aging reports, click the **Reports Center** icon in the navigation bar, and then click **Customers & Receivables**. You can choose to see images of sample reports or a list of the reports with a description.

Some businesses run these reports daily; others do so maybe once a month. Part 8 covers reports in depth, including how to create them, customize them, filter them, and so on. Here, I just explain the different types of aging reports, which you can use to help you track customer balances.

A/R Aging Summary: How much each customer owes you and how much of each customer's balance is overdue.

A/R Aging Detail: All the unpaid invoices and statement charges by due date. The Aging column shows you the number of days past due.

Other reports are similar to aging reports and can help you view transactions grouped by customer:

Open Invoices: All the unpaid invoices and statement charges, grouped by customer and job.

Collections Report: All the overdue invoices and statement charges, also grouped by customer and job. This handy report includes the customer contact information so that you can call each customer on the report and beg for your money.

Customer Balance Summary: Unpaid customer balances, grouped by customer and job.

Customer Balance Detail: Individual transactions, grouped by customer and job, along with the unpaid balances for each customer.

Now that you can easily find unpaid balances and overdue balances, you need to decide about finance charges. The next section covers how to deal with finance charges.

Handling Finance Charges

Assessing finance charges is one tactic to get customers to pay their overdue balances. Because assessing finance charges is not exactly customer-friendly, you might first want to try to get the customer to pay using a collections reminder email from the Collections Center. You should also make it clear to your customers from the beginning that you will assess finance charges at some point (say, after 60 days) of not receiving a payment.

Before assessing finance charges, you'll need to set up your finance preferences.

Setting Finance Charge Preferences

You first need to figure out the interest rate you'll charge and at what point you want the assessments to begin.

To set finance charges, follow these steps:

1. Go to the **Edit** menu and click **Preferences**.

2. Click **Finance Charge** in the left panel, and then click the **Company Preferences** tab (see Figure 15.4).

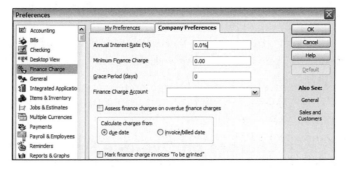

Figure 15.4: *Finance charge preferences.*

3. In the **Annual Interest Rate** field, type in the percentage you want to charge on an annual basis. QuickBooks prorates the annual interest charge based on the number of days the payment is overdue.

4. (Optional) In the **Minimum Finance Charge** field, type the minimum dollar amount you'll charge so that you can recoup some of the expenses you incur by having to assess finance charges in the first place—like that nasty $10 fee my bank charges me for each overdraft protection transaction.

5. In the **Grace Period** field, type the number of days you are willing to give your customers beyond the due date before you start assessing finance charges.

6. Choose the account you use to track finance charges—for example, the Other Income account. If QuickBooks did not create an account to track finance charges, you'll need to add a new income account. Click **Add New** and choose **Other Income** as the account type.

7. Leave the Assess Finance Charges on Overdue Finance Charges check box blank. Besides being a mean thing to do, it could be illegal. Check with your accountant; in some states, assessing finance charges on overdue finance charges is illegal.

8. Choose when you want QuickBooks to begin calculating finance charges: from the due date or from the invoice/billed date. Using the due date is the most common (and less greedy) method.

9. When you assess finance charges, QuickBooks automatically creates an invoice, but by default, those invoices are not marked to be printed—they will appear on the monthly reminder statements you send. Click the Mark Finance Charge Invoices As "To Be Printed" check box if you want to print them during your next printing session.

10. Click **OK** to save the finance charge preferences.

Assessing Finance Charges on Overdue Balances

You should assess finance charges just before sending reminder statements. Also, make sure that you've applied all payments or credits before you assess finance charges. When you open the Assess Finance Charges window, customers who have unapplied payments or credits appear with an asterisk next to their names. Fix those before assessing finance charges.

To assess finance charges, follow these steps:

1. Go to the **Customers** menu and choose **Assess Finance Charges**, or from the Home page, click the **Finance Charges** icon. Figure 15.5 shows the Assess Finance Charges window.

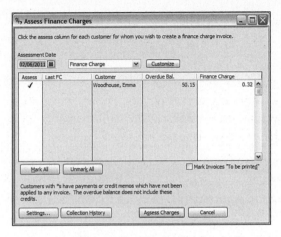

Figure 15.5: *The Assess Finance Charges window shows all customers who have overdue balances.*

2. Change the date in the Assessment Date field to the date you want to impose the charge. (This is typically the last day of the month, if you send out monthly reminder statements.) If you change the date and press **Tab** to move to the next field, QuickBooks recalculates the charge based on the new date.

3. QuickBooks automatically puts a check mark in the Assess column for all customers; click to remove any customers you do not want to charge. For example, if this is the first time one particular customer is overdue, you may want to give this customer the benefit of the doubt. Notice the **Mark All** and **Unmark All** buttons. Depending on how many customers you want to deselect (or select), these buttons may make it easier.

   The Last FC column shows the previous date you assessed finance charges for a customer.

4. To change the finance charge amount for a particular customer, click in the **Finance Charge** column and type the new amount.

5. To view a customer's history to make sure you should really be assessing a finance charge, click the customer to select it and then click **Collection History**. You can double-click a transaction to open the original transaction, to view the details and decide whether the charge is warranted.

6. Click the **Mark Invoices "To Be Printed"** check box if you want to send the invoices to the customers. (Most businesses will not do this, but will send monthly reminder statements with the finance charges added instead.)

7. Click **Assess Charges** when you've made sure everything is correct.

QUICKTIP

If you want to stay on friendly terms with your customers, you don't want to send them an invoice *and* a reminder statement each month.

Now, when you create your monthly reminder statements, the finance charges will appear.

Creating Reminder Statements

Besides sending emails via the Collections Center, you can nudge a customer with an overdue balance with an e-mail or print and mail a monthly reminder statement of the balance due. The reminder statement lists recent invoices you've already billed, any payments received, and any credits applied. They show how much a customer owes currently and how long the balances have been outstanding.

Before you create reminder statements, you should assess any finance charges, as described earlier in this chapter.

Reminder statements are useful for nagging customers who have an overdue balance and to keep a record of a customer's transactions. So even though you may use invoices to bill customers, use reminder statements to remind customers that their payments are overdue.

There's nothing for you to do to prepare for statements; QuickBooks tracks invoices, payments, and credits as you work, which is all you need to create reminder statements. All you do is print them.

The steps to produce and print reminder statements are the same for creating billing statements (some businesses use statements instead of invoices). See Chapter 13 for information on creating statements.

Printing Collection and Other Letters

QuickBooks provides yet another way to nudge customers who are behind in paying you. The Collections Center (described earlier in this chapter) gives you a way to e-mail collection notices. You can also print collection letters from within the Customer Center for mailing to customers.

QuickBooks also supplies several other types of standard letters, on topics ranging from bounced checks, birthday wishes, and denying a credit application, among others.

To print letters from within QuickBooks, you need to have Microsoft Word installed on your computer.

To print collection letters, follow these steps:

1. Click **Customer Center** in the navigation bar.

2. Click the **Word** menu at the top of the Customer Center.

3. Click **Prepare Collection Letters**.

4. Select the options to choose the customers you want to send letters to. You can specify by number of days the payment is overdue. Click **Next**.

5. QuickBooks shows you a list of customers who match the options you selected. Make sure the customers you want to send the letter to have a checkmark next to them. Click **Next**.

6. Choose the type of collection letter you want to send. QuickBooks offers several templates that vary in sternness and tone, as shown in Figure 15.6.

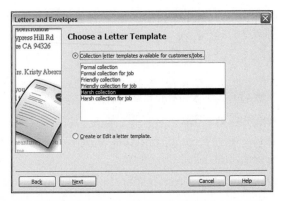

Figure 15.6: *QuickBooks offers several styles of collection letters.*

7. Type your name and title as you want it to appear at the end of the letter. Click **Next**.

8. QuickBooks creates the letter and, if any information is missing (the salutation, for example), displays a message. Once the letter appears on the screen, you can edit the missing information. You can also edit any of the text.

9. From within Word, print the letter.

To print other kinds of letters, such as a bounced check letter, follow these steps:

1. Click **Customer Center** in the navigation bar.

2. To print a letter to one customer, highlight the customer in the Customers & Jobs tab.

3. Click the Word menu at the top of the Customer Center.

4. Click the first menu item, **Prepare Letter for <customer name>**.

5. In the list of letter templates, highlight the one you want to print and click **Next**.

6. Type your name and title as you want it to appear at the end of the letter. Click **Next**.

7. QuickBooks creates the letter and, if any information is missing (the salutation, for example), displays a message. Once the letter appears one the screen, you can edit the missing information. You can also edit any of the text.

8. From within Word, print the letter.

To create and print letters to multiple recipients, click **Prepare Customer Letters** from the Word menu.

The Least You Need to Know

- Use the Collections Center to see at a glance who has past-due invoices and almost-due invoices. You can send one or more e-mail reminders and keep notes to record your collection efforts.

- Use aging reports and customer snapshots to keep on top of overdue balances.

- Assess finance charges to get your customers' attention when they have overdue balances.

- Send out monthly reminder statements to customers with overdue balances.

- Prepare collection letters for overdue customers from the Customer Center. QuickBooks offers several templates that vary by harshness and tone.

Money Going Out

Paying bills isn't nearly as much fun as receiving payments. In this part you learn how to track bills you owe to your vendors. If you need to track sales tax for your business, you can use QuickBooks to handle that facet of running a business.

Chapter 16 walks you through the process of entering and paying your bills. You learn about setting up reminders to pay your bills, as well as setting up recurring bills and applying vendor credits and discounts. You also learn how to record handwritten checks.

Chapter 17 tells you what you need to know about tracking and paying sales tax. First, you set up sales tax preferences and then assign tax codes to your customers and the items you sell. You also learn how to generate sales tax reports and pay your sales tax agencies.

Paying Bills

In This Chapter

- Setting up bill preferences
- Entering bills
- Memorizing recurring bills
- Applying discounts and credits
- Paying bills
- Writing checks to pay bills without entering bills

I sort through my mail every day and hope that the stack of checks from customers is taller than my stack of bills. Of course, I open the checks first and decide that I need to mop the floor before I face the stack of bills. There's always something more fun to do than pay those bills. I psyche myself up and feel grateful at least that QuickBooks makes it easier, if not less painful.

About Bills and Accounts Payable

Bills come from your vendors, which could be your cell phone company, your suppliers, or your cleaning service, among others. QuickBooks offers a couple ways to track and pay your bills. You could use the easy way: when the pile of bills gets high enough, you sit down and write checks to the vendors and assign the amounts to expense accounts one by one. Or you could use a two-step process, in which you first enter the bill when it arrives and then pay the bill when it's due. One advantage of the two-step process is that QuickBooks can track your payables in the Accounts Payable (A/P) account so that you'll always know how much you owe at any given time. Another advantage is that QuickBooks can remind you when your bills are due.

There are names for the type of accounting each method represents, and I introduced those concepts in Chapter 4: cash accounting and accrual accounting. The pile-up-the-bills-and-pay-them-when-you-feel-like-it method is cash accounting. The two-step method (enter bills, then pay bills) is the accrual method. No matter which way you choose, QuickBooks can create the appropriate financial reports (cash or accrual) for tax purposes.

Setting Up Bills Preferences

You can set a couple of preferences for entering bills and paying bills. You can choose how many days after you receive a bill it's due. And you can have QuickBooks warn you about duplicate bill numbers from the same vendor.

To open the Bills preferences, go to the **Edit** menu and click **Preferences**. In the left panel, click **Bills**; then click the **Company Preferences** tab (see Figure 16.1).

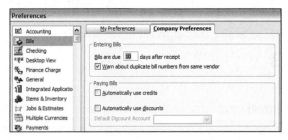

Figure 16.1: *Set preferences for entering bills and paying bills.*

You'll see the following options:

Bills Are Due X Days After Receipt: QuickBooks enters 10 as the number of days, but you can change that if you want. When that due date arrives, QuickBooks adds the bill to your reminders list. Using 10 days as an example, if you enter the bill on July 18, the bill would be due on July 28. QuickBooks uses the number you enter when the vendor has not specified any payment terms. So if your payment terms with a particular vendor is Net 15, your bill would be due on August 2.

Warn About Duplicate Bill Numbers from the Same Vendor: Keep the check box checked if you want QuickBooks to warn you about duplicate bill numbers. This is handy to avoid paying the same bill twice.

Automatically Use Credits: If you check this check box, QuickBooks will apply any credits you have with the vendor to the bill you are paying (using the Pay Bills window).

Automatically Use Discounts: If you check this check box, QuickBooks will apply any discounts you have with the vendor to the bill you are paying (using the Pay Bills window). For example, if the vendor terms are 2% 10 Net 30 and you pay within 10 days, QuickBooks will automatically calculate the 10 percent and apply it against the bill.

Default Discount Account: If you checked **Automatically Use Discounts**, choose the account you use to track vendor discounts (don't choose a discount account you may have created for customer discounts). This account can be either an income account or an expense account. Click **<Add New>** if you haven't set up the account yet. Create a discount account as an income account if you consider the early payment discount as money you've earned. Create a discount account as an expense account if you consider the discount as money you've saved on expenses; this reduces your total expenses.

Entering a Bill for Expenses

The next couple sections talk about the accrual method of handling bills: the two-step process of first entering bills and then paying them. If you want to use the cash method, see "Paying with Checks" or "Paying with Credit Cards," later in this chapter.

When you receive a bill, you should record it using the Enter Bills window as soon as you can so that you can take advantage of early payment discounts, if any. And QuickBooks can remind you when bills are coming due so you can avoid any late payments or irate calls from your vendors.

This chapter covers entering and paying bills for things other than inventory. If you told QuickBooks that you want to track inventory, you'll see two additional icons on your Home page: Receive Inventory and Enter Bills Against Inventory. Chapter 19 covers entering and paying bills for inventory.

To enter a bill for expenses, follow these steps:

1. Go to the **Vendors** menu and choose **Enter Bills**, or click the **Enter Bills** icon in the Vendor section of the Home page. If you're already in the Vendor Center, click **New Transactions** and then click **Enter Bills**. Figure 16.2 shows the Enter Bills window.

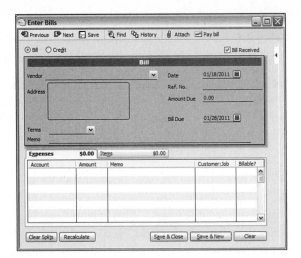

Figure 16.2: *The Enter Bills window (History pane is closed).*

2. Click the down arrow on the Vendor field to open the menu to choose a vendor (or click **<Add New>** if this bill is from a new vendor). QuickBooks fills in much of the information for you from the vendor record.

3. If you use purchase orders (explained in Chapter 19) and you have a purchase order open with the vendor you selected, QuickBooks asks you if you want to receive against the purchase order. This will most likely be the case if you track inventory, which is covered in Chapters 18 through 20.

4. In the Date field, choose the date of the bill so that QuickBooks can accurately track when the bill is due (and fill in the Bill Due field, too).

5. In the Ref. No. field, enter the reference number of the vendor bill (or invoice number), if any. It's a good idea to enter the reference number because it can later help you distinguish between this bill and a similar bill from the same vendor.

6. In the Amount Due field, type in the total amount of the bill.

7. If QuickBooks has not automatically filled in the Terms, choose the terms that the vendor arranged with you. If your terms offer a discount for early payment, QuickBooks adds a Discount Date field, which shows when the bill must be paid in order to receive the discount.

8. Type a memo about the bill, if you want.

9. On the Expenses tab, click in the Account column and click the down arrow that appears; choose the expense account you want to assign to the bill.

10. If you're assigning the amount to more than one expense account, change the amount QuickBooks entered for you in the Amount column.

11. If you plan to pass on the amount to a customer as a reimbursable expense, or if you just want to track job costing, choose the Customer:Job.

12. QuickBooks puts a check mark in the Billable column after you choose the customer/job. Click to remove the check mark if you don't plan on being reimbursed for the expense. If you see something that looks like a tiny bill, you've already billed the customer for the expense.

13. If you track classes, choose the class by clicking in the column, clicking the down arrow, and choosing the class.

14. Repeat steps 9 through 13 as needed to split the bill amount among different expense accounts. For example, your credit card bill might cover several expense accounts.

15. For information on the Items tab, see Chapter 19.

16. Click **Save & New** to save the bill and enter a new one, or click **Save & Close** to save the bill and close the window.

Entering a Vendor Credit

If a vendor gives you a credit, entering the credit is similar to entering a bill, only with fewer fields to fill in.

To enter a vendor credit, follow these steps:

1. Go to the **Vendors** menu and choose **Enter Bills**, or click the **Enter Bills** icon in the Vendor section of the Home page.

2. Click the **Credit** button above the Vendor name. Figure 16.3 shows the credit window.

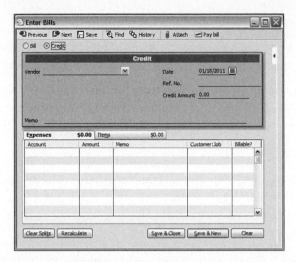

Figure 16.3: *The Enter Bills window changes to show credit-related fields.*

3. Click the down arrow in the Vendor field to open the menu to choose a vendor. QuickBooks fills in much of the information for you from the vendor record.

4. In the Date field, choose the date of the credit memo.

5. In the Ref. No. field, enter the credit memo number.

6. In the Credit Amount field, type in the total amount of the credit memo.

7. On the Expenses tab, choose the account to credit and change the amount, if necessary.

8. On the Items tab (if the credit is for inventory items), choose the item, the quantity, and the cost.

9. Click **Save & Close.**

Setting Up Recurring Bills

Most likely, you have bills that you pay every month, such as rent, utilities, cell phone, and so on. You can enter the bill and then memorize it to make it easier to enter each month.

Memorizing a Vendor Bill

In the Enter Bills window (see Figure 16.2), fill out the vendor information like normal. If the bill amount is the same every month, you can enter that amount. If the bill amount varies, you can leave the Amount Due field empty. Before you save the bill, have QuickBooks memorize it by pressing **Ctrl+M** or by choosing **Memorize Bill** from the **Edit** menu. In the Memorize Transaction window (shown in Figure 16.4), choose the following options:

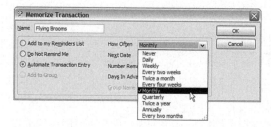

Figure 16.4: *The Memorize Transaction window.*

Remind Me: Select this to have QuickBooks remind you when it's time to enter the bill. From the **How Often** menu, choose how frequently you want to be nagged.

Don't Remind Me: If you select this, QuickBooks won't tell you to enter the bill and won't add it to your Reminders list.

Automatically Enter: Select this, and QuickBooks will automatically enter the bill for you. From the **How Often** menu, choose how often you want QuickBooks to enter it. In the **Next Date** field, enter the date the next bill is due. You can skip the **Number Remaining** field if the bill will be ongoing. In the **Days in Advance to Enter** field, type the number of days before the bill is due that you want QuickBooks to enter the bill.

Click **OK** to save your settings. You don't have to save the bill you entered to have QuickBooks memorize it unless you want QuickBooks to add it to your accounts payable. So just close the Enter Bills window and, when QuickBooks asks if you want to save it, click **No**.

Using a Memorized Vendor Bill

If you didn't indicate that QuickBooks should enter the bill automatically, you'll need to open the memorized bill and turn it into a bill that is due.

To open a memorized bill, follow these steps:

1. Go to the **Lists** menu and click **Memorized Transaction List** (or press **Ctrl+T**).

2. In the Memorized Transaction List, select the memorized bill and click **Enter Transaction** (or simply double-click the bill).

3. Make any changes, including the amount, if the field is empty.

4. Click **Save & Close**. QuickBooks adds it to your accounts payable.

Paying Bills

The second part of the accrual method of bill payment (entering bills and then paying them) is, go figure, actually paying the bills. But before we get into that, you can arrange to have QuickBooks remind you when it's time to pay some bills.

Setting Bill Reminders

When running your own business, you can have a lot going on and time can fly. Before you know it, you've missed a couple due dates. QuickBooks to the rescue! You can set reminders for paying bills (among a bunch of other things). You do this through Reminders Preferences.

To set bill pay reminders, follow these steps:

1. Go to the **Edit** menu and click **Preferences**.

2. In the left panel, click **Reminders**.

3. On the My Preferences tab, click the **Show Reminders List When Opening a Company File** check box if you want an "in your face" reminder each time you start QuickBooks. You can always turn it off later if you find it too annoying. And if you don't turn on this preference, you can go to the **Company** menu and click **Reminders** to see the list.

4. Click the **Company Preferences** tab (see Figure 16.5).

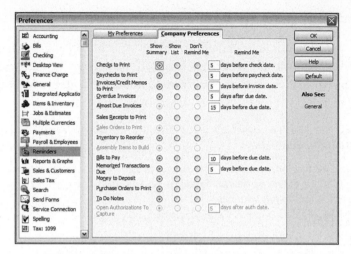

Figure 16.5: *The company preferences for reminders.*

5. For the Bills to Pay reminder, make sure you select either **Show Summary** (shows a one-line summary and total for all bills coming due) or **Show List** (shows each bill and the amount coming due). (You'll see a lot of other reminders here; some may be "dimmed," which means your version of QuickBooks doesn't have that feature.)

6. In the **Days Before Due Date** field, type the number of days before bills are due that you want to have QuickBooks remind you. (For me, being a procrastinator, the default of 10 days is just too long—just gives me all the more time to procrastinate.)

7. Click **OK**.

Viewing Your Unpaid Bills

If you want to see a list of bills that are due before you decide which ones to pay, you can generate a report. Go to the **Reports** menu, go to **Vendors & Payables**, and click **Unpaid Bills Detail**. The report displays an Aging column so you can see at a glance which bills need some attention.

Choosing Which Bills to Pay

Sometimes you may not have enough to pay all your bills that are due. Do you pay off your major vendors who supply things required to keep you in business, like utilities? Or do you pay a smaller amount to all your vendors, to keep everyone in your good graces?

> **NUMBERS HAPPEN**
>
> Vendors that you should never skip or not pay in full are your government vendors: taxes and payroll withholdings. And never, in a pinch, dip into payroll withholdings to pay your bills.

In QuickBooks, you can choose which bills to pay and you can choose to pay them in full or make a partial payment. Sometimes it might help to make partial payments to more vendors than to pay off fewer vendors.

To pay your bills, go to the **Vendors** menu and choose **Pay Bills**, or click the **Pay Bills** icon in the Vendor section of the Home page. Figure 16.6 shows the Pay Bills window. Or, in the Enter Bills window, click the **Pay Bill** button at the top of the window.

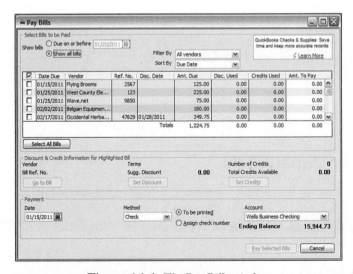

Figure 16.6: *The Pay Bills window.*

Due on or Before: Click this option to change which bills are shown. Change the date to show more or fewer bills that are due.

Show All Bills: Click this option to show all bills without taking the due date into consideration. This option might be better because you can see which bills offer a discount (the discount date); those bills won't necessarily show up if you choose to show by the due date.

Filter By: Choose to see all bills from one vendor or see all vendors.

Sort By: Change the order of the bills in the window. You can choose to sort by Due Date (oldest first), Discount Date, Vendor, or Amount Due (largest first).

To choose which bills to pay, click in the check mark column for the vendor you want to pay. To select all the vendor bills, click **Select All Bills.**

Changing the Amount to Pay

When you select a bill, QuickBooks assumes that you want to pay the bill in full, so it enters the full payment amount in the Amt. to Pay column.

To change the amount to pay on a bill, type the amount in the **Amt. to Pay** column and press **Tab** to update the total. When you don't pay the full amount, QuickBooks keeps the bill in the Pay Bills window, showing the unpaid amount.

Applying Discounts and Credits

When you highlight a vendor in the list of bills, you can display the actual bill by clicking the **Go to Bill** button. When you highlight a vendor, you can see whether you can apply any discounts or credits to apply, as shown in Figure 16.7.

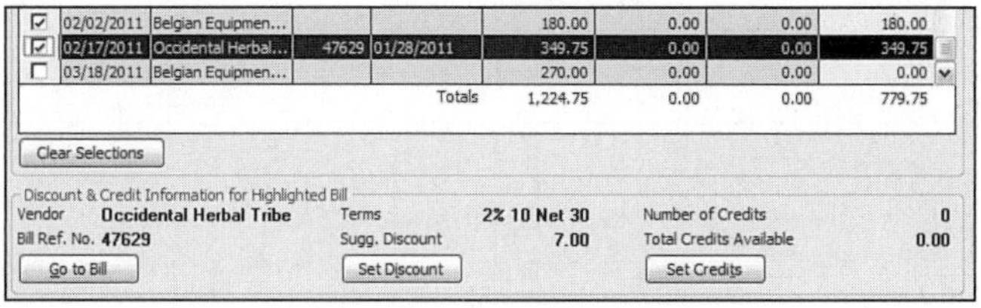

Figure 16.7: *When you highlight a vendor bill, the Discounts & Credits section shows any available discount or credits.*

In Bills preferences (described earlier in this chapter), you can indicate whether you want QuickBooks to apply discounts and credits automatically. If so, the amounts shown in the Amt. to Pay column for a selected bill take the discount or credit automatically. But you have the option of changing that setting in the Pay Bills window for a particular bill.

When you check a bill to pay, the **Set Discount** and **Set Credits** buttons become active (or "clickable"). See Figure 16.7.

If you plan to make a partial payment on a bill with a discount for early payment, you can adjust the discount amount accordingly. Also, some businesses take the discount even if the payment isn't early. If the discount date has passed, QuickBooks won't apply the discount; you have to apply it manually. Other businesses give themselves a discount even if the terms do not specify a discount. In all cases, to adjust the discount amount, click **Set Discount**. Enter the amount; depending on your Preference settings, you may need to choose the discount account and a class (if you use class tracking). Click **Done**. You'll see the discount amount in the Disc. Used column.

If you have any credits with the selected vendor, you can choose the credits to apply (or not apply). If QuickBooks automatically applied a credit and you want to save the credit for later, click **Set Credits** and click to remove the check mark next to the credit. You can also change the amount of the credit to use: click in the **Amt. to Use** column and adjust the amount. Click **Done**.

Choosing the Payment Options

After selecting the bills to pay, changing amounts, and applying discounts and credits, you're ready to pay the bills. Figure 16.8 shows your payment options.

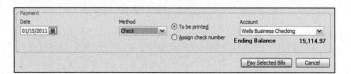

Figure 16.8: *The lower portion of the Pay Bills window is where you choose payment options.*

Payment Date: This date will appear on your checks (defaults to today's date). To predate or postdate the checks, change the date here.

Method: Choose the payment method to pay the bills—Check or Credit Card. (If you subscribe to one of the bill payment services, you will see Online Bank Pmt. as a method as well.)

If paying by Check, select **To Be Printed** to put the checks in the printing queue. If you pay using handwritten checks, select **Assign Check Number**. After you click **Pay Selected Bills**, you can type the starting check number to use.

Account: Choose the checking or credit card account to use to pay the selected bills.

Paying the Bills and Producing Checks

To pay the selected bills, click **Pay Selected Bills**. QuickBooks adds transactions to the appropriate register (check or credit card) and displays a Payment Summary window. If you selected To Be Printed, you'll see a **Print Checks** button. Click the button to print the checks right now, or click **Done** and print the checks later. Click **Pay More Bills** to pay other bills by a different payment method.

If you're paying by check, you'll need to either print them and sign them before mailing, or write the checks by hand. Chapter 5 covers printing checks. If you're writing the checks by hand, all you need to do is write them; QuickBooks has already recorded the check payments for you using the check numbers you specified.

Paying with Checks Without Entering Bills

If you use the cash basis method of accounting, you write your checks directly to the vendors, without having to go through the two steps of entering bills and then paying the bills.

Even if you use the two-step process, sometimes you may need to write a check to a vendor (the one who camped outside your door demanding payment right then and there), without going through the process of first entering the bill.

NUMBERS HAPPEN

Important! Do not use the Write Checks window to write a check for a bill you have already entered. This will mess up your accounts payable.

The next sections explain how to enter handwritten checks into QuickBooks.

Using the Write Checks Window

Paying your vendors by check without using the Enter Bills/Pay Bills process is called direct disbursement. You have two ways to write direct disbursement: writing a check by hand and recording it, or entering a check into QuickBooks to print it.

To write a direct disbursement check, follow these steps:

1. Go to the **Banking** menu and click **Write Checks**, or, on the Home page, click the **Write Checks** icon.

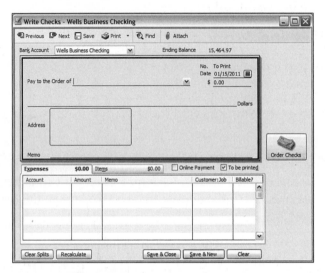

Figure 16.9: *The Write Checks window.*

2. In the Write Checks window (see Figure 16.9), choose the Bank Account to use for the check.

3. If you're entering a handwritten check, deselect the **To Be Printed** check box (below the check on the right). QuickBooks changes the No. field to show the next check number, which you can change to match the paper check, if needed.

4. Click the down arrow in the **Pay to the Order Of** field and choose the vendor to pay. QuickBooks warns you if you've already entered a bill for the vendor and nudges you to go to the Pay Bills window. If you're paying a different bill, you can choose to write a check anyway.

5. Fill in the amount of the check and press **Tab**. QuickBooks writes out the amount for you.

6. Enter an optional Memo. This prints on the checks if you're printing them.

7. On the Expenses tab, assign the check amount to one or more expense accounts. (If the check is for purchasing items for inventory, click the **Items** tab and assign the amounts and enter the quantities purchased. This places the items into inventory. Part 5 covers managing inventory and using the Items tab in more detail.)

8. If you're being reimbursed for this check or you just want to track expenses by job, choose the customer/job. If it is billable, click in the **Billable** column to put a check mark in it.

9. Click **Save & Close** to record the check and close the Write Checks window, or click **Save & New** to record the check and write another one.

The following list describes some of the buttons on the Write Checks window:

Clear Splits: Removes all the expense accounts and amounts, or items and quantities. QuickBooks puts the total amount in the Amount column on the Expenses tab.

Recalculate: Adds the amounts on both the Expenses tab and the Items tab, and changes to amount on the face of the check, if needed.

Online Payment: If you've signed up for online banking (extra fees apply), click to select the check box. This tells QuickBooks to make the payment online instead of printing the check.

Clear: Erases everything on the check including the vendor. If you're editing a check previously entered, you'll see **Revert** instead of Clear.

The Items tab has more buttons, but we talk about those in Part 5.

If you're writing a direct disbursement check for printing (instead of recording a handwritten check, follow the previous steps, except for step 3). Make sure the **To Be Printed** check box is checked. This puts the check in the printing queue for later printing.

Recording a Handwritten Check

If you're at the big box store buying a bunch of supplies, you may choose to write a check for the items at the store. When you get back, you'll have to record that handwritten check into your check register. The steps are the same as for writing a direct disbursement check, described in the previous section.

Printing Checks

Chapter 5 covers printing, but I'll give you a brief description here. To print a single check from the Write Checks window, click the **Print** icon at the top of the window.

To print a batch of checks you've entered into the Write Checks window, make sure the **To Be Printed** check box is selected for the checks. When you're ready to print the checks, go to the **File** menu, go to **Print Forms,** and click **Checks**. In the Select Checks to Print window (see Figure 16.10), double-check the check number and change it, if necessary; then select the checks to print.

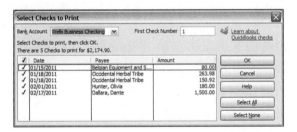

Figure 16.10: *The Select Checks to Print window.*

The Least You Need to Know

- For paying bills, you can choose the accrual method (first entering bills and then paying them) or the cash method (paying a bill directly by writing a check).
- You can have QuickBooks memorize vendor bills for quick data entry.
- Set bill reminders so QuickBooks can alert you when bills are coming due.
- If a vendor offers discounts for early payment or if you have a credit with a vendor, you can apply the discount or credit to the bill, reducing the amount you owe.

Tracking and Paying Sales Taxes

In This Chapter

- Setting up sales tax preferences
- Creating sales tax items and sales tax groups
- Setting up sales tax codes
- Assigning tax codes to customers and items
- Finding out how much you owe
- Paying your sales tax agencies

If you run a retail store, for sure, you'll need to collect sales tax on the things that you sell. Even if you don't sell through a public location, you may be liable for collecting tax on services you provide and on products you purchase and pass on to your customers. The rules for collecting sales tax vary by state. For example, clothing in New Jersey is not taxable. You'll need to check with your tax agency to learn what's taxable and what's not. Even if you're not a retail store, you may have to collect taxes. Check with your accountant to make sure.

To further complicate things, you may have customers who are taxable, customers who are out-of-state, and others—such as wholesale customers—who are exempt from taxes.

After collecting the taxes, you'll need to remit them to your tax agencies at certain intervals.

About Sales Tax in QuickBooks

QuickBooks can help you track and pay sales tax, but you'll need to perform a few steps to do this:

1. **Set up sales tax in QuickBooks:** Set up sales tax preferences, create sales tax items and rates, tell QuickBooks which items and customers are taxable (or not taxable), set up your tax agency as a vendor, and set up a payment schedule.

2. **Enter the opening balance for your sales tax:** If you currently owe sales tax to your tax agency, you'll need to enter the balance in the sales tax payable account.

3. **Charge tax on sales:** When you sell taxable items to taxable customers, you'll need to use sales tax items so QuickBooks can calculate the taxes on the sale.

4. **Pay your tax agency at regular intervals:** When your sales taxes are due, run a sales tax liability report to find out how much you owe.

Each of these steps is detailed in the sections that follow.

Setting Up Sales Tax Preferences

When you set up your company file, QuickBooks asked whether you collect sales tax or turned it on by default based on your business. This turned on the sales tax features in QuickBooks. If you need to collect tax and you don't see the sales tax features (for example, if you don't see the Manage Sales Tax icon on the Home Page), you'll need to turn on the sales tax feature.

To enable sales tax, follow these steps:

1. Go to the **Edit** menu and click **Preferences**.

2. In the left panel of the preferences window, click **Sales Tax** and then click the **Company Preferences** tab.

3. Click **Yes** to answer the question Do You Charge Sales Tax? Figure 17.1 shows the sales tax preferences.

4. Read the following sections for how to set up taxes using the Sales Tax preferences window.

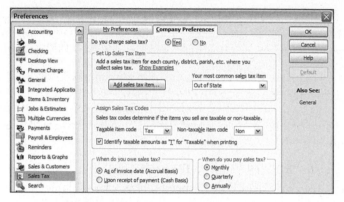

Figure 17.1: *Sales Tax Preferences window.*

Adding Sales Tax Items

In QuickBooks, you create items for sales tax to help you keep accurate records about the sales taxes that you collect and need to remit. You can add sales tax items directly from the Sales Tax preferences window. Before you add a sales tax item, you'll need to find out the sales tax rates for your state, county, and city.

To add a sales tax item, follow these steps:

1. Right there on the Sales Tax Preferences panel, click the **Add Sales Tax Item** button. Figure 17.2 shows the Add New Sales Tax Item window.

Figure 17.2: *Sales Tax Item window.*

2. In the New Item window, click in the Sales Tax Name field and type a name for this sales tax item. You can include the tax location and rate—for example, "Napa County 9.25%." This name will be listed in the Tax field menu on your invoices and sales receipts.

3. In the Description field, type a name for the tax, to make it clear to the customer what this tax covers—for example, "Napa County sales tax." This is how it will appear as a line item on an invoice or sales receipt.

4. In the Tax Rate field, type the tax rate percentage (including the % sign)—for example, "9.25%."

5. In the Tax Agency field, click **<Add New>** to add a record for the agency you remit this tax to.

6. Click **OK** to return to Sales Tax preferences.

Repeat these steps to add other sales taxes you're responsible for collecting. You'll need a sales tax item for each district in which you do business. Say you have a retail store in one county and you also sell your wares at the annual harvest festival in another county. You'll need to add a new sales tax item for that county.

To update the sales tax rates when taxes go up, go to the **Lists** menu, click **Item List**, and then double-click the sales tax item and make the changes.

Creating a Sales Tax Group Item

Let's say your business is in a district that charges an additional tax on top of the county rate, and you remit the district and county taxes to different agencies. To handle this, you can create a sales tax group item. This way, the customer sees only one sales tax item on the invoice or sales receipt, but you can track the taxes separately. Before you can create a sales tax group, you need to create a sales tax item for each tax: for example, one for the county, one for the district, and one for the city.

QUICKTIP

Create a sales tax group item only if you pay more than one agency. Check with your tax agency; some agencies split your single payment among the appropriate agencies.

Follow the preceding steps to set up the sales tax items you need. Then create the sales tax group item to group them together.

In the Sales Tax Preferences panel, click the **Add Sales Tax Item** button. In the New Item window, choose **Sales Tax Group**. Then click in the **Tax Item** column to choose the individual sales tax items, as needed. As shown in Figure 17.3, the sales tax group includes the state and local county tax that is paid to the state agency and a special assessment tax paid to the city tax agency.

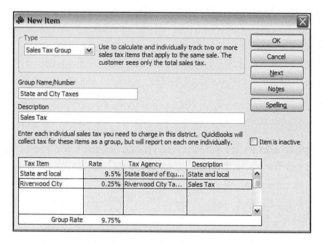

Figure 17.3: *Sales Tax Group Item window.*

The next section explains how to set up and use sales tax codes.

Setting Up Sales Tax Codes

QuickBooks uses sales tax codes to identify whether a product or service that you sell is taxable. You also use tax codes to determine whether a customer is taxable. QuickBooks sets up two sales tax codes for you when you turn on sales tax: TAX is used for taxable items and customers, and NON is used for nontaxable items and customers. Examples of customers who aren't taxable include nonprofit organizations, wholesale customers, or out-of-state customers.

For most businesses, the two tax codes are sufficient. However, some states require more detail on nontaxable sales, such as the reason for the nontaxable status. You can create additional codes for this and run reports for the agencies that require more detail.

Some additional sales tax codes you might need to set up include a code for out-of-state sales and customers, a code specifically for wholesale customers, a code specifically for nonprofits, and another code for government agencies. This depends on the requirements of your tax agencies, so be sure to check with them.

To add a new nontaxable tax code, in the Sales Tax preferences window, click the field next to **Nontaxable Item Code** and choose **<Add New>**. Enter a code, using up to three characters—for example, WHL for wholesale. Since the three-letter code may be a little cryptic, type in a description to explain what the code is used for—for example, "Wholesale customers." Click **OK** to save the new tax code. To add a new taxable sales code, in the Sales Tax preferences window, click the field next to **Taxable Item Code** and choose **<Add New>**. Enter the code and description, and click **OK**.

QUICKTIP

If your state requires you to report on out-of-state sales, you'll need to create an "out of state" tax code (OOS) and create a sales tax item with a 0 percent rate.

You can also add tax codes at any time from the Sales Tax Code List. Go to the **Lists** menu and click **Sales Code Tax List**. Just press **Ctrl+N** when the window is open and fill in the fields.

Setting Preferences for Paying Sales Tax

You can set two preferences for paying sales tax:

When Do You Owe Sales Tax?: Select the appropriate basis for your sales tax reports: cash or accrual. What you select here overrides the accounting basis you set up for your business. Some agencies may require payment on accrual, others on a cash basis. Check with your tax agency.

When Do You Pay Sales Tax?: Choose the tax payment schedule. If you don't know what it is, check with your tax agency. If you collect a lot of sales tax, the agency may want you to pay monthly; if you collect a little, the agency may want annual payments.

Click **OK** to save the Sales Tax preferences.

Assigning Tax Codes to Customers and Items

You need to tell QuickBooks which customers and items are taxable and which are not taxable. You can do this at the time you create the customer record or item, or you can edit existing customer records or items to assign the tax codes.

Assigning Tax Codes to Customers

When adding a new customer or editing an existing customer, you can indicate the customer's taxable status and assign the usual sales tax item you use with the customer.

To assign sales tax information to customers, follow these steps:

1. Open an existing customer record (go to the Customer Center, highlight the customer, and click **Edit Customer**) or create a new customer record (choose **New Customer** in the upper left).

2. On the Additional Info page, choose a tax code from the Tax Code menu to assign the customer a code. See Figure 17.4.

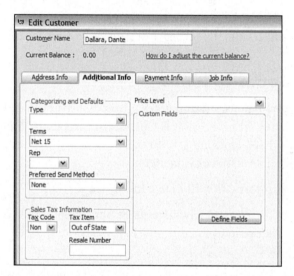

Figure 17.4: *Assigning sales tax information to customers.*

3. If you always use the same tax rate for this customer, choose the tax rate from the Tax Item menu.

4. If the customer is a reseller or wholesale customer, enter the customer's resale number.

5. Click **OK**.

QUICKTIP

The customer tax code takes precedence over an item tax code. If a nontaxable customer purchases an item that is taxable, the item will not be taxed.

What if you have a billion customers and you don't want to open each customer record, change the tax status, and save it? Here's a trick: you can use the Add/Edit Multiple List Entries window. In the Customer Center, right-click the **Customers & Jobs** tab and choose **Add/Edit Multiple Customers:Jobs**. You'll see a list of your customers. On the far right of the window, click **Customize Columns**. In Available Columns, click **Tax Code** and then click the **Add** button. Click the **Add** button again to add a Tax Item column. Click **OK**. You'll see (you may have to scroll a bit) the two columns you added. Click in the Tax Code and Tax Item fields and choose the options for the current row (each customer is a row). When you're done, click **Save Changes**. This trick works for items, too. Just right-click in the Item List and choose **Add/Edit Multiple Items**. The Sales Tax Code column should already be in the list.

Assigning Tax Codes to Items

When adding a new item or editing an existing item, you can indicate whether the item is taxable. States differ on what is considered taxable. In some states, food items are not taxed; in others, clothing is not taxed. Check with your state for the rules. You can set the taxable status of your items.

To assign sales tax information to items, follow these steps:

1. Open an existing item (click **Items & Services** on the Home page and double-click the item to edit) or create a new item (open the Item List and press **Ctrl+N**).

2. In the Sales Information section, choose a tax code from the Tax Code menu to assign the item a code. See Figure 17.5.

Figure 17.5: *Assigning sales tax information to items.*

3. Click **OK**.

Applying Tax to Your Sales

If you've assigned your items and customers a tax status, QuickBooks will automatically calculate the sales taxes for taxable customers on invoices, sales receipts, and estimates.

> **BEHIND THE SCENES**
>
> When you make a taxable sale, the amount of the tax appears in the Sales Tax Payable account.

If you're selling to out-of-state customers and you created an "out of state" tax code, QuickBooks doesn't charge sales tax. You can create a report that shows your nontaxable, out-of-state sales when you pay your taxes.

Managing Your Sales Taxes

Depending on how much sales tax your business charges, your payment schedule can vary. You may be required to pay sales taxes monthly, quarterly, or annually.

QuickBooks provides a streamlined way to manage your sales taxes. On the Home page, click the **Manage Sales Taxes** icon. Figure 17.6 shows the Manage Sales Tax window, where you can perform many of the sales tax tasks.

Figure 17.6: *Manage your sales tax tasks from one window.*

Generating Sales Tax Reports

Filling out sales tax forms can be a less than joyous occasion (okay, a major pain), but QuickBooks provides a couple of reports to make it a little easier. From the Manage Sales Tax window, you can click links to generate the following two tax reports when you need to pay your taxes:

Sales Tax Liability report: Summarizes the sales tax you've collected and what you currently owe to the tax agencies. This report shows both taxable and nontaxable sales for each tax code. QuickBooks uses the payment schedule you set in sales tax preferences to set the date range for the report. If you need to change the date, from the Dates menu, choose the date range to match your payment schedule—for example, Last Month if you pay monthly, or Last Calendar Quarter if you pay quarterly. Or you can manually enter the dates in the From and To fields. Initially, QuickBooks uses the accrual basis; if your agency requires cash basis, click **Modify Report** and click **Cash**.

Sales Tax Revenue Summary: Shows you a summary of taxable and nontaxable sales by tax agency. This summary also shows total sales by tax code, and those figures can help you fill out the tax forms. If you collect sales tax for more than one district (for example, County and City), QuickBooks shows each district separately. Initially, QuickBooks uses the accrual basis; if your agency requires cash basis, click **Modify Report** and click **Cash**.

Paying Your Sales Tax Agencies

Once you've generated the reports and filled out those forms, you're ready to remit your sales taxes.

To remit sales taxes, follow these steps:

1. From the Manage Sales Tax window, click **Pay Sales Tax** (or go to the Vendors menu, go to Sales Tax, and click **Pay Sales Tax**). Figure 17.7 shows the Pay Sales Tax window.

2. Choose the bank account to use to write the check.

3. Look at the Show Sales Tax Due Through date to make sure it corresponds to the end date of the reporting period (the last date for the end of the previous month, for example).

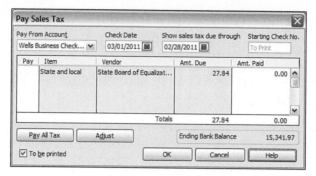

Figure 17.7: *Pay Sales Tax window.*

4. If the Starting Check No. field shows To Print, the **To Be Printed** check box is selected. If you're writing a handwritten check, click to remove the check mark in **To Be Printed** and type in the actual check number. If you're transferring money from your account online to the tax agency, put EFT (for Electronic Funds Transfer) in the Starting Check No. field.

5. In the Pay column, click to put a check mark next to the taxes you're paying with this check. Click **Pay All Tax** if all the tax agencies are on the same schedule, which is not likely.

6. If you procrastinate like me and you owe a fine, click the **Adjust** button and type in the amount of the fine or other adjustment, such as a credit, discount, penalty, interest, or rounding error. Click **OK**.

7. Click **OK** to record the payment.

Don't use the Write Checks or Pay Bills windows to pay your sales taxes. If you do, your payments won't be applied correctly and bookkeeping and reporting errors will result.

The Least You Need to Know

- In QuickBooks, you create items for sales tax to help you keep accurate records about the sales taxes you collect and need to remit.
- QuickBooks uses sales tax codes to identify whether a product or service you sell is taxable. You also use tax codes to determine whether a customer is taxable.

- To update sales tax rates when taxes go up, go to the **Lists** menu, click **Item List**, and then double-click the sales tax item and make the changes.

- Generate sales tax reports to help you fill out those painful sales tax forms.

- After you've generated the reports and filled out those forms, remit your sales taxes using the Pay Sales Tax window, not the Write Checks or Pay Bills windows.

Managing Inventory

Read the chapters in this part if your business carries and tracks inventory. You learn how to manage all your inventory tasks using QuickBooks Pro, including tracking, purchasing, and receiving inventory. This part also covers reporting on inventory and counting inventory.

Chapter 18 prepares you for tracking inventory. It explains how inventory works in QuickBooks, how to set up inventory preferences and accounts, and how to set up inventory items.

Chapter 19 goes into the nitty-gritty of purchase orders. It also tells you what to do when the inventory you've ordered arrives.

Chapter 20 helps you create inventory valuation and inventory stock status reports. It walks you through the process of taking an inventory count, preparing for the count, and making adjustments to the count.

Tracking Inventory

In This Chapter

- Understanding how QuickBooks values inventory
- Learning about inventory items
- Setting up inventory preferences
- Setting up inventory accounts
- Creating inventory items

Not all businesses track inventory, but if you want to, QuickBooks can help you manage it. If you keep things on hand to sell to customers, you'll want to track inventory. You set up items to represent the things you sell so QuickBooks can track the values and quantities behind the scenes. QuickBooks can help you figure out when it's time to reorder or which items you have too much of. Here's the deal: if you buy or make things to resell to customers, you'll want to track inventory. This means a retail store, a distributor, or a manufacturer will likely want to track inventory.

About Inventory

Inventory represents the items sitting on your backroom shelves (or retail shelves) waiting to be sold. You track them by creating inventory items for the goods you keep in inventory. You don't create an inventory item for each single thing you stock; an inventory item represents the entire stock of the item. For example, you sell widgets: you wouldn't create an inventory item for each widget, but you create inventory items by type of widget—Large Widgets and Small Widgets.

LIFO, FIFO, and Average Cost

You may have heard the terms LIFO and FIFO (by the way, wouldn't those make amusing names for a pair of poodles?). LIFO and FIFO are the popular kids on the block for tracking inventory. LIFO stands for last in, first out; FIFO stands for first in, first out. These are standard costing methods of inventory valuation. However, that's not how QuickBooks Pro works. QuickBooks Pro uses the simpler *average cost* method to figure out the value of your inventory. It takes the total cost of each item you have in stock and divides the total cost by the number of items. It does this for each inventory item you keep in stock and then totals all the results to get the value of your inventory. The value of your inventory is important because it is considered an asset and can affect the worth of your business. If you need to use the FIFO method, upgrade your QuickBooks version to QuickBooks Enterprise Solutions with Advanced Inventory. That version also supports tracking serial/lot numbers and multiple locations.

DEFINITION

The **average cost** method calculates the value of inventory you have in stock based on the sum of the cost of those items divided by the number on hand.

Behind the scenes, QuickBooks is busy recalculating the average cost each time you buy more of an inventory item. It adds the new cost total for the new items to the previous cost of older items, and divides by the total number of old and new items. This gives you the average cost for each item.

About Inventory Items

For each item that you keep in stock for resale, you create an inventory part item. The items can be things you manufacture, like hand-crafted greeting cards or cell phone covers; or a product you buy already manufactured. The key point is that you have these inventory part items on hand for the purpose of reselling to customers.

QuickBooks uses the inventory part item to track the quantity on hand, the costs and value, and your *cost of goods sold* (COGS). See "About the Cost of Goods Sold Account," later in this chapter.

When you set up an inventory part item, you can enter a "reorder point" amount. When QuickBooks determines that the item has reached that number, you'll see a message saying it's time to reorder the item.

> **DEFINITION**
>
> The **Cost of Goods Sold** account (when abbreviated, it's pronounced like *cogs* in "wheels and cogs") tracks how much you paid for items (the cost) that you had in inventory and then sold.

Setting Inventory Preferences

You can set a couple of preferences for inventory tracking, including turning on the feature and setting reminders. If QuickBooks has not turned on the inventory feature based on your answers when you set up your company file, you can do so now.

Turning On Inventory Tracking

To turn on inventory tracking, go to the **Edit** menu and click **Preferences**. In the left panel, click **Items & Inventory**, and then click the **Company Preferences** tab. (See Figure 18.1.)

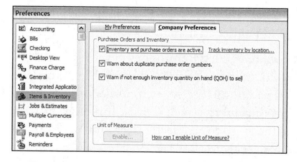

Figure 18.1: *The Items & Inventory preferences.*

If you don't see a check mark in the **Purchase Orders and Inventory** check box, click it to turn on inventory features. When you turn on inventory, you also turn on purchase orders, although you don't have to use them. When inventory is turned on, you'll see inventory and purchase order icons on the Home page, you'll be able to create inventory part items, and you'll be able to generate inventory reports.

The two links on the page lead to upsell opportunities: if you want to do those things, you'll have to upgrade your QuickBooks edition.

The two inventory options you do have control over are described below and selected by default:

Warn About Duplicate Purchase Order Numbers: If this option is checked, QuickBooks lets you know whether a P.O. number already exists in your company file. This helps avoid confusion later. If you don't use purchase orders, you can click to remove the check mark.

Warn If Not Enough Inventory Quantity on Hand (QOH) to Sell: If this option is checked, QuickBooks warns you when you enter an item on a sales form and you don't have enough on hand to fulfill the order. You can go ahead and save the sales form anyway, but QuickBooks Pro doesn't handle backorders (you have to upgrade to get backorder tracking). Also, all QuickBooks does is warn you that you don't have enough quantity on hand; you have to order more from the vendor.

Next, you can set inventory reminders, so don't click OK to close the Preference window.

Setting Inventory Reminders

One inventory reminder preference might be useful to you. QuickBooks can remind you when it's time to reorder an item.

In the Preference window, click **Reminders** in the left panel. When QuickBooks asks whether you want to save the changes you made to the Items & Inventory preferences, click **Yes**. For the Inventory to Order option, select how you want to be reminded: **Show Summary** (you'll see just Inventory to Reorder) or **Show List** (you'll see a list of the items to reorder). Select **Don't Remind Me** if you want to rely on your memory. Click **OK** to close the Preference window.

Setting Up Accounts Needed for Inventory

You'll need a few accounts to track inventory, and QuickBooks creates a couple of them for you in your chart of accounts: an Inventory Asset account to track the current value of your inventory, and a Cost of Goods Sold (COGS) account to track how much you paid for your inventory items and subsequently sold.

First, I'll describe what the COGS account does for you; then I'll go over other accounts you might want to create.

About the Cost of Goods Sold Account

While an item sits on the shelf in your store or backroom, QuickBooks tracks its value in the Inventory Asset account. When you sell an item, QuickBooks takes the value out of the Inventory Asset account and puts it into the COGS account. QuickBooks multiplies the quantity you sold by the average cost of the item and tracks that value in COGS. QuickBooks needs to track this cost so it can determine your profit on the items you sell. To calculate your gross profit before expenses, QuickBooks subtracts the costs of the items you've sold from your total income. You can see this on a Profit and Loss report.

QUICKTIP

You can create additional COGS accounts as subaccounts of the COGS account to track costs for different types of inventory—for example, one to track products you sell and another to track materials you sell.

When you sell an inventory item to a customer, QuickBooks decreases your Inventory Asset account and increases your Cost of Goods Sold account (that debit/credit thing).

Creating Other Inventory Accounts

One account you'll want to create is an Inventory Adjustment account. This is where you can track any adjustments you make to inventory quantities. Let's say you've taken a physical count of your inventory and discovered that you have quite a bit more rubber duckies than you thought. You'll also have to adjust for that carton of soap bars that got damaged by a water leak. In these cases, you'll adjust the inventory asset account up for the duckies and down for the soap. But you need to have an account to balance those adjustments—hence, the Inventory Adjustment account.

The inventory adjustment account you create can be either an expense account or a COGS account. Check with your accountant about which one you should use. To create the account, go to the **Lists** menu and click **Chart of Accounts**. In the Chart of Accounts window, press **Ctrl+N**. Select the account type as either an Expense account or a Cost of Goods Sold account (see Figure 18.2). Click **Continue** and give the account a name, such as Inventory Adjustment. Talk to your accountant to figure out which tax line to assign to this account. Click **Save & Close**.

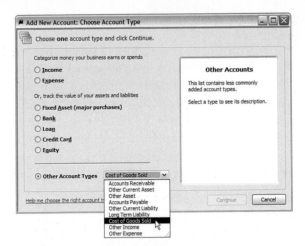

Figure 18.2: *The New Account type window.*

As mentioned earlier, you can create subaccounts of the COGS account to track different types of inventory. Say you own a retail cooking store. You sell food items, equipment, and cookbooks. You could create a subaccount for each category of items. This will give you more detail and could help you determine what is most profitable for you.

To create a subaccount, go to **Lists** and click **Chart of Accounts**. Press **Ctrl+N** to add a new account. Click **Other Account Types** and then choose **Cost of Goods Sold**. Click **Continue** and enter a name for the subaccount. Click the **Subaccount Of** check box and then choose **Cost of Goods Sold** as the parent account. Click **Save & Close**.

Setting Up Inventory Items

Before you can track inventory, purchase inventory, or sell inventory, you need to create the inventory items.

BEHIND THE SCENES

When you order and receive inventory items, QuickBooks increases the on-hand quantities and value of inventory, and adjusts the average costs. When you sell inventory items, QuickBooks decreases the on-hand quantities and value of inventory, and increases the cost of goods sold.

To create an inventory item, follow these steps:

1. Go to the **Lists** menu and choose **Item List**, or click the **Items & Services** icon in the Company section of the Home page.

2. Click the Item button at the bottom left of the list and click **New**, or press **Ctrl+N** to open the new item window. Figure 18.3 shows the New Item window.

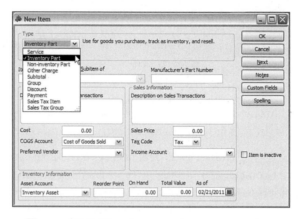

Figure 18.3: *Creating a new inventory part item.*

3. Click in the **Type** field and choose **Inventory Part**.

4. Click in the **Item Name/Number** field and type a unique identifier for the item.

   When you create an invoice or purchase order, this is the name you will see as a choice on the line item menu.

5. (Optional) To make this item a subitem, click the **Subitem Of** check box to put a check mark in it, and then choose the parent item (or click **<Add New>**).

6. (Optional) If you purchase this inventory part item from a vendor and the vendor has a part number, click in the **Manufacturer's Part Number** field and type the number. This is useful when writing a purchase order for the item because the vendor will know exactly what you want to order.

7. For Purchase Information:

   • Click in the **Description** field for Purchase Information and type the description you want to appear on purchase transactions.

   • Click in the **Cost** field for Purchase Information and type the cost of the item, or leave it blank and fill in the cost on the purchase order (or when you enter the vendor's bill and pay with a check).

   • From the COGS Account menu, choose the cost of goods sold account to which you want to post the cost when you sell it.

   • If you have a preferred vendor for this item, choose the vendor name.

8. For Sales Information:

   • Click in the **Description** field and type the description of this item that you want to appear on invoices, estimates, and sales receipts.

   • Click in the **Sales Price** field and type the price you charge for this item. (You can change the price, if needed, when you create a sales transaction, or you can leave the price blank and type a price when you create an invoice, estimate, or sales receipt.)

   • From the Tax Code menu, choose whether this item is taxable. (You'll see the Tax Code menu only if you charge sales tax.)

   • From the Income Account menu, choose the income account to use to track the income from the sale of this item.

9. For Inventory Information (see Figure 18.4):

Figure 18.4: *Entering inventory information.*

• QuickBooks has already created an Inventory Asset account for you and has entered it in the Asset Account field.

• Click in the **Reorder Point** field and type the minimum number of items you want to keep in stock. QuickBooks will add a reminder to the Reminders List (which you enabled earlier in this chapter) to order more.

- Leave the On Hand and Total Value fields empty. QuickBooks will come up with these values when you receive the items into inventory (see Chapter 19) or when you make an inventory adjustment (see Chapter 20).

10. Click **OK** to save the inventory part item and close the window, or click **Next** to save it and create a new one.

QUICKTIP

If you have to enter a lot of inventory items, it may be faster to use the Add/Edit Multiple List Entries window. In the Item List, click **Item**, then click **Add/Edit Multiple Items**. This opens a spreadsheet-like view where each row represents an item.

Creating Parent and Subitems

Creating parent and subitems can be helpful for grouping similar items and reporting on them in sales reports and graphs. For example, a retail fishing store might want to group flies by type. So a parent item could be Fly Fishing Flies and subitems could be Dry Flies, Nymph Flies, Salmon Flies, and so on.

To create a parent item, follow the steps above in "Setting Up Inventory Items," skipping step 5.

Keep the following in mind when creating parent and subitems:

- The parent item is the "umbrella" item; the subitems will be grouped under the parent item.

- The subitems must be the same item type (inventory part) as the parent item.

- For the parent item, you don't need to enter the description, cost, price, re-order point, or on-hand amount.

- For both the parent item and the subitems, you must enter the COGS account, income account, and asset account.

- To make an item a subitem of the parent item, click the **Subitem Of** check box and then choose the parent item.

Creating Inventory Groups

QuickBooks Pro isn't designed to track manufactured items (you need QuickBooks Premier or Enterprise Solutions to track inventory assemblies). But you can create groups, which can be made up of inventory part items, as well as other item types, and then "manufactured" and sold as a group.

Before creating the inventory group, create the items that will go into the group. A group item can contain any other item types except other group items.

To create an inventory group, follow these steps:

1. Go to the **Lists** menu and choose **Item List,** or click the **Items & Services** icon in the Company section of the Home page.

2. Click the **Item** button at the bottom left of the list and click **New** or press **Ctrl+N** to open the new item window.

3. Click in the **Type** field and choose **Group**. Figure 18.5 shows the New Group Item window.

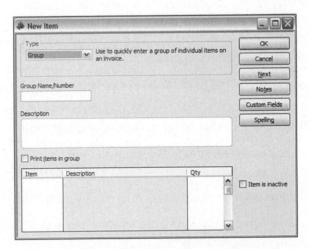

Figure 18.5: *Creating a group item for inventory.*

4. Type a name or number for the group.

5. Type a description for the group. This description will appear on sales forms.

6. If you want the customer to see the items that make up the group, click the **Print Items in Group** check box. If you don't check the box, the customer sees only the name of the group.

7. Click in the **Item** column and choose an item that is part of the group. In the Qty column, type how many of this item goes into the group.

8. Repeat step 7 for each item in the group. You can enter up to 20 items.

9. Click **OK**.

When you sell a group item, QuickBooks adjusts the quantity on hand for each item in the group.

The Least You Need to Know

- QuickBooks uses the Average Cost method to figure out the value of your inventory. It takes the total cost of each item you have in stock and divides the total cost by the number of items.

- For each item that you keep in stock for resale, you create an inventory part item. The items can be things you manufacture or products you buy already manufactured. The key point is that you have these inventory part items on hand for the purpose of reselling to customers.

- Use the Reorder Point field in the inventory part item window to tell QuickBooks the minimum number of the item you want to keep in stock. QuickBooks will add a reminder to the Reminders List to order more.

- Use a group item to mimic a product you assemble from other inventory parts or items.

Purchasing and Receiving Inventory

In This Chapter

- Understanding purchase orders
- Writing purchase orders
- Receiving inventory with a bill
- Receiving inventory without a bill
- Purchasing inventory over the counter

Sometimes my memory is like a sieve … I'm wondering, "Did I order those ceramic tiles already?" and "What about those picture frames—how many did I order?" Once again, the miracle of QuickBooks saves the day. When I use QuickBooks' purchase orders, I can keep track of those pesky little details.

About Purchase Orders

Probably most of your suppliers of materials and inventory items will want you to issue a purchase order to order from them. Using purchase orders is optional but is standard business practice. Even if you order over the phone or Internet, you'll want to create a purchase order. Besides being the "way things work," the main purpose of purchase orders is to keep track of things you've ordered.

When you turned on the inventory feature, you also turned on purchase orders. Inventory and purchase orders go hand-in-hand. When you create your first purchase order, QuickBooks creates a new account called Purchase Orders. This is a *nonposting* account, which means any amounts on the purchase order are not posted and do not affect your income statement or balance sheet.

DEFINITION

A **nonposting** account does not affect your profit or loss and does not affect your financial reports.

Use purchase orders when you order something that you will receive and pay for later. If you buy supplies or inventory items in person at a store, you don't need to create a purchase order. You can also use purchase orders to buy things that are not inventory items, such as fixed assets or services that are not set up as inventory. When you receive the items, you can compare the shipment with the purchase order to make sure you received the correct items in the correct amounts.

Creating Purchase Orders

As mentioned previously, QuickBooks tracks inventory from the time you purchase items to the final sale to customers.

Purchasing and receiving inventory involves a few steps, which QuickBooks tracks for you in various accounts. The first step starts with creating a purchase order. QuickBooks tracks the purchase order in the Purchase Orders account. The second step is receiving the inventory and entering the bill (or *item receipt*, if you didn't receive the bill with the inventory). When you receive the inventory, QuickBooks increases the accounts payable based on the bill amount, adds the value of the inventory to your Inventory Asset account, increases the on-hand amount of the item, and recalculates the average cost. The third step is paying the bill.

DEFINITION

An **item receipt** tracks inventory you receive without a bill. Convert the item receipt into a bill when you actually receive the bill from the vendor.

When you sell the item, QuickBooks tracks the sale in an income account and the cost in a COGS account, and tracks the value of the remaining inventory in the Inventory Asset account.

If you don't see the Purchase Orders icon on the Home page or on the Vendors menu, you need to turn on the inventory features, as explained in Chapter 18.

The purchase order form will probably look familiar to you; it looks like an actual vendor bill.

To create a purchase order, follow these steps:

1. Open the purchase order form by going to the **Vendors** menu and click **Create Purchase Orders**, or click the **Purchase Orders** icon on the Home page.

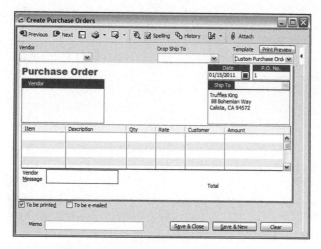

Figure 19.1: *The Purchase Order form.*

2. On the purchase order form (see Figure 19.1), click the down arrow in the Vendor field to open the menu to choose a vendor (or click **<Add New>** if this purchase order is for a new vendor). QuickBooks fills in much of the information for you from the vendor record.

3. If you use classes in tracking inventory, choose the class from the Class menu. (If you haven't turned on class tracking, you won't see the Class menu.)

4. If you want to ship the order directly to someone else, click the Drop Ship To menu and choose the person or company you want to ship the order to.

5. Look in the Date field and P.O. No. fields and change the date or number, if necessary. If this is your first purchase order, QuickBooks starts numbering from 1. If you don't want to appear as a "newbie" to your vendor, you can change the purchase order number to something higher. From then on, QuickBooks increases that number by one.

6. Click in the Item field and choose the item you're purchasing with this purchase order.

7. Type a description if QuickBooks didn't fill out that field.

8. Click in the Qty column and type the quantity you're ordering.

9. If you're purchasing the item for a customer or job, choose the Customer:Job.

10. Repeat steps 6 through 9 as needed to add more items to the purchase order.

11. In the Vendor Message box, type an optional note for the vendor.

12. Indicate whether the purchase order should be e-mailed or printed. Click the appropriate check box to put a check mark in it.

13. In the Memo field at the bottom, type a brief note to yourself on what the purchase order is for. The note can help you later associate the purchase order with the bill.

14. Click **Save & New** to save the purchase order and enter a new one, or click **Save & Close** to save the purchase order and close the window.

QUICKTIP

To check the on-hand amount for an inventory item, open the Item List (click **Items & Services** on the Home page) and check the Total Quantity On Hand column for the inventory item.

Receiving Inventory

When you receive a shipment, you'll want to compare the shipment with your purchase order and add the items to your inventory. The process differs slightly depending on whether you receive the items with or without the bill. This section covers four scenarios for receiving inventory: you receive a bill at the same time as the inventory, you receive the inventory first and the bill comes later, you receive the bill before receiving inventory, or you purchased inventory items over the counter and need to account for the purchase.

Receiving the Bill with the Inventory Items

When items are shipped with the bill, either you open the shipment box and, right there staring you in the face is the bill, or the bill is in an envelope attached to the outside of the box. In QuickBooks, this is a one-step process.

To receive the bill with the inventory, follow these steps:

1. Go to the **Vendors** menu and click **Receive Items and Enter Bill**, or, in the Vendors section of the Home page, click **Receive Inventory** and then choose **Receive Inventory with Bill**. See Figure 19.2.

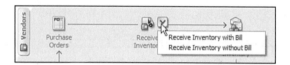

Figure 19.2: *Receive inventory on the Home page.*

2. In the Enter Bills window (see Figure 19.3), choose the vendor.

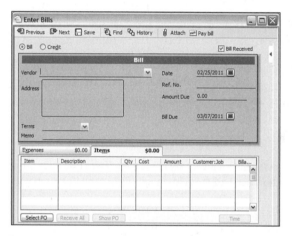

Figure 19.3: *Enter Bills window with Items tab showing.*

3. After you choose the vendor and the vendor has a purchase order open, QuickBooks asks if you want to receive against one or more purchase orders. Click **Yes** to receive against the purchase order.

4. This is where that memo you wrote to yourself on the purchase order comes in handy. In the Open Purchase Orders window (see Figure 19.4), click the check mark column to select the purchase order you want to receive against.

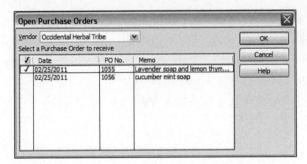

Figure 19.4: *Select the purchase order to receive against.*

5. QuickBooks fills out the rest of the bill for you. This is where you check that the quantities received match the quantity you ordered. Change the quantity amount, if necessary.

6. Click **Save & New** to save the bill and enter a new one, or click **Save & Close** to save the bill and close the window.

When you save the bill, QuickBooks adds the items to inventory and posts a bill transaction to your accounts payable.

QUICKTIP

You can enter a bill for inventory items even if you don't use purchase orders. Just type the amount due and manually fill out the Items tab with the items you received.

If you received a partial shipment against a purchase order, QuickBooks changes the purchase order based on the quantities received. The purchase order is still considered "open" and the remaining items are still on order.

At the bottom of the Bill or Item Receipt window (see Figure 19.3), you'll see three buttons: Select PO, Clear Qtys/Receive All (If you have a quantity in the Qty field, Receive All changes to Clear Qtys), and Show PO.

Select PO: Shows you a list of open purchase orders with the vendor. Click the purchase order to fill in the line items in the Items tab from that P.O.

Clear Qtys/Receive All: Click **Clear Qtys** if you didn't receive everything on the P.O. in this shipment. QuickBooks erases all the quantities. Click **Receive All** to put the original quantities back, to indicate that you've received all the items in full.

Show PO: Click a line item to select it, and then click **Show PO** to see the purchase order the line item came from. This is useful if you're receiving against more than one P.O. at the same time.

Receiving the Inventory Items Without a Bill

When items are shipped without the bill, you may not want to wait until you receive the bill to put the stuff into inventory so you can sell it. To put the stuff into inventory, you need to tell QuickBooks that the items have been received. You do this by creating an item receipt. Receiving inventory without a bill is a two-step process: create an item receipt and then later, when you receive the actual bill, enter the bill.

To receive inventory items without a bill, follow these steps:

1. Go to the **Vendors** menu and click **Receive Items**, or, in the Vendors section of the Home page, click **Receive Inventory** and then choose **Receive Inventory Without Bill**.

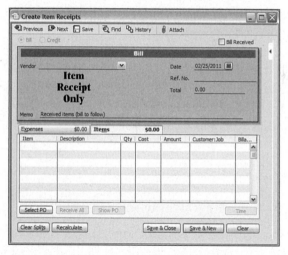

Figure 19.5: *Fill out the Item Receipt window (History panel hidden).*

2. In the Item Receipt window (see Figure 19.5), choose the vendor.

3. After you choose the vendor, if the vendor has a purchase order open, QuickBooks asks if you want to receive against one or more purchase orders. Click **Yes** to receive against the purchase order and then click to select the purchase order. (If there is no purchase order, you can fill out the item receipt manually.)

4. If there is a purchase order, QuickBooks fills out the rest of the item receipt for you. This is where you compare that the quantities received match the quantity you ordered. Change the quantity amount, if necessary. (If there is no purchase order, you can fill out the item receipt manually.)

5. Click **Save & New** to save the item receipt and enter a new one, or click **Save & Close** to save the item receipt and close the window.

When you save the item receipt, QuickBooks adds the items to inventory and posts an item receipt type transaction (instead of a bill) to your accounts payable.

When you receive the actual bill, you'll need to enter the bill. See "Entering a Bill for Items Received," next.

Entering a Bill for Items Received

The second step in receiving inventory items without a bill is to record the bill when it does arrive. To record the bill, don't use the Enter Bills window (this will cause a double posting to your accounts payable). Instead, follow the steps in this section.

To enter a bill for items received, do this:

1. Go to the **Vendors** menu and click **Enter Bill for Received Items**, or, in the Vendors section of the Home page, click **Enter Bills Against Inventory**.

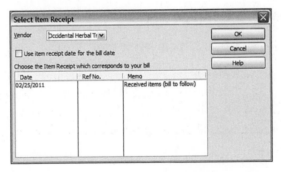

Figure 19.6: *Select the item receipt against which you want to enter the bill.*

2. In the Select Item Receipt window (see Figure 19.6), click to select the item receipt that goes with the bill and click **OK**.

3. Click in the "Use item receipt date for the bill date" check box to change the date of the bill to the date of the item receipt. Generally, companies invoice the same date they deliver the goods. Since this is usually in the past and the bill form defaults to the current date, selecting this check box saves a little time.

4. QuickBooks prefills most of the bill. Change any quantities or amounts, if needed.

5. If you need to add any shipping charges or sales tax, click the **Expenses** tab and add a shipping expense item (and/or sales tax item) and amount.

6. Click the **Recalculate** button to update the Amount Due if you changed or added items.

7. Click **Save & Close**. QuickBooks asks if you're sure you want to save the transaction (even if you didn't make any changes). This is because the transaction is being changed from an item receipt to a bill. Click **Yes** to save the changes.

NUMBERS HAPPEN

There's a chance of a double-posting to the accounts payable account, especially if someone in the warehouse records the receipt of the item and someone else records the bill. QuickBooks tries to prevent this from happening by alerting the person recording the bill if the wrong enter bill window is used.

Receiving the Bill Before You Receive Inventory

Even if you receive the bill before you receive the inventory items you ordered, it's a good idea to wait until you actually receive the items before you pay the bill. For example, if you ordered something online, you might receive the bill by e-mail before the shipment arrives. In fact, QuickBooks doesn't provide a way to pay for inventory before you receive it.

Paying by Check or Credit Card

You can also receive inventory by paying the bill using a check or credit card, or you can receive inventory when you purchase items over the counter.

Occasionally, my local framing shop has phenomenal deals on frames when buying multiples; it's often cheaper than wholesale mail order prices, taking into account not having to pay for shipping. But I still need to "receive" those items into inventory.

You can receive the items by recording either a check or a credit card purchase. To receive against a purchase order instead of recording an over-the-counter purchase, just choose the appropriate purchase order when QuickBooks asks you.

To write a check, follow these steps:

1. Click **Write Checks** on the Home page to open the Write Checks window.

2. Fill out the top portion of the check. (If the vendor you choose has open bills, QuickBooks alerts you that you should use Pay Bills instead of Write Checks. If this is an additional purchase not already covered by the open bills, click **Continue Writing Check**.)

3. If the vendor you select has open purchase orders, QuickBooks asks you to select the purchase order to receive against. Skip this step if you're purchasing items over the counter.

4. On the check, click the **Items** tab.

5. In the line item area, enter the items you've purchased and the quantities.

6. Click **Save & Close** to save the check.

NUMBERS HAPPEN

If you choose a vendor on the check and there are outstanding bills for the vendor, QuickBooks warns you that you should use the Pay Bills window instead of the Write Checks window. This is to prevent inaccuracies in your accounts payable balance.

To pay by credit card, follow these steps:

1. Click **Enter Credit Card Charges** on the Home page.

2. Check the Credit Card menu to make sure the correct credit card is selected.

3. Fill out the top portion of the credit card window. (If the vendor you choose has open bills or item receipts, QuickBooks alerts you that you should use Pay Bills or Enter Bill for Received Items. Click **OK** to remove the warning.)

4. If the vendor you select has open purchase orders, QuickBooks asks you to select the purchase order to receive against. Skip this step if you're purchasing items over the counter.

5. Click the **Items** tab.

6. In the line item area, enter the items you've purchased and the quantities.

7. Click **Save & Close** to save the check.

Checking Your Open Purchase Orders

Back to my mind being a sieve … more often than I like to admit, I forget whether or when I've placed an order for inventory items. Lucky for my addled brain, QuickBooks can help in several ways.

To see a list of all outstanding purchase orders, go to the **Reports** menu, go to **Purchases**, and click **Open Purchase Orders**. Alternatively, click the **Vendors** button on the Home page, click the **Transactions** tab, and click **Purchase Orders**. From the Filter By menu, choose **Open Purchase Orders**. Double-click a purchase order to open it.

To see a list of purchase orders for an item, click **Items & Services** on the Home page. Click the item, go to the **Reports** menu, and click **QuickReport**. Double-click a purchase order to open it.

To see how much of an item you have on hand and on purchase orders, double-click the item in the Item List. At the bottom of the window, you'll see the quantity on hand and the number of items currently on open purchase orders (see Figure 19.7).

Figure 19.7: *The Inventory Information gives you an at-a-glance look at quantities.*

To see on-hand, on order, and reorder point quantities for all items at a glance, customize the Item List. Go to **Lists** and click **Item List**. In the Item List window, click **Item** and then click **Customize Columns**. In Available Columns, select **Quantity on Purchase Order**, click **Add**, select **Reorder Point**, and click **Add**. You can move them up or down on the list to determine what position they appear in the Item List. Click **OK**.

The Least You Need to Know

- Use purchase orders when you order something that you will receive and pay for later.
- When you receive a shipment, you'll want to compare the shipment with your purchase order and add the items to your inventory, which you can do with or without the bill.
- You can also receive inventory by paying the bill using a check or credit card, or you can receive inventory when you purchase items over the counter.
- When you save a bill or item receipt, QuickBooks adds the items to inventory and posts a transaction to your accounts payable.

Periodic Inventory Tasks

In This Chapter

- Using inventory reports
- Preparing for an inventory count
- Counting inventory
- Adjusting inventory

The trick behind managing inventory is this: keep enough of an inventory item on hand so that it's there when your customers want it, avoid being overstocked to the point that you can't sell the item as it becomes passé. Do you have a box of go-go boots in the corner of your warehouse that you can't even give away? That's what you want to avoid.

QuickBooks offers several inventory reports to help you analyze trends and pricing. If the value of your inventory is growing faster than your sales, it's time to think about what's not selling and why. Priced too high? Have today's fashionistas shunned go-go boots? What decade is this, anyway? QuickBooks can also help you write off those "what was I thinking" items that no longer sell.

Preparing Inventory Valuation Reports

Inventory valuation reports tell you how much your inventory is currently worth. QuickBooks can generate two different reports to find the value of your inventory: Inventory Valuation Summary and Inventory Valuation Detail.

Inventory Valuation Summary

To generate an inventory valuation summary report, go to **Reports**, go to **Inventory**, and then choose **Inventory Valuation Summary** (see Figure 20.1).

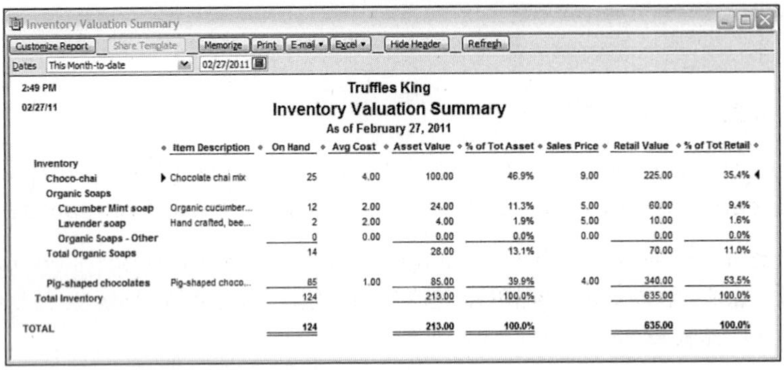

2:49 PM
02/27/11

Truffles King
Inventory Valuation Summary
As of February 27, 2011

	Item Description	On Hand	Avg Cost	Asset Value	% of Tot Asset	Sales Price	Retail Value	% of Tot Retail
Inventory								
Choco-chai	Chocolate chai mix	25	4.00	100.00	46.9%	9.00	225.00	35.4%
Organic Soaps								
Cucumber Mint soap	Organic cucumber...	12	2.00	24.00	11.3%	5.00	60.00	9.4%
Lavender soap	Hand crafted, bee...	2	2.00	4.00	1.9%	5.00	10.00	1.6%
Organic Soaps - Other		0	0.00	0.00	0.0%	0.00	0.00	0.0%
Total Organic Soaps		14		28.00	13.1%		70.00	11.0%
Pig-shaped chocolates	Pig-shaped choco...	85	1.00	85.00	39.9%	4.00	340.00	53.5%
Total Inventory		124		213.00	100.0%		635.00	100.0%
TOTAL		124		213.00	100.0%		635.00	100.0%

Figure 20.1: *The Inventory Valuation Summary report.*

The Inventory Valuation Summary provides a quick view of the value of your inventory for the date range you choose (the default is Current Month to Date). The report columns include these:

Item Description: The description you entered when you set up the item for purchase transactions.

On Hand: The quantity of the item currently in stock. QuickBooks takes the number of the item you've received into inventory and subtracts the number you've sold. If the number is negative, you've sold more stock than you have. Time to order more or to record the receipt of inventory.

Avg Cost: The average cost that you've paid for each item over time. Each time you buy more of an item, QuickBooks recalculates the average cost.

Asset Value: The total value of the item; QuickBooks multiplies the quantity on hand by the average cost.

% of Tot Asset: A higher percentage may mean that you have too many on hand and that the item isn't selling. This could mean the item is obsolete. If the item is selling, the higher percentage could mean you just have too many in stock and that you should think about not ordering as many or as often.

Sales Price: The price that you sell the item for. This is the sales price you entered when you set up the item. If it shows $0.00, you didn't specify a sales price.

Retail Value: This is the sales price multiplied by the number you have on hand.

% of Tot Retail: This is the percentage of the total retail value of all your inventory items represented by the item's retail value.

Inventory Valuation Detail

This report shows each individual transaction that increased or decreased your inventory (each purchase and sales transaction) for the time period you specify.

To generate an inventory valuation summary report, go to **Reports**, go to **Inventory**, and then choose **Inventory Valuation Detail** (see Figure 20.2). You can double-click a transaction to open it.

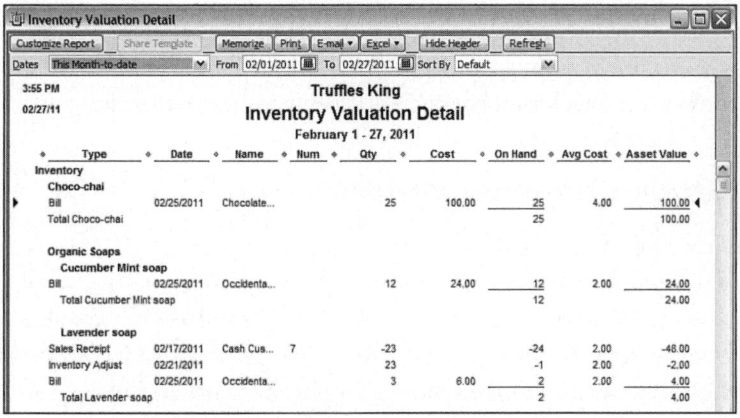

Figure 20.2: *The Inventory Valuation Detail report.*

The report shows the type of transaction (bill, item receipt, sales receipt, invoice, inventory adjustment, and so on). It also shows the date, name, and number of the transaction, as well as the quantity and cost. In addition, it shows the on-hand quantity of the item after the transaction, the average cost, and asset value.

Preparing Inventory Stock Status Reports

Stock status reports show you the current state of your inventory. Two stock status reports exist: Stock Status by Item and Stock Status by Vendor. The reports are similar and include the reorder point (you enter the reorder point when you set up the item), the on-hand amount, whether the number is less than the reorder point, the number of items on a purchase order, the next delivery date, and the average sales per week.

QUICKTIP

Be sure to add a reorder point to your inventory items so you won't get caught short and not have the items in stock to sell to your customers.

Inventory Stock Status by Item

The Inventory Stock Status by Item report groups the report by item. This is useful for seeing, based on your average sales per week, whether you have enough of the item in stock or on purchase orders to fulfill customer demands.

Inventory Stock Status by Vendor

The Inventory Stock Status by Vendor report (see Figure 20.3) groups and subtotals the report by vendor. This report can tell you at a glance whether you're running low on an item (a check mark appears in the Order column to indicate that the quantity on hand is lower than the reorder point you set) and tell you which vendor to order from. You can check the number shown on purchase orders (in the On PO column) to see if those orders will be enough to restock.

Dates This Month-to-date ▾ From 02/01/2011 ▤ To 02/27/2011 ▤

4:29 PM			**Truffles King**				
02/27/11			**Inventory Stock Status by Vendor**				
			February 1 - 27, 2011				
	◦ Item Description ◦	Reorder Pt ◦	On Hand ◦	Order ◦	On PO	◦ Next Deliv	◦ Sales/Week ◦
Chocolate World							
Choco-chai	▶ Chocolate chai mix		25		0		0 ◀
Pig-shaped chocolates	Pig-shaped choco...	10	85		40	02/25/2011	0
Total Chocolate World			110		40		0
Occidental Herbal Tribe							
Cucumber Mint soap	Organic cucumber...	4	12		0		0
Lavender soap	Hand crafted, bee...	10	2	✓	3	02/25/2011	6
Total Occidental Herbal Tribe			14		3		6

Figure 20.3: *The Inventory Stock Status by Vendor report.*

If you're placing an order for one item from a vendor, you can use the report to check the stock of other items you order from the vendor. Then, you can see if you can get a price break or discount with a higher volume purchase or simply save on shipping.

Inventory Item Report

You can get a report on a single inventory item. Click **Items & Services** on the Home page. In the Item List window, highlight the item, click **Reports**, and then click the QuickReport (see Figure 20.4).

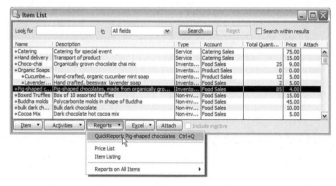

Figure 20.4: *Create a QuickReport on a single item from the Item List.*

This report shows the sales and purchase transactions for the selected item. It shows the on-hand amount and the amount currently on purchase orders and bills (see Figure 20.5), as well as quantities sold from invoices and sales receipts. If you see a negative number in the Qty column, that number represents the number you've sold to the customer; since the items have been sold, the on-hand quantity for the item decreases.

The total shows you the number of items you'll have in stock after you receive the items on the purchase order(s).

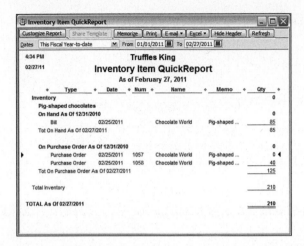

Figure 20.5: *A QuickReport showing the on-hand and on-order amounts for a single item.*

Counting Inventory

Sooner or later, you'll have to put on your dust mask and take a physical count of your inventory. Why? So you can be sure the numbers in QuickBooks are accurate. QuickBooks does a great job of tracking your purchases and sales of items, but QuickBooks isn't psychic. It doesn't know that your uncle helped himself to a case of wine, or that a pack of mice got into those gourmet cheese puffs.

QuickBooks can help by providing a blank worksheet you can use during your inventory count.

Preparing for a Physical Inventory

If you have a large warehouse that might make counting inventory seem overwhelming, you can create a custom field for inventory items, for example, to specify the location or bin number where the item is stored.

To add a custom field, follow these steps:

1. Click **Items & Services** on the Home page.

2. In the Item List, double-click an inventory part item to open it.

3. Click the **Custom Fields** button.

4. On the window that appears, click **Define Fields**.

5. Click in the Label field and type the name. Then click to check the **Use column**, as shown in Figure 20.6.

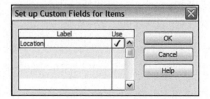

Figure 20.6: *Type a label name for the field and click in the Use column.*

6. Click **OK** until you see the Custom Field window with an empty field ready to be filled in.

7. Type the bin number or location, such as Aisle 2, and click **OK**.

8. Click **OK** to go back to the Item List.

9. Back at the Item List, double-click each inventory part item to add the information to the new custom field. In the item window, click **Custom Fields**, type the location, and click **OK**.

10. Click **OK** to save the edited item.

11. Repeat steps 9 through 10 for each inventory part item.

QUICKTIP

It may be faster to use the Add/Edit Multiple List Entries window to edit your items to add data to the custom field. In the Item List, click **Item**, then click **Add/Edit Multiple Items**. Click **Customize Columns**, locate the custom field, and click **Add**. Click **OK** and then edit the items.

Now, when you create the Physical Inventory Worksheet, you can add the custom Location or Bin Number field to the worksheet and sort by that field so your counters can easily and efficiently find the items.

During the physical count, you'll want to "freeze" your inventory so you won't affect the counts during that time. You'll need to handle your transactions differently to ensure an accurate count. Keep the following in mind when counting inventory:

- Make sure to record the receipt of items in QuickBooks that are already on your shelves, if you haven't already. And record any sales of items in QuickBooks that aren't already recorded. This ensures the on-hand quantities are current and correct.

- Don't fill out an item receipt or enter a bill for received items until after the inventory count is completed.

- If you receive any inventory items during the count, leave them in their boxes; don't unpack and place them on the shelves.

- Hold off on shipping items to customers until after the count.

- If you enter invoices or sales receipts during the count, mark them as "pending." Before saving the invoice or sales receipt, go to the **Edit** menu and click **Mark Invoice As Pending** (or **Mark Sales Receipt As Pending**). Then save the form. When you've completed the inventory count, edit the invoice or sales receipt and then go to **Edit**. There, click **Mark Invoice As Final** (or **Mark Sales Receipt As Final**).

- If you run a retail store, perform the inventory count during off hours or slow periods.

Just before you're ready to start the count, you can generate and print the worksheet.

Generating the Physical Inventory Worksheet

You can use the Physical Inventory Worksheet as you walk around your backroom or warehouse to count the inventory you have. The worksheet lists your items and has a place where you can write down the actual count.

You can customize the worksheet, for example, to remove the Preferred Vendor column—there's really no point in having it there. You can remove the Quantity On Hand column to spare your counters from the temptation of taking any extras they find. You can add a custom field as a column, such as the Location field described in the preceding section. And you can sort the report by item name or by some other column, if you organize your stock alphabetically or numerically.

QUICKTIP

Modify the worksheet to remove the Quantity on Hand column if you're not doing the inventory yourself. The counters don't need to know the amount on hand, and it may tempt them to pocket any items over the amount instead of accounting for them.

To generate and customize the Physical Inventory Worksheet:

1. Go to **Reports**, go to **Inventory**, and then choose **Physical Inventory Worksheet**.

2. To change the columns that appear on the report, click **Customize Report** at the top left of the report.

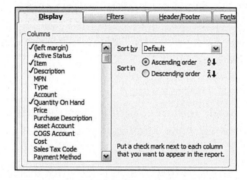

Figure 20.7: *The Modify Report window.*

3. On the Display tab (see Figure 20.7), click a column name to add or remove it from the worksheet. A check mark indicates that the column will appear in the report. To remove the Quantity on Hand column, click it so that it doesn't have a check mark next to it.

4. Custom fields are listed at the bottom, so scroll down to the bottom of the list of columns. Put a check mark next to the custom column(s) you want to appear in the worksheet. (You might find two columns named the same if you set up a custom field—for example, Location may appear twice. Pick the one closest to the bottom of the list.)

5. To sort the worksheet alphabetically, click the **Sort By** menu and choose the column to alphabetize—for example, By Item if you organize your stock room by item name (see Figure 20.8).

Figure 20.8: *Choose the column to sort the worksheet by.*

6. Click **OK** to display the worksheet with your new settings (see Figure 20.9).

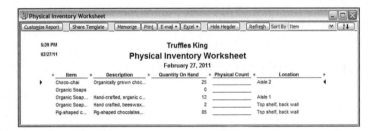

Figure 20.9: *The Physical Inventory Worksheet.*

7. When you're ready to start counting, click the **Print** button to print the worksheet to give to your counters. Type the number of copies you need.

Note that, by default, the worksheet shows only active inventory items. If you want to also include both active and inactive items, you need to change the setting. In the **Modify Reports**, **Status** filter, click **All**.

About Inventory Adjustments

After you complete the inventory count, print another Physical Inventory Worksheet with the On Hand Quantity showing and consolidate all worksheets onto the new blank worksheet. Compare the quantities in the Physical Count column with the amounts in the On Hand column.

Discrepancies could occur from items being broken or otherwise damaged, or from theft. You'll have to account for the discrepancies in QuickBooks by making an inventory adjustment and offsetting the amount in an inventory adjustment account.

Setting Up an Inventory Adjustment Account

To account for the cost of the inventory adjustment, you'll need to create an inventory adjustment account. This can be either an expense account or a subaccount of the COGS account. Ask your accountant which type you need to set up. However, QuickBooks doesn't like it when you choose a COGS account for inventory adjustment and will nag you each time you choose the account.

To create an inventory adjustment account, click **Chart of Accounts** on the Home page. Press **Ctrl+N**. In the Add New Account: Choose Account Type window, click **Expense** and then click **Continue**. Type a name for the account, such as Inventory Adjustment. Click **Save & Close**.

Making Inventory Adjustments

Now that you have your master physical inventory worksheet with the counts for all the items on it, you can make corrections. For each item for which the quantity on hand differs from the actual count, you'll need to make an adjustment for the item.

To make an inventory adjustment, follow these steps:

1. Go to the **Vendors** menu, go to **Inventory Activities**, and click **Adjust Quantity/Value on Hand** (see Figure 20.10).

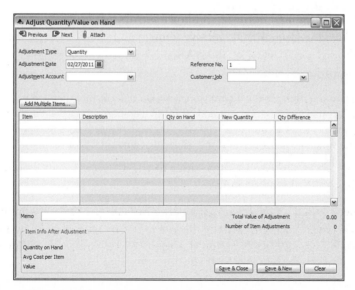

Figure 20.10: *The Adjust Quantity/Value on Hand window.*

2. Keep the Adjustment Type as Quantity because you will be entering quantities from your inventory count.

3. Choose the Inventory Adjustment account you set up to track inventory adjustments.

4. Do one of the following:

    • If you're adjusting just a few items, click in the Item column and, from the menu, choose the first item you're adjusting. QuickBooks fills in the description and current quantity on hand.

    • If you're adjusting a lot of items, click **Add Multiple Lines**. Click in the checkmark column for each item or click **Select All**. Then click **Add Selected Items**.

5. Click or Tab to the New Quantity column and type the new quantity, if needed, from the inventory count.

6. Press Tab. QuickBooks calculates the difference, as either a positive or negative number.

7. Repeat steps 4 through 6 as needed to complete the inventory count adjustments.

8. In the Memo field, type why you're making the adjustment, such as "Quarterly inventory count."

9. Click **Save & Close**.

BEHIND THE SCENES

When you decrease the quantity on hand, QuickBooks increases the inventory adjustment expense account and offsets that amount with a decrease in the inventory asset account. An increase in the quantity decreases the inventory adjustment expense account and offsets that amount with an increase in the inventory asset account.

Adjusting for Obsolete Inventory

Remember those go-go boots? You can dispose of them and get the wretched things out of your warehouse *and* write off the amount as an expense.

You'll need to create an expense account to track obsolete items, such as Obsolete Inventory. Follow the steps in "Setting Up an Inventory Adjustment Account" to create the account. Then follow the steps in "Making Inventory Adjustments," except choose the obsolete inventory account you just created. Choose the item to write off and enter **0** (zero) as the New Quantity. Click **Save & Close**.

The Least You Need to Know

- Inventory valuation reports tell you how much your inventory is currently worth.
- Stock status reports show you the current state of your inventory. Two stock status reports exist: Stock Status by Item and Stock Status by Vendor.
- Create a custom field for inventory items—for example, to specify the location or bin number where the item is stored. This makes counting inventory more efficient.
- During the physical count, most businesses "freeze" their inventory so that on-hand amounts will not be affected.
- Create an inventory adjustment account to track the cost of the inventory adjustment.
- In addition to adjusting quantities after an inventory count, you can make adjustments to write off obsolete inventory.

Day-to-Day Banking Tasks

Part

6

This part covers some typical banking activities you perform during the course of your business day or week. You learn how to use account registers, make deposits, and reconcile your bank accounts.

Chapter 21 goes over basic checking transactions, including how to use both account registers and customer registers. You also learn how to use QuickBooks to perform other banking tasks, such as transferring money, making deposits, and voiding or deleting checks.

In Chapter 22, you find out how to reconcile your bank accounts and locate the source of any discrepancies. QuickBooks even has a feature that undoes a previous reconciliation if things have become hopelessly messed up. This chapter also explains how to reconcile and pay your credit card bill.

Chapter 23 covers miscellaneous banking tasks. Hopefully, you won't often have to deal with bounced checks, but this chapter helps you set up QuickBooks items you'll need in case a customer check bounces, handle any bank fees, and re-invoice the customer. This chapter also tells you how to set up and track petty cash.

Basic Checkbook Transactions

In This Chapter

- Using account and customer registers
- Voiding and deleting transactions
- Transferring money between accounts
- Making deposits and getting cash back
- Viewing the Undeposited Funds account register

Remember those balance sheet accounts from Chapter 4? QuickBooks creates a register for each of those accounts except the Retained Earnings equity account. The registers look a lot like a checkbook register, and they show a list of transactions that occurred in the account.

QuickBooks also creates a register for each of your customers that shows only the transactions associated with that customer.

Every time you enter a transaction, such as a bill payment or a deposit, QuickBooks makes an entry into the appropriate register. So if you make a payment on a credit card, QuickBooks logs the payment in the credit card register; if you write a check to pay a bill, QuickBooks logs the check in the register for the checking account you used.

Using Registers

If you prefer, you can enter transactions directly into registers. For example, instead of using the Write Checks or Make Deposit windows to enter a transaction, just enter it directly into the *bank account register*. Some might find the direct method is faster.

> **DEFINITION**
>
> A **bank account register** can be a checking, savings, money market, or petty cash account.

In addition, instead of using the Enter Bills window to enter a transaction, just enter it directly into your accounts payable (A/P) register.

Sometimes you'll want to work directly in a register to enter a debit card transaction or transfer funds between accounts, just because it's easier.

Opening a Register

QuickBooks offers a couple ways to open registers, depending on the type of register.

To open a balance sheet account, go to the **Banking** menu and click **Use Registers**; then choose the account to open. Alternatively, go to the **Lists** menu, click **Chart of Accounts**, and double-click the account to open; or right-click the highlighted account and choose **Use Register**; or highlight the account, go to **Banking**, and click **Use Register**. How could you ever get bored having so many ways to open a register?

Income and expense accounts aren't considered balance sheet accounts, but you can still open them to see a list of transactions. Double-clicking an income or expense account opens a QuickReport instead of a register. You can view the transactions, but you can't edit them or enter new ones in the report itself. You can, however, double-click a transaction to open it for editing.

If you want to open a register for a customer, click **Customer Center** on the navigation bar. On the Customers tab, right-click the customer or job and click **Use Register**.

Using Account Registers

Each account register shows a record of all transactions that affect the account's balance. You can use your account registers to create, edit, and delete transactions and maintain the account (make adjustments, void transactions, and so on).

All the registers work the same way for all types of accounts, but the column headings change depending on the type of account. Figure 21.1 shows a checking account register.

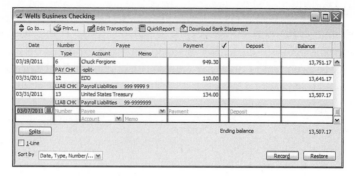

Figure 21.1: *A checking account register.*

Now I'll briefly go over ways to navigate in a register. Some registers have a subset of what is listed here.

Go To: Click to search in the current register only. Search by payee, transaction number, memo, or amount.

Edit>Find: Go to **Edit** and click **Find** to search across several accounts.

=: In an amount field of a new transaction, press the equals sign (=) on your keyboard to open a minicalculator. Press **Enter** to put the result into the field, or press **Esc** to leave the calculator without inserting the amount.

Tab: Press the **Tab** key on your keyboard to move from one field to the next.

Edit Transaction: Click on a transaction and click **Edit Transaction** to open the original transaction or make changes you can't make directly in the register.

PgUp/PgDn: Press the **PgUp** key to jump up in the register several transactions at a time; press **PgDn** to jump down in the register.

Home/End: Press the **Home** key on your keyboard to move to the beginning of the current field. Press **Home** twice to move to the first field of the current transaction. Press **Home** three times to move to the beginning transaction of the register. The **End** key works the same, only in reverse.

+/-: In a Date or Number field of a new transaction, press the **Plus** sign (+) on your keyboard to increase the date or number; press the **Minus** sign (-) on your keyboard to decrease the date or number. Another good trick for Date fields is to type **t** on your keyboard to automatically enter today's date.

Splits: Click **Splits** to open the transaction so you can split the amount of the transaction between two or more accounts. Figure 21.2 shows a transaction with Splits open. Click Splits again to close. Splits works only for expenses on checks and credit card charges. To enter splits on other transactions, click **Edit Transaction**.

Date	Number	Payee		Payment	✓	Deposit		Balance	
	Type	Account	Memo						
01/15/2011	Number	Flying Brooms		123.00		Deposit		15,761.13	▲
	CHK	Repairs and Maint	Memo						

Account	Amount		Memo	Customer:Job	Billable?			Close
Repairs and Maintenance		100.00		Darcy, Colin	☑	▲		
Equipment and supplies	▼	23.00			▼			Clear
						▼		Recalc

Splits		Ending balance	13,507.17

Figure 21.2: *Assign the amount of a transaction to one or more accounts in the splits area.*

1-Line: Click to put a check mark in the 1-Line check box to display more transactions in the register. Each transaction is shown on one line instead of two.

Sort by: Choose how you want to sort the transactions in the register.

Restore: Removes any changes you've made and restores the transaction to its original state.

Record: Saves the new transaction or saves the changes you made to an existing transaction.

One more thing … the Checkmark column in a register tells you the cleared status of the transaction. A check mark means the transaction has been reconciled and cleared. An asterisk means you marked the transaction as cleared, but you haven't finished the reconciliation yet.

Using Customer Registers

Each customer has a register that lists all the transactions with the customer, including invoices, payments received, credit memos, refund checks, statement charges, discounts applied, and finance charges—all accounts receivable transactions. The register doesn't list sales receipts—the customer pays in full at the time of purchase, so there's no accounts receivable to track.

Use the customer register to view all transactions that affect the customer's balance. You can also enter statement charges (if you use billing statements) directly in the register.

Voiding and Deleting Transactions

If you need to void a check, deposit, or funds transfer, you can void it or you can delete it. For example, if you wrote the incorrect amount on a handwritten check, you can void the check and write a new one. If you need a blank check to establish an automatic funds transfer, you void the check, but keep the blank check in the register so you know why there's a missing check number.

When you void a transaction, QuickBooks changes the amount to zero and indicates that the transaction is void. If you delete a transaction, it's gone from your records. Voiding a transaction is better than deleting one because it still shows in your records. It doesn't have any affect on the financials, but keeping it around may prove useful in the future when your accountant is going over your books.

To void a transaction, click it in the register, go to the **Edit** menu, and click **Void Transaction**. Click **Record**. To delete it, click **Delete Transaction** instead. Click **OK** to confirm.

Transferring Money Between Accounts

If you have two bank accounts, you can transfer money between them. For example, when your checking account gets precariously low, you can transfer money from your savings account.

Before you can transfer funds, you have to have set up the accounts involved. Go to **Lists** and click **Chart of Accounts**. Press **Ctrl+N**, choose **Bank** as the account type, and fill out the new account information. Click **Save & Close**.

To transfer money, go to **Banking** and click **Transfer Funds**. Choose the accounts and the amount of the transfer. Click **Save & Close**. Figure 21.3 shows the Transfer Funds window.

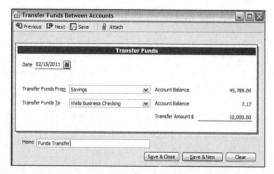

Figure 21.3: *The Transfer Funds window.*

Depositing Payments from Customers

When you receive customer payments, you record them in the Receive Payments window (Chapter 14 covered customer payments). But where do those payments go? QuickBooks puts them in the Undeposited Funds account (unless you specified a different account), and there they hang out until you make a deposit.

To make a deposit from customer payments, follow these steps:

1. Go to the **Banking** menu and click **Make Deposit**.

2. In the Payments to Deposit window (see Figure 21.4), click in the check mark column to select a payment to deposit.

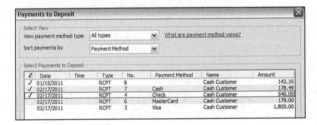

Figure 21.4: *The Payments to Deposit window.*

3. Click **OK**.

4. In the Make Deposits window (see Figure 21.5), verify that the Deposit To account is correct and that the date matches the date you actually make the deposit at the bank.

5. Add any other deposits to include, such as a wad of cash or a refund. If you're making credit card deposits, you might want to enter credit card fees as a negative amount. For each deposit you add, choose the person who gave you the money (Received From), the account to use to track the money, the payment method, and the amount.

Note that if you're depositing a refund, you choose the vendor name in Received From. If the refund is from an overpayment, choose the expense account where the original expense was posted. If it's for the return of goods purchased with a bill, choose the Accounts Payable account.

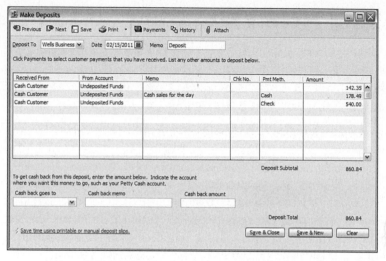

Figure 21.5: *The Make Deposits window.*

6. If you want cash back from the deposit, choose a petty cash or "cash drawer" account from the Cash Back Goes To menu. Type an optional memo and enter the cash back amount. Note that if you're a sole proprietor, you can get cash back for yourself. Just choose the Owner's Draw account instead of Petty Cash (see Figure 21.6).

Figure 21.6: *Recording a cash back from deposit.*

7. To print a deposit slip to take with you to the bank, click the arrow next to the **Print** button and choose **Deposit Slip**.

8. Click **Save & Close**.

QUICKTIP

When making a deposit, select transactions that are the same type—for example, all American Express payments or all cash and checks—and make separate deposits for each type. This makes reconciliation easier if your bank groups deposits by type.

Depositing Money Not from Customers

Some examples of deposits not from customers include a refund or rebate check from a vendor, and money you're putting into the business. If you're depositing money from a loan, first create a liability account to track the loan (see Chapter 8 for how to create an account). Then deposit the loan.

You can use a check register for a single deposit or use the Make Deposits window for multiple deposits.

Using the Check Register

If you want to make a deposit that isn't from customer payments, you can simplify your life by entering the deposit transaction directly in the check register if you're making only a single deposit. You can also use the Make Deposits window as described in the following section if you're making multiple noncustomer deposits.

To make a deposit not from customer payments, follow these steps:

1. Go to the **Banking** menu and click **Use Register**. Figure 21.2 shows a register.

2. Go to the bottom of the register and click in the blank transaction.

3. Click in the Date column and choose the date you actually make the deposit.

4. Press **Tab** to move to the Payee field. For deposits, you don't have to enter a payee, but you can type something to remind you about the deposit. It will appear on reports that include the deposit transaction. If you're depositing a bank loan, you enter the bank as a vendor and use the bank as the payee. If the money comes from an owner or partner, enter the person's name (which should already be in your Other Names list).

5. Press **Tab** to move to the Deposit field and type in the amount of the deposit. QuickBooks changes the number in the Num field to DEP, for "deposit."

6. Press **Tab** to move to the Account field and choose the account that is the source of the money. If you're depositing a bank loan, choose the liability account you set up to track the loan. If the money comes from an owner or partner, choose an equity account. If you're depositing a refund from a vendor, choose the expense account associated with the original transaction. If you sold an asset for cash, choose the original asset account. Are you

screaming "TMI! TMI? Too much information!"? When in doubt, choose **Ask My Accountant**.

7. Click **Record**. (You could also just press the **Tab** key to record it and move to the next transaction line in the register.)

Using the Make Deposits Window

If you're depositing money that's not related to customer payments and you're depositing more than one item, use the Make Deposits window instead of the register. The steps are almost identical to those described in the section titled "Depositing Payments from Customers," earlier in this chapter.

Viewing the Undeposited Funds Account

Just for fun, do you want to look at the Undeposited Funds account? I knew you would! This looks just like a register and lists all the funds hanging out waiting to be deposited, as shown in Figure 21.7. It works just like a register, too, so read "Using Registers," earlier in this chapter, for more information.

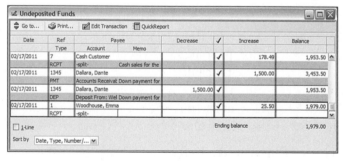

Figure 21.7: *Viewing the Undeposited Funds account.*

To view the account, go to the **Lists** menu and click **Chart of Accounts**. Highlight the Undeposited Funds account, click the **Activities** button, and choose **Use Register**.

The Least You Need to Know

- You can enter transactions directly into registers. For example, instead of using the Write Checks or Make Deposit windows to enter a transaction, just enter it directly into the bank account register.
- Each customer has a register that lists all your transactions with that customer. Use the customer register to view all transactions that affect the customer's balance.
- When making a deposit, select transactions that are the same type—for example, all American Express payments or all cash and checks—and make separate deposits for each type. This makes reconciliation easier if your bank groups deposits by type.
- If you want to make a deposit that isn't from customer payments, you can simplify your life by entering the deposit transaction directly in the check register if you're making only a single deposit.

Balancing Your Checking and Credit Card Accounts

In This Chapter

- Reconciling your bank accounts
- Finding and fixing reconciliation problems
- Generating reconciliation reports
- Undoing a previous reconciliation

QuickBooks can actually make reconciling your checking and credit card accounts almost fun. Okay, maybe not. But at least QuickBooks relieves some of the boredom (or terror, depending on your state of mind). A lot of the transactions are already in QuickBooks, so you don't have to enter much data.

When you reconcile an account, you compare the transactions entered in QuickBooks in a bank account with the bank's record of the same account. The bank sends you a statement that includes checks written, interest, bank fees, and deposits. Most likely, the statement won't match your current balance until you account for checks and deposits that haven't yet cleared the bank. Reconciling your accounts helps ensure the accuracy of your accounting records. You can reconcile bank accounts and credit card accounts.

Reconciling a Checking Account

Reconciling an account in QuickBooks is a two-step process: beginning the reconciliation, where you enter balance information, charges, and interest from your bank statement; and completing the reconciliation, where you mark transactions that match the bank statement.

Preparing to Reconcile

Before you start, make sure you've entered all the transactions, such as checks, bills paid, deposits, and transfers, to keep QuickBooks as up-to-date as possible. Also make sure the opening balance in your register matches the ending balance on the first bank statement you will reconcile. If the beginning balance is different from the balance on the bank statement, you need to figure out the discrepancy before you reconcile. Maybe you missed entering a historical transaction (described in Chapter 11). But no worries if you can't track down the discrepancy; you can have QuickBooks create an adjustment transaction so your opening balance matches the balance on the statement at the end of the reconciliation.

> **NUMBERS HAPPEN**
>
> If you end up making an adjustment to your opening balance, tell your accountant so the adjustment can be accounted for at year-end closing.

Starting a Reconciliation

The first part of reconciling is where you compare beginning balances, enter the ending balance, and enter service charges or interest. The second part (described in "Comparing Transactions," in the following section) is where you mark cleared checks and deposits.

To start reconciliation, follow these steps:

1. Go to the **Banking** menu and click **Reconcile**, or, on the Home page, click **Reconcile**.

2. In the Begin Reconciliation window (shown in Figure 22.1), choose the account to reconcile.

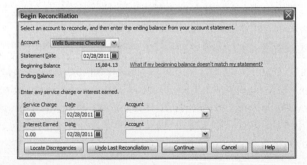

Figure 22.1: *Enter information from your bank statement in this window.*

3. Enter the date of the statement.

4. Compare the beginning balance on the statement (some banks call it starting balance) with the balance in your account. If it doesn't match, click the **What If My Beginning Balance Doesn't Match My Statement?** link and read the help topic that appears.

5. In the Ending Balance field, type the ending balance shown on the bank statement.

6. In the Service Charge field, type in the bank's service charge, choose the date of the charge, and then choose the expense account you use to track service charges. If you already entered the service charge in the bank register, don't also enter it here.

7. In the Interest Earned field, type the bank interest income, if any. Choose the date of the interest and choose the income account you use to track interest. If you already entered the interest in the bank register, don't also enter it here.

8. Click **Continue**.

The next section describes how to mark transactions that have cleared.

Comparing Transactions

The next step in reconciliation is to compare individual transactions with those on your bank statement. You'll mark which checks and deposits have cleared the bank.

If, during the reconciliation, you come across a deposit, check, or withdrawal that shows up in the bank statement but doesn't show up in the Reconcile window, you probably just forgot to record the transaction. Click **Leave** and fix the problem. When you come back to reconcile, everything will be as it was when you left. See "Changing or Adding a Transaction During Reconciliation," later in this section.

To mark transactions that have cleared, follow these steps:

1. In the Reconcile window (shown in Figure 22.2), compare what you see with your bank statement. If you see a deposit on the statement that matches one listed in Deposits and Other Credits, click in the check mark column to mark it as cleared. Be sure to verify that the amounts and dates match. If they don't match and they should, see "Changing or Adding a Transaction During Reconciliation," later in this section.

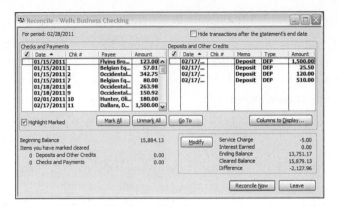

Figure 22.2: *Compare checks, payments, and deposits shown with your bank statement.*

2. For each check or payment on the bank statement that matches one in the Checks and Payments section, click in the check mark column to mark it as cleared. Be sure to verify that the amounts and dates match. If they don't match and they should, see "Changing a Transaction During Reconciliation," later in this section.

3. Look at the difference shown on the bottom right of the Reconcile window:

   • If the difference shows zero, today is your lucky day and you should go buy a lottery ticket. Click **Reconcile Now**.

   • If the difference is not zero, go back and verify that all the amounts match. Or maybe you marked something as cleared that didn't really clear—click the check mark to remove it. Maybe you didn't enter a transaction in QuickBooks—a check you wrote by hand and forgot about or a deposit you made but didn't record. See "Changing or Adding a Transaction During Reconciliation," later in this section.

   • If the difference is small and you're not a perfectionist, click **Reconcile Now** anyway and have QuickBooks create an adjustment transaction for you.

   • If the difference is too large to ignore, take a breather and click the **Leave** button. Sometimes coming back to it later is a good idea—fresh eyes and brain, and all. But if you're eager to solve this riddle, see "Locating Discrepancies," later in this chapter.

4. If you're good, QuickBooks asks if you want to print a reconciliation report. You can print now or later. Previous reconciliation reports appear in Banking Reports.

> **BEHIND THE SCENES**
>
> When you choose to let QuickBooks make an adjustment so that the account will reconcile, QuickBooks creates an expense account called Reconciliation Discrepancies to track reconciliation differences.

Changing or Adding Transactions During Reconcile

If you notice a difference between a transaction on the bank statement and what the transaction shows in QuickBooks—for example, numbers were transposed as 26.26 instead of 26.62—you can open the transaction right from the Reconcile window. Just double-click the transaction. Make the change to correct the error and click **Save & Close**. Back in the Reconcile window, put a check mark to mark the transaction as cleared.

Sometimes you're not able to make changes to the transaction. If this happens, you'll need to dig through your bills and deposits to find the source of the transaction amount. You likely entered an incorrect amount into QuickBooks. It might be easier to delete the offending bill payment or deposit and start over.

If you discover a missing transaction (one that appears in your bank statement but not in QuickBooks), click **Leave**. You can stop the reconciliation process and come back to it later. Open the register for the bank account and add the missing transaction. Go to **Banking**, click **Use Register**, and choose the account. In the blank transaction at the bottom of the register, type the transaction details. Click **Record**. Go back to the reconciliation by choosing **Banking** and clicking **Reconcile**. Click **Continue** and, in the Reconcile window, mark the transaction as cleared.

Locating Discrepancies

If you want to track down any discrepancies, click Leave to stop the reconciliation temporarily. Go back to the **Banking** menu and click **Reconcile**. In the Begin Reconciliation window (see Figure 22.1), click **Locate Discrepancies**.

Generating a Reconciliation Report

In the Locate Discrepancies window (see Figure 22.3), click **Discrepancy Report** to see a report that shows cleared transactions that have changed since the last reconciliation. So if the bank statement shows a different beginning balance, it could mean that a previously cleared transaction was changed in the check register.

Figure 22.3: *Use this window to explore the source of discrepancies through reports.*

In the Type of Change column in the report, you can see whether the amount was changed on the transaction, whether the transaction was deleted, or whether it was marked as "uncleared" (the check mark was clicked in the register). Changing the cleared status affects the beginning balance for the current reconciliation.

The Effect of Change column shows how the amount affected the beginning balance. So if the amount of the beginning balance is off by the amount in the Effect of Change column, you've found the transaction that is causing the discrepancy. Double-click the transaction in the report to restore it to the correct amount (shown in the Reconciled Amount column).

If a transaction has been deleted (you see "Deleted" in the Type of Change column), the only thing you can do is re-create the transaction. You can't double-click the transaction in the report because it no longer exists.

Tricks for Finding Discrepancies

If the reports don't help, here are a few tricks:

- Check that the account you're reconciling is the same account as shown on the statement. If you have several accounts with one bank, it could be an easy mistake to make, especially if you're tired or overly caffeinated.

- Look through the transactions on the bank statement. It's easy to forget to record in QuickBooks a debit card transaction, a cash withdrawal, or any automatic payments you've set up. Add the missing transaction and, when you return to reconcile, mark them as cleared.

- Check the discrepancy amount and see if it matches a transaction amount exactly. Maybe you incorrectly marked it as cleared or uncleared.

- Look for transactions that may have been entered backward—for example, you recorded a deposit as a withdrawal. In the Reconcile window, the amount will be correct but the transaction will appear in the wrong section.

- Look for duplicate amounts in the Reconcile window. Maybe you entered a transaction twice. Go to the register and find transactions that have the same date, payee, and amount. Delete one of the transactions.

- Look for transactions that are half the amount of the discrepancy. So if the discrepancy is $750, look for a transaction with the amount of $375. This could indicate that you entered a payment as a deposit, or you entered a deposit as a payment. This sounds weird, but the discrepancy is double because, for example, a check for $375 is missing and an extra deposit appears for $375 instead.

- Look for typing errors in your QuickBooks transactions, such as transposed numbers.

- In the Reconcile window, QuickBooks keeps a running total of Deposits and Other Credits and Checks and Payments you have marked as cleared. Your bank statement may also show these totals. You can compare the Reconcile window totals to the bank statement totals to see where the difference is. If the running total for Deposits and Other Credits matches, then the difference is likely a payment or check.

QUICKTIP

Now here's a real trick to amaze your friends. If you can divide a reconciliation difference by 9, that tells you that a transposed number is the likely suspect.

Undoing a Previous Reconciliation

If you're at a loss and you can't find the discrepancy, it may be in a previous reconciliation, which you can undo and start over. In the Begin Reconciliation window, click **Undo Last Reconciliation**.

QuickBooks tells you what will happen (transactions will be uncleared, including service charges and interest). Click **Continue**. Read the message that appears and click **OK**. Start the whole reconciliation process again. But don't re-enter the service charges or interest on the Begin Reconciliation window; those still exist in the register, they've just been marked as uncleared.

Reconciling and Paying Your Credit Card Bill

The steps for reconciling a credit card are identical to those for reconciling a checking account. The only difference is that, at the end of the reconciliation, QuickBooks asks if you want to pay all, part, or none of the bill. You can tell QuickBooks that you want to write a check or enter a bill for the payment.

The Least You Need to Know

- When you reconcile an account, you compare individual transactions with those on your bank statement. You'll mark which checks and deposits have cleared the bank.

- You can stop a reconciliation at any time and come back to it later. Click **Leave** and fix the problem or take a breather. When you come back to reconcile, everything will be as it was when you left.

- If the account doesn't reconcile and the amount is so small that you don't care about it, QuickBooks can create an adjustment transaction for you for the amount of the difference.

- To help you find discrepancies, QuickBooks has a report that shows cleared transactions that have changed since the last reconciliation.

Handling Other Banking Tasks

In This Chapter

- Handling NSF or bounced checks
- Reinvoicing customers
- Dealing with bank fees
- Tracking petty cash

No matter what they're called—bounced checks, nonsufficient funds (NSF), insufficient funds, or rubber checks—these checks aren't fun to deal with. And it takes quite a few steps to fix the situation in QuickBooks. But hopefully this won't happen to you often.

Another banking task that you may not need to deal with often, or at all, is handling petty cash. It's pretty easy just to grab a wad of cash or get cash back from a deposit, but you also have to remember to track it.

Handling Checks That Bounce

You've got a check from a customer that bounced. You're probably a bit miffed, and your customer is probably embarrassed. In any event, you need to do quite a few things to handle a single bounced check. You have to create two items: an "other charge" item to remove the amount of the check from your account, and an "other charge" item for a service charge. Then you'll need to reinvoice the customer and include the service charge. Finally, you'll need to enter any fees the bank charged you in your account register and reduce your account by the amount of the check.

Setting Up Items for Bounced Checks

You'll need to set up two "other charge" type items to track the bounced check and fees. Chapter 9 covered creating items, so here I'll just give a brief summary.

To create "other charge" items for the bounced check amount and bounced check fees, click **Items & Services** on the Home page and press **Ctrl+N**. Choose **Other Charge** as the item type. Type a name for the item, such as Bad Check or Bad Check Processing Fees. Leave the Amount or % field blank, choose **Non** as the tax code, and then choose the bank account you use to deposit checks. For the fees, choose the expense account you use for bank service charges. Click **OK**.

Reinvoicing the Customer

Next, you'll create an invoice that includes the other charge items you just created. When you use the Bad Check item on the invoice, QuickBooks reverses the original transaction amount from the bank account.

BEHIND THE SCENES

Because you linked the bad check item to your bank account, QuickBooks reduces your bank account by the amount of the bounced check—it appears as a payment and the amount goes back into Accounts Receivable.

Create a new invoice for the customer. In the line item area, choose the "bad check" item you created. In the Amount field, type the amount of the original check. In the next line, choose the "bounced check service charge" item you created. In the Amount field, type the amount your bank charged you (or you can make the amount larger, to account for your pain and suffering—but check with your accountant first because this could be illegal in your state). (See Figure 23.1 for an example.) Type an optional customer memo and click **Save & Close**.

Keep your fingers crossed that the check for this invoice doesn't bounce, too.

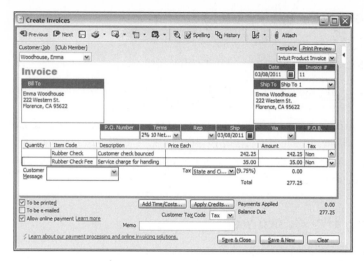

Figure 23.1: *Reinvoicing for a bounced check.*

Entering the Bank Fees

Your bank charged you a fee for the hassle of the bounced check, so you'll need to record that fee in your bank account. The fastest way to do this is through the account register.

Go to **Banking** and click **Use Register**. Choose the bank account that charged the fee. Go to the bottom of the register and choose the date that the bank charged the fee. Press **Tab** and delete the number QuickBooks puts in the Num field. You can leave the Payee field blank. In the Payment field, type the amount the bank charged you. Click the **Splits** button. For the account, choose the **Bank Service Charges** account. Type a memo that includes the name of the customer and maybe the check number of the bounced check. From the Customer:Job menu, choose the customer who wrote the bounced check. Deselect the Billable check box, because you already billed the customer for the charge when you reinvoiced. See Figure 23.2 for an example.

Special note if you use Billing Statements: Instead of choosing the Bank Service Charges expense account, choose the Accounts Receivable account so it will show up on the customer's statement.

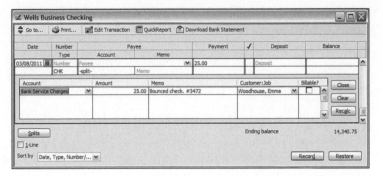

Figure 23.2: *Recording the bank fee for a bounced check.*

Click **Record** to enter the transaction into your register.

> **QUICKTIP**
>
> QuickBooks supplies a "canned" letter you can print out and mail to the customer whose check has bounced. See Chapter 15 for more information.

Tracking Petty Cash

If you keep a jar of cash around to use for minor purchases, such as a Choco-Chai from the vendor down the street, you'll need to track those amounts because all those little expenses affect your business finances.

You'll need to do a few things to track petty cash: create a petty cash account to track the transactions, record an initial "deposit" to the cash account, and record any purchases you make using petty cash.

Creating a Petty Cash Account

Open your chart of accounts (press **Ctrl+A**) and check to see if a petty cash account has already been set up. If not, press **Ctrl+N** and add a new account. The account type should be **Bank**. Enter a name for the account, such as Cash or Petty Cash. Leave the opening balance at zero, unless you've already got the cash; in that case, click **Enter Opening Balance** to record the amount.

To put money into the account, take cash out of your checking account, write a check to "Cash," and, in the Account field, choose the Petty Cash account. Go to the bank and cash the check. When you get back, put the cash in the jar.

If you use a debit card instead of a check to take money out of the ATM, do a "funds transfer." See "Transferring Money Between Accounts" in Chapter 21.

If you got cash back from a deposit to put into your petty cash, record the cash transaction in the Make Deposits window. In the Cash Goes Back To field, choose the **Petty Cash** account. Type a memo and enter the amount of cash. See Figure 23.3 for an example.

Figure 23.3: *Recording the cash back from a deposit.*

Recording Petty Cash Purchases

Whenever you or someone else takes cash from the jar, you need to account for the cash taken. An easy way to do this is to just enter the transaction in the Petty Cash register.

Open your Chart of Accounts (press **Ctrl+A**) and double-click the petty cash account. This opens the register. In the blank transaction at the bottom of the register, choose the date that the cash was taken. Press **Tab** and delete the number QuickBooks puts in the Num field. You can leave the Payee field blank. In the Payment field, type the amount spent (not the amount taken out, but the amount spent on whatever was purchased, because any change should go back into the jar). For the account, choose the expense account. If you need to divide the amount between two or more accounts, click the **Splits** button and choose the appropriate accounts for the split amounts. Click **Record**.

The Least You Need to Know

- You'll need to create a couple items to handle bounced checks and reinvoice the customer, adding a service charge to be reimbursed for the bank fee.
- Your bank charged you a fee for the hassle of the bounced check, so you'll need to record that fee in your bank account. The fastest way to do this is through the account register.
- Create a petty cash account if you keep a jar of cash around to use for minor purchases.
- Whenever you or someone else takes cash from the jar, you need to account for the cash taken. An easy way to do this is to enter the transaction in the Petty Cash register.

Managing Your Business

This part covers some activities you need to do from time to time in the course of running your business. This isn't stuff you do every day, and some businesses might never perform some of these tasks. You learn how to do things like track time and mileage, track payroll, record owners equity, and manage your company file.

If you have employees, turn to Chapter 24 to find out how to set up for payroll using the manual payroll process (without using a fee-based payroll solution). You learn to set up your employees, salary, benefits, and payroll taxes. In addition, this chapter explains how to run payroll and how to pay your payroll liabilities.

If you or your employees need to track time, Chapter 25 describes how to set up for time-tracking, how to enter time for a single activity or using a weekly timesheet. You also learn how to track business mileage, including adding business vehicles, adding items to track mileage, entering actual miles driven, and generating mileage reports.

Chapter 26 explains the ins and outs of owners equity and owners draw accounts, which track the money owners invest, take out, and earn.

Finally, Chapter 27 covers the important task of backing up your company file.

Setting Up and Using Payroll

In This Chapter

- Turning on manual payroll
- Setting up payroll with the wizard, including compensation and benefits
- Processing payroll and paying employees
- Paying 1099 vendors
- Paying payroll tax liabilities and nontax liabilities
- Preparing tax forms

I'm just going to come right out and say it: payroll can be really complex and tricky, and you could end up with a hot mess. If you have just one or two employees, or if you just occasionally hire a subcontractor, doing payroll by yourself won't be too bad. But you might want to think about using one of QuickBooks' payroll services or a service like Paychex, especially if you have more employees. Of course, those services cost money. So in this chapter, I'm assuming that you're a really small company and you want to do your payroll manually (and keep a bottle of extra-strength headache medicine around).

About Payroll

QuickBooks recommends that you subscribe to one of its payroll services, and your accountant might want you to as well. Check the Appendix B for a link to QuickBooks payroll services and options. But I'm here to explain how to process your payroll without using a service.

Currently, you may be using handwritten checks to pay employees, and you may keep track of the various payments using a spreadsheet or a handwritten form. You probably calculate the various tax and benefits deductions tediously by hand. Now that you have QuickBooks, you can still calculate payroll manually, but you can set up payroll items and accounts so you can print paychecks that show the amounts and deductions. QuickBooks will also keep track of the amounts and deductions.

Here's what you need to do:

- Make sure you have the up-to-date payroll tax tables for both the feds and your state.

- Calculate withholdings and deductions by hand for each paycheck.

- Enter the amounts into QuickBooks.

- Print (or handwrite) the paychecks.

- Manually keep track of your payment schedules.

- Periodically pay your payroll tax liabilities.

- Manually fill out and file required forms.

Setting Up Your Company to Process Payroll Manually

Setting up your company so you can do manual payroll is a little like going down the rabbit hole (almost like QuickBooks doesn't want you to do it).

To process payroll manually, go to the **Help** menu and choose **QuickBooks Help**. Click the **Search** tab and type **Manual Payroll**. In the list of topics that appears, click **Process Payroll Manually (Without a Subscription to QuickBooks Payroll)**. In step 1, click **Manual Payroll Calculations**. At the bottom of that help topic, click **Set My Company File to Use Manual Calculations**. Click **OK** to confirm.

Phew! Did you leave a trail of breadcrumbs to get back?

Setting Up for Payroll

You need to prepare for payroll before you write the first paycheck. This involves adding payroll accounts to your chart of accounts, setting up payroll items, setting up your employees and/or 1099 vendors, setting up employee deductions (such as health insurance), and setting up the taxes you have to withhold.

The easy way to do this is to use the Payroll Setup Wizard, which is discussed next.

Using the Payroll Setup Wizard

The Payroll Setup Wizard helps you set up payroll taxes, employees, employee compensation and benefits, and year-to-date payroll amounts.

To start the Payroll Setup Wizard, go to the **Employees** menu and click **Payroll Setup**. (If you don't see the Payroll Setup menu item, follow the steps in the previous section to indicate that you want to do payroll manually. If you already did that and you don't see the menu item, go to **Edit**, click **Preferences**, and click Payroll & Employees. Click **Company Preferences** and click **Full Payroll**.) Figure 24.1 shows the Welcome page of the wizard.

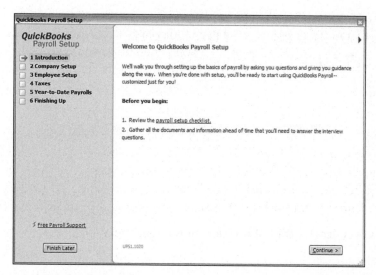

Figure 24.1: *Set up payroll items and employees with the Payroll Setup Wizard.*

Make sure you are connected to the Internet and click the link for **Payroll Setup Check List** to download a free PDF to help you gather the information you'll need. Click **Continue** to move from one setup stage to the next. To complete the wizard at another time, click **Finish Later**. The next time you open the wizard, QuickBooks starts where you left off.

The following sections explain each step of the wizard.

Setting Up Compensation and Benefits

In the Company Setup stage, QuickBooks asks about how you compensate your employees (such as salary, hourly wages, bonuses, commissions, and so on). Then it asks you about the benefits you provide (such as health insurance, retirement, and vacation and sick leave). These become your *payroll items*.

> **DEFINITION**
>
> **Payroll items** track compensation, tax, and deduction amounts on a paycheck and accumulate year-to-date wage and tax amounts for each employee, as well as items used when making a payroll tax payment.

To set up compensation, click **Compensation** under **Company Setup.** (Or just click **Continue** from the previous setup page.) Figure 24.2 shows the options for compensation. Put a check mark for each type of compensation you offer. (Click a blank box to put a check mark in it, or click a checked box to remove the check mark.) Click **Finish**.

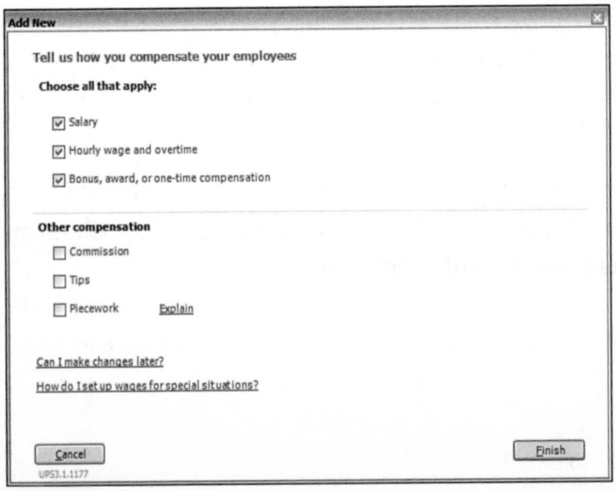

Figure 24.2: *Choose the compensation options you provide.*

Back on the Company Setup wizard page, you'll see a list of payroll items QuickBooks has set up based on your compensation options.

To move on to company benefits, click **Continue** or click **Employee Benefits** under **Company Setup**. QuickBooks walks you through setting up insurance, retirement, paid time off, and other benefits. Click **Continue** to go through page by page.

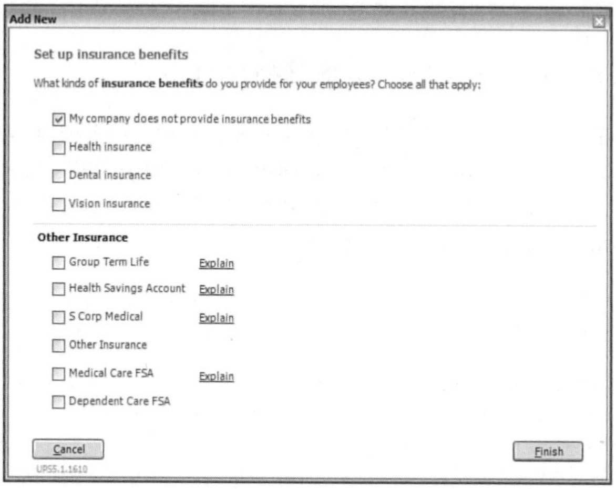

Figure 24.3: *The Set Up Insurance Benefits page.*

Figure 24.3 shows the options for insurance. Put a check mark for each type of insurance you offer. (Click a blank box to put a check mark in it, or click a checked box to remove the check mark.) Click **Finish** and then click **Continue** to move on to the retirement benefits page.

Each benefit page works similarly: you check the benefits you provide and then click **Finish** and **Continue** to move on. After you've gone through the benefits pages, all your payroll items for compensation and benefits will have been set up. The next step is setting up your employees.

If you need to edit the payroll items later, go to the **Employees** menu and click **Manage Payroll Items**, and then click **View/Edit Payroll Item List**. Or create new ones by clicking New Payroll item here.

Setting Up Employees with the Wizard

Employees are people who work for you and who are on staff. So that means owners shouldn't be set up as employees. Subcontractors should be set up as 1099 vendors.

For each employee, you specify the taxes and benefits. Each page is summarized here:

Employee information: Type the employee's name, address, and other basic information. If a field is required, it has an asterisk next to it. This information is needed for preparing W2s.

Hiring information: Choose the employee type (click **Explain** for help on the types). Enter the employee's Social Security number and hire date (other information is optional). If you've fired an employee (QuickBooks prefers to call it "released"), type in the date of "release." Even though the employee doesn't work for you anymore, you'll need to issue a W2 for the time worked.

Wages and compensation: Choose how frequently the employee gets paid and how the employee is compensated (hourly, salaried, or commission only). If hourly, enter the hourly rate. Select the check boxes for other wages (overtime and bonuses) and enter the optional amounts that are applied per paycheck.

Benefits: Indicate which benefits to include for the employee by putting a check mark in the box. Enter the amounts (or percentages—type the % sign) per paycheck deducted for this employee's benefits.

Sick: Indicate how much sick time the employee earns, maximum amounts, and current balances.

Vacation: Indicate how much vacation time the employee earns, maximum amounts, and current balances.

Direct Deposit: Indicate whether you use direct deposit for this employee—if so, enter the bank account information. Using direct deposit requires an extra fee. To sign up, click **Finish Later** in the Payroll Wizard. Make sure you are connected to the Internet, go to the **Help** menu, and click **Add QuickBooks Services** if you want to subscribe to the add-on.

State Tax: Indicate where the employee lives and works.

Federal Tax: Indicate the employee's filing status, number of allowances, and withholding information. Also indicate whether the employee is subject to Social Security, Medicare, unemployment taxes, or earned income credit.

State Tax (the sequel): Indicate the employee's filing status, number of allowances, and withholding information. Also indicate whether the employee is subject to unemployment, training, and disability taxes.

Wage Plan Code: (California) Choose the wage plan code from the menu. (This code is used only for e-filers.)

Yay! Click **Finish.** QuickBooks displays the employee in the list. If something is missing, you'll see an exclamation mark. If there's a problem, you'll see a red X. Read the Summary column for the details. Select the employee and click **Edit** to locate and fix the problem.

Well, you're not finished if you still have more employees. Click **Add New** to add another employee.

Later, if you need to add new employees or update existing employments, click **Employee Center** in the navigation bar.

Setting Up Payroll Taxes with the Wizard

Next, you provide QuickBooks with information to help you set up the federal and state taxes, tax agencies, payees, and payment frequency.

QuickBooks shows you the federal and state payroll items set up for you. If you need to make changes, select the item and click **Edit.**

On the remaining Tax setup pages, QuickBooks guides you through supplying any missing information. If you see the message that the federal EIN is missing, click **Finish Later.** Go to the **Company** menu and click Company Information. In the Company Identification field, type your nine-digit EIN number. Click **OK** and return to payroll setup by going to **Employees** and clicking **Payroll Setup.**

Next, QuickBooks prompts you to specify Payee and Payment frequency for 940/941/944 payments.

Entering Payroll History with the Wizard

If you haven't paid any employee yet (you are a new business and you just hired your first employee) or if you haven't processed payroll this calendar year, you don't need to enter payroll history. But if you've issued any paychecks through a service, through another financial software package, or manually, you need to enter year-to-date payroll amounts. QuickBooks shows you a table you can use to enter paychecks, tax payments, and nontax payments, such as health insurance and retirement plans.

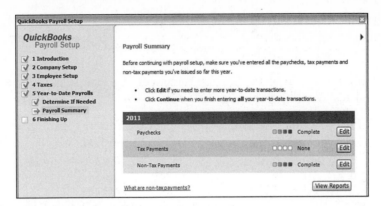

Figure 24.4: *Enter all year-to-date paychecks and payroll liability payments.*

Figure 24.4 shows the Payroll Summary page for entering historical payroll. Click the **Edit** button for **Paychecks**, **Tax Payments**, and **Nontax Payments** (such as health insurance, garnishments, and retirement plans) to enter year-to-date amounts.

> **QUICKTIP**
>
> If it's close to the end of the year, it might be easier to wait until January 1 to start using QuickBooks for payroll. That way, you won't have to enter historical payroll.

You can't pay employees until you've entered the history (if required). QuickBooks needs to know the year-to-date information to calculate taxes correctly.

Finishing Up

The last page of Payroll Setup asks if you want to back up your company file—after all this work, that might be the prudent choice. Click **Back Up** to back up your company file, or click **Go to Payroll Center**.

Running Payroll

Now that you have your payroll items set up, you can write paychecks for your employees. Because you'll be calculating the deductions for payroll items manually for each pay period, make sure you have the latest payroll tax tables from the IRS before you process payroll each time. You'll also need to know the limits on taxes, such as FUTA (Federal Unemployment Tax) and Social Security.

To run payroll, follow these steps:

1. Go to the **Employees** menu and click **Pay Employees**.

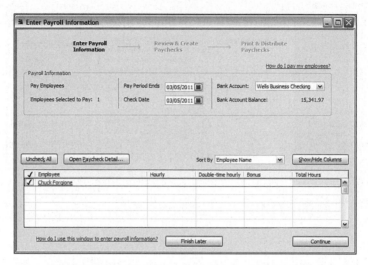

Figure 24.5: *The Enter Payroll Information window.*

2. In the Enter Payroll Information window (see Figure 24.5), check that the dates and accounts are correct and put a check mark next to the employees you want to pay.

3. For hourly employees, enter the total number of regular hours worked during the pay period (that is, not overtime hours). If the employee worked any overtime hours, enter the number of overtime hours. (When you set up an employee, you can choose the payroll items and rates to use for his earnings: Salary, Hourly, Double-time Hourly, Overtime (×1.5) hourly, and Bonus. Each payroll item appears as a column in the Enter Payroll Information window. The columns you see depend on which payroll items you've set up for all your employees; so if you haven't indicated, for example, that a certain employee is eligible for Double-time hourly, you can't enter the hours in the Double-time hourly column.) Add an optional bonus amount (if the Bonus column appears) for this paycheck, if you're feeling generous. Press **Tab**; QuickBooks calculates the total number of hours.

4. Click **Open Paycheck Detail**. You'll notice that (as shown in Figure 24.6) there are still a lot of zeros. This is because you're calculating all those figures manually; if you subscribed to a service, QuickBooks would have calculated those numbers for you.

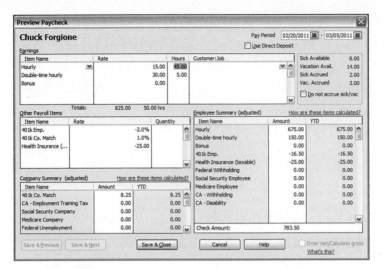

Figure 24.6: *The paycheck detail for the selected employee.*

5. Calculate all the "zero" amounts, as needed (using either a spreadsheet or a calculator and napkin), and enter the amounts in the appropriate fields.

6. Click **Save & Next** to move on to the next paycheck, or click **Save & Close**.

7. When you're back at the Enter Payroll Information window, click **Continue** to print and review the paychecks.

8. Select how you want to produce the paychecks: **Print Paychecks from QuickBooks** or **Assign Check Numbers to Handwritten Checks** and enter the check number to use. You might want to use a handwritten check if your printer is on the fritz or if you "released" someone and are in a hurry to give him a final check.

9. If everything seems okay, click **Create Paychecks**.

10. In the next window, choose **Print Paychecks** to print a physical check that the employees can take to the bank. (If you're paying for the direct deposit add-on, choose **Print Pay Stubs** so your employees have a record of the check.)

11. In the Select Paychecks to Print window (see Figure 24.7), put a check mark next to each check you want to print. Make sure that the account is correct and that the check number matches the next check in the printer.

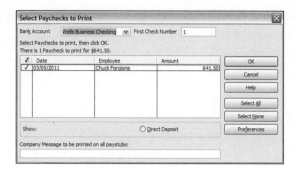

Figure 24.7: *Select the paychecks you want to print.*

12. Load the printer with the checks from the account you use to pay employees.

13. Click **OK** and choose the check style options (depending on the type of checks you use, such as voucher, standard, or wallet).

14. Click **Print**.

15. Check to make sure that the checks printed correctly; if they did, click **OK** in the Print Checks Confirmation window. If something is amiss, click the link **What If My Checks Printed Incorrectly?** to read through the plethora of things that could go wrong and fix them.

At any time, you can review employee paychecks by going to the Employee Center.

Paying 1099 Vendors and Owners

If you employ subcontractors (1099 vendors), you need to take a few actions. First, create an expense account to track the 1099 vendor payments, called something like Outside Services or Subcontractor Payments. Next, make sure you've set up preferences to track 1099 vendors. Go to the **Edit** menu and click **Preferences.** In the left panel, click **Tax: 1099.** On the Company Preferences tab, click **Yes** to the question Do You File 1099-MISC Forms? Next, map the category (most companies need to map only Box 7, Nonemployee Compensation) to the expense account you set up to track 1099 vendor payments (see Figure 24.8).

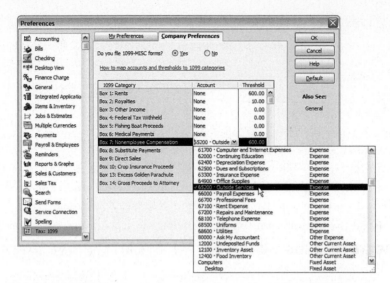

Figure 24.8: *Map the expense account to use to track 1099 vendor payments.*

Then set up the subcontractor as a vendor and indicate 1099 status. See "Entering Additional Information" in Chapter 7.

Each time you pay a 1099 vendor, QuickBooks tracks the amount; at the end of the year, you must send a 1099-MISC form to the vendor if the total payments are greater than the current threshold (currently $600). To view who needs to get a 1099, go to the **Reports** menu, go to **Vendors & Payables**, and click **1099 Detail**.

When you're ready to print 1099s (and a 1096, which is a total of all 1099s), go to the **File** menu, go to **Print Forms**, and click **1099s/1096**. Follow the steps in the wizard to double-check that everything is correct, make sure the preprinted 1099 forms are in the printer, and click **Print 1099s**.

BEHIND THE SCENES

Owners and business partners are not on the business payroll. You pay them through an owner's draw. See Chapter 26 for more information.

Paying Payroll Liabilities

When you set up payroll, QuickBooks automatically creates two accounts: *Payroll Liabilities* and Payroll Expenses. It links the payroll items to these two accounts.

DEFINITION

The **Payroll Liabilities account** tracks the federal, state, and local withholding taxes deducted from your employee paychecks, as well as Social Security and Medicare.

Payroll taxes and withholdings can vary from state to state, and the federal government has its own schedule. Contact your tax agencies or accountant to check what the payment schedules are and what payments you're liable for. For example, some states may require disability insurance and unemployment. Because you're not using a payroll service, you have to keep track of what you owe and the payment schedules; QuickBooks won't automatically remind you when they are due.

Paying Payroll Taxes

Each time you process paychecks, you deduct tax withholdings for state, local, and federal taxes, along with withholdings for other agencies (Medicare, health, and so on). These amounts are tracked in the Payroll Liabilities account until you pay the various agencies based on their payment schedules. To determine when to pay, use the tax schedules provided by the IRS and your state and local tax agencies.

To pay payroll taxes, follow these steps:

1. Go to the **Employees** menu, go to **Payroll Taxes and Liabilities**, and click **Pay Payroll Liabilities**.

2. In the Select Date Range for Liabilities window, choose the date range that your payment covers—for example, Last Month or Last Calendar Quarter. Check with the tax agencies if you're not sure how often you need to remit the payments.

3. Click **OK**.

4. In the Pay Liabilities window (shown in Figure 24.9), deselect the **To Be Printed** check box if you're writing a check by hand.

5. Choose the bank account you want to use to pay the liabilities, and choose the date for the check.

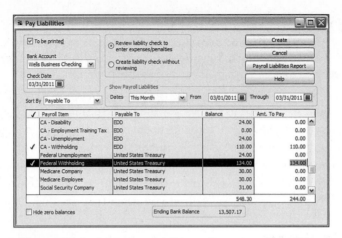

Figure 24.9: *Select the payroll item that you need to pay now.*

6. In the list of payroll items, click to put a check mark next to the ones you want to pay. If you selected more than one liability payable to the same vendor, QuickBooks creates one check, which means that the vendor won't know that the payment covers more than one item. It's a good idea to create a separate check for each payroll item for the same vendor. Repeat steps 1 through 6 for each payroll item so you'll have separate checks to the same vendor.

7. Click **Create** to create checks for the selected payments.

8. Click **Next** and **Previous** to cycle through the checks to verify them.

9. Click **Save & Close**.

Paying Nontax Liabilities

If you provide insurance, retirement, or other benefits, you also have to remit payments to the appropriate agencies or companies.

> **NUMBERS HAPPEN**
>
> Don't use the Write Checks window to write a check for nontax liabilities. You must use the Pay Liabilities window, or you'll wreak havoc with your accounting.

To pay nontax liabilities, follow the same steps just described in "Paying Payroll Taxes," but select the appropriate agencies/companies you want to pay.

Printing Payroll Liability Checks

If you selected the To Be Printed check box in the Pay Liabilities window, QuickBooks places the checks in the printing queue.

To print the checks, go to the **File** menu, go to **Print Forms**, and click **Print Checks**. Choose the account to use and enter a check number to match the first check in the printer. Select the liability checks you want to print, and click **OK**. Select the style of check and other printing options; then click **Print**.

The tax agencies send coupons for your scheduled payments, so fill out the appropriate coupon and send it with the check.

Preparing Tax Forms

As an employer, you are required to submit forms (such as Forms 941, 944, 943, and 940) that document how much payroll taxes and withholdings you have collected and owe, and how much you have remitted year-to-date. Check with the tax agencies to learn how often you need to file these forms; some are required quarterly, others annually. You'll also need to generate W2/W3 forms to document the annual payments per employee.

Because you don't use a payroll service, you need to fill out these forms manually. But QuickBooks can help with the figures you need to complete the forms manually.

Go to the **Employees** menu, go to **Payroll Tax Forms and W2s**, and click **Tax Form Worksheets in Excel**. Select the tax form you're filling out and click **Create Report** (see Figure 24.10).

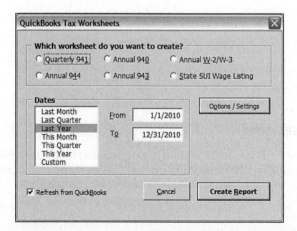

Figure 24.10: *Select the worksheet for the tax form you're filling out.*

The Least You Need to Know

- Use the Payroll Setup Wizard to make easy work of creating payroll items, recording employees, and entering historical payroll.

- Contact your tax agencies or accountant to check your tax liability payment schedules and determine payments you're liable for.

- The deductions and tax withholdings are tracked in the Payroll Liabilities account until you pay the various agencies based on their payment schedules.

- As an employer, you're required to submit forms that document how much payroll taxes and withholdings you have collected and owe, and how much you have remitted year-to-date.

Tracking Time and Mileage

In This Chapter

- Tracking track time and mileage
- Setting up time tracking and mileage items
- Entering time for a single activity or on weekly timesheets
- Generating time and mileage reports
- Adding a vehicle
- Entering a vehicle mileage record

Tracking time and mileage can be useful in many ways, most importantly so you can get reimbursed by your customers when working on their jobs. Companies track time for a variety of reasons. Service-based businesses have customers who pay for those services, so tracking time needs to be fairly precise. Also, tracking time on projects can help when scheduling jobs and generating estimates in the future. Product-based companies may have employees and want to track their time for payroll. And, of course, you can deduct the miles you put on your company vehicle in the course of doing business, as an expense to reduce your taxes. But that requires documentation, which QuickBooks can help provide.

About Tracking Time in QuickBooks

QuickBooks has a few ways you can keep track of time:

- Enter time while you're doing the work on a project using the built-in stop-watch, which logs your hours as you work.

- Fill out a single activity or weekly timesheet for your employees or 1099 vendors.

- Use the separate QuickBooks Timer program and install the software on your workers' computers. Your employees track time in this separate software program, and you can import the time data into QuickBooks.

Another way to track time costs money. It's a tool that lets your employees and contractors input their time online. To learn more, go to **Employees** menu, go to **Enter Time**, and click **Let Your Employees Enter Time**.

To track time, you'll need to turn on the time-tracking features.

Turning On Time Tracking

When you set up your company file, QuickBooks might have turned on time tracking based on your type of business or if you indicated you want to track time. If you want to track time using the QuickBooks Timer, you need to make sure the feature is turned on in Preferences. You also need to set a couple of preferences for billable time and expenses, if you didn't do that in Chapter 13.

To open the Time & Expenses preference, go to the **Edit** menu and click **Preferences**. Scroll down to the bottom of the left panel, click **Time & Expenses**, and then click the **Company Preferences** tab (see Figure 25.1).

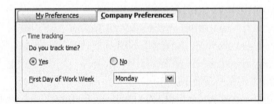

Figure 25.1: *Turn on time tracking.*

To track time, answer **Yes** to the question **Do You Track Time?** Then choose the day you want to start with on weekly timesheets.

If you're only tracking time and don't want to set up for reimbursable expenses, you're done. If you do want to set up for reimbursable expenses, see the "Invoicing for Reimbursable Expenses" section in Chapter 13 to learn about setting up the remaining preferences on this page.

Setting Up People Who Track Time

If you have employees, you set them up in Chapter 24. If you have 1099 vendors, you probably set them up in Chapter 7. Refer to those chapters if you haven't set up employees or 1099 vendors.

If you're a sole proprietor or you have co-owners or partners, you need to add yourself or co-owners to the Other Names list. As a sole proprietor or co-owner, you don't get paid through a paycheck; instead, you take what's called an "owner's draw." Chapter 26 explains this.

To add a name to the Other Names List, go to the **Lists** menu and click **Other Names List**. Press **Ctrl+N** and fill out the form.

Setting Up Service Items for Tracking Time

You probably already set up some service items if you provide service to customers (see Chapter 9) and those service items can be billable to your customers. But you might want to create a few service items to use internally on timesheets that aren't billable. For example, if you want to track how much time you or your employees spend doing certain tasks, create service items for those tasks. If you want to track the time spent on administrative tasks, create a service item called Admin Tasks. Other examples include marketing, training, maintenance and repairs, bookkeeping, meetings, and shelf stocking.

To set up an internal, nonbillable service item, click **Items & Services** on the Home page and press **Ctrl+N**. Choose **Service** as the item type and give the item a name. Leave the Rate field empty because you're not actually going to charge anyone for this service. In the Account field, click **<Add New>** to create a fake income account (fake because nothing will get posted to the account—you're not selling these services to customers). Give the account a name, such as Task Tracking or Nonbillable Tasks.

If this nonbillable service is being performed by a 1099 vendor, create a separate service item following the steps in the previous paragraph, except check the **This Service Is Performed by a Subcontractor, Owner, or Partner** check box. This way, you can assign the costs to an expense account and also keep track of the subcontractor's time.

One more thing: because tracking time is associated with customers and jobs, you need to create a fake customer to use for nonbillable tasks. Give the "customer" a name, such as Company Tasks or Internal. All you need to enter is the name; you don't need to fill out any other fields in the fake customer record.

Entering Time for a Single Task

QuickBooks has a stopwatch that makes it easy to record time spent on a task as you perform it. For example, if you're a lawyer and you want to track a phone conversation with your client, you can start the stopwatch at the start of the call and stop it at the end of the call. You get to the stopwatch through the Time/Enter Single Activity window (see Figure 25.2).

QUICKTIP

When entering time in the Duration field, you can use either hh:mm (hours, minutes) or decimal format (2.5 for 2 hours, 30 minutes). Choose the format you prefer in General Preferences. If you're using the stopwatch, QuickBooks converts the hh:mm:ss it records to your preferred format when you leave the field.

You can also use this window to enter details about one task on one date. If you're working on several jobs on the same date, you need to record your activities separately for each job.

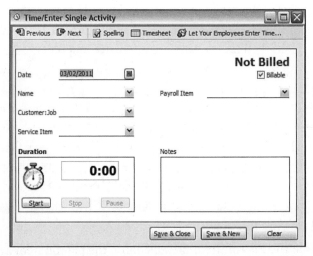

Figure 25.2: *Use the stopwatch to record time as you work, or enter details about a single task.*

To enter time on a single activity, follow these steps:

1. Go to the **Employees** menu, go to **Enter Time**, and click **Time/Enter Single Activity**. Or, in the Employees section on the Home page, click **Enter Time** and then click **Time/Enter Single Activity**.

2. In the Time/Enter Single Activity window (see Figure 25.2), change the date if you're recording time on a previous day. Note that you can't use the stopwatch if you change the date from today's date.

3. Click in the Name field and choose the person performing this activity. The names come from the Employees list, the Vendors list, and the Other Names list. If you select an employee name, QuickBooks asks if you want to use the time data during payroll creation and adds a Payroll Item field (determines compensation rate).

4. In the Customer:Job field, choose the customer and job that this time is associated with, even if it's not billable to the customer. If you're recording time spent on administrative tasks, choose the fake customer you created in the previous section.

5. In the Service Item field, choose the service item associated with the task performed. If you're recording time for internal, nonbillable tasks, choose the item you set up for that purpose in the previous section.

6. Click **Start** to begin tracking time as you work, using the stopwatch, and click **Stop** when you're finished. Alternatively, you can enter the time spent directly in the Duration field using hh:mm (2:15) or decimal format (2.25). When you leave the field, QuickBooks converts the time to the preferred format you set up in General Preferences.

7. If the time spent is billable to the customer, make sure the Billable check box is checked. If the time is nonbillable, click the check box to remove the check mark. Even though the time isn't billable, it will appear on reports on this job.

8. If you see the Payroll Item menu, choose the payroll item associated with the task, such as hourly wages. If you don't see the Payroll Item menu, you haven't turned on the payroll features, the person you selected is either not an employee, or the employee hasn't been linked to track time. For example, if the name you selected comes from the Other Names list, you won't see the Payroll Item menu.

9. If you track classes, choose the class associated with this task.

10. Type any details or comments in the Notes field. These notes can appear on invoices and on job reports.

11. Click **Save & Close**.

BEHIND THE SCENES

When you mark time as billable, QuickBooks adds the time spent to the list of billable hours for the job. When you later invoice the customer, QuickBooks reminds you that you can add some billable hours to the invoice.

Entering Time Using Weekly Timesheets

The weekly timesheet (see Figure 25.3) is similar to the single activity form, except that you fill in a week at a time. One person can fill out the weekly timesheet and associate the time spent with one or more jobs.

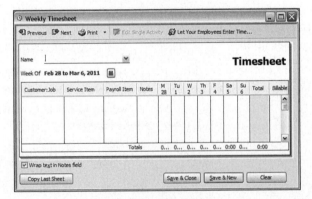

Figure 25.3: *Use the weekly timesheet to record time spent on multiple jobs over a week's time.*

To enter time on a weekly timesheet, follow these steps:

1. Go to the **Employees** menu, go to **Enter Time**, and click **Use Weekly Timesheet**. Or, in the Employees section on the Home page, click **Enter Time** and then click **Use Weekly Timesheet**.

2. In the Weekly Timesheet window (see Figure 25.3), click in the Name field and choose the person this timesheet belongs to. The names come from the Employees list, the Vendors list, and the Other Names list. If you are filling out timesheets for several employees or vendors working on the same job with the exact same hours, you can save time by choosing **Multiple names (non-payroll) or Multiple names (payroll)**. Note that if you choose Multiple names (payroll), the "Use time data to create paychecks" checkbox must be selected in the employee record for the employee to appear on the list. Select the employees and click **OK**.

3. Change the week dates if you're recording time on a previous week.

4. In the Customer:Job field, choose the customer and job that this time is associated with, even if it's not billable to the customer. If you're recording time spent on administrative tasks, choose the fake customer you created for that purpose.

5. In the Service Item field, choose the service item associated with the hours worked. If you're recording time for internal, nonbillable tasks, choose the item you set up for that purpose.

6. If you see the Payroll Item menu, choose the payroll item, such as hourly wages. If you don't see the Payroll Item menu, you haven't turned on the payroll features, the person you selected is not an employee, or the employee has not been linked to track time. For example, if the name you selected comes from the Other Names list, you won't see the Payroll Item menu.

7. Type any details or comments in the Notes field. These notes can appear on invoices and on job reports.

8. If you track classes, choose the class associated with this task.

9. Click in the Day of the Week column to enter the hours spent on that day.

10. Enter the time spent in hh:mm (2:15) or decimal format (2.25). When you leave the field, QuickBooks converts the time to the preferred format you set up in General Preferences.

11. If the time spent is billable to the customer, make sure the Billable check box in the Billable? column is checked. If the time is nonbillable, click the check box to remove the check mark. Even though the time isn't billable, it will appear on reports on this job.

12. Repeat steps 9 through 11 to fill out the remaining days in the week for this customer/job. Keep in mind that each row represents one customer/job. So if you perform the same service item for more than one customer or for more than one job with the same customer, enter each customer/job in its own row.

13. Click **Save & Close**.

QUICKTIP

If you usually work on the same customer/job, perform the same tasks, and enter the same hours, you can copy a previous timesheet—just click the **Copy Last Sheet** button. You can adjust the hours as needed.

Printing Timesheets

You can print timesheets so that employees or other workers can have copies of their timesheets for their own records or so that they can give a timesheet to a manager for a signature.

To print timesheets, go to the **File** menu, go to **Print Forms**, and click **Timesheets**. In the window, change the date range if you need to (the default date range is the current week). Make sure there's a check mark next to each name whose timesheet you want to print. If you want to print all the text in the note field, click **Print Full Activity Notes**. Otherwise, only the first line is printed. Click **OK** and then click **Print**.

QUICKTIP

If you have workers or subcontractors who don't have access to your QuickBooks, you can print a blank timesheet for them to fill out by hand. Open a new timesheet, click the arrow to the right of the **Print** button, and choose **Print Blank Timesheet**.

Generating Time Reports

Time reports can show you time spent on jobs, by item or by name. Before you pay your workers or before you bill a customer, you can review time spent in reports.

To generate a time report, go to the **Reports** menu, go to **Jobs, Time & Mileage**, and choose one of the following time reports:

Time by Job Summary: Shows the time spent on each customer or job, listed by the service item. Use this report to get a quick overview of time spent. You can use it to catch excessive hours or hours charged to the incorrect service item.

Time by Job Detail: Shows each service item performed for a particular customer or job and the time spent by each worker. If you double-click a service item, you can see the Time/Enter Single Activity window for those hours and date. Use the Billing Status column to see quickly whether the time spent was set appropriately as billable or nonbillable. If the time is billable but not yet billed, you will see "Unbilled."

Time by Name: Shows each worker and the time spent on each customer or job. If the hours seem too low, you can check the timesheets to see if some are missing.

Time by Item: Shows the total time spent for each service item, listed by customer or job. Use this report to figure out whether too many activities are unbillable or whether you need to increase staff.

Using QuickBooks Timer

QuickBooks offers a software program, which you can install on any computer, even without QuickBooks. The workers can enter their time without needing access to your QuickBooks file. After entering time (either using the stopwatch feature or entering the hours upon completion), the workers can send the time data to you. You can import it into your QuickBooks file to use for payroll or for billable time.

Describing how to use the Timer is beyond the scope of this guide. You can install the Timer by clicking the Windows **Start** menu, going to **All Programs**, **QuickBooks**, and clicking **Install QuickBooks Timer**. You'll need the QuickBooks CD to install it. After you install it, check the Help feature for further instructions.

Tracking Mileage

Whether the miles you put on your company vehicle are billable or unbillable, you should keep track so you can deduct the mileage from your taxes. If your customers will be reimbursing you, they expect you to keep accurate records, as do your pals at the IRS.

To track mileage, you need to add a company vehicle, set the mileage rate, and record the miles driven. The following sections cover each of these.

Adding a Vehicle

Before you can track mileage, you need to enter a record for a company vehicle.

To add a vehicle, follow these steps:

1. Go to the **Lists** menu, go to **Customer & Vendor Profile Lists**, and click **Vehicle List**.

2. In the Vehicle List (see Figure 25.4), press **Ctrl+N** to add a vehicle.

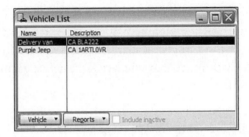

Figure 25.4: *Add a company vehicle so you can track mileage.*

3. In the New Vehicle window, type a name for the vehicle (or use the license plate number).

4. Type an optional description—for example, the year, model, make, insurance policy number, or VIN number.

5. Click **OK**.

Setting the Mileage Rate

You need to keep up with the IRS mileage rates to take advantage of the latest rates. Check with www.irs.gov to get the latest rates.

To enter the rates, go to the **Company** menu and click **Enter Vehicle Mileage**. Click **Mileage Rates**. Click in the Effective Date column and choose the date the rate became effective. Click in the Rate column and enter the IRS rate. Click **Close**.

Creating an Other Charge Item for Mileage

If you want to be reimbursed by your customers for mileage, you need to create a mileage item. Create an Other Charge item for mileage. Chapter 9 explains adding items in more detail, so I'll just give you a reminder here.

In the Item List window, press **Ctrl+N** to add a new item. Choose **Other Charge** as the item type. Enter a name for the item. Check the **This Item Is Used in Assemblies or Is a Reimbursable Charge** check box. From the Expense Account menu, choose the expense account you want to post the cost to. In the Cost field, type in the current IRS mileage rate, which you will have to update from time to time when the rate changes. From the Income Account menu, choose the income account you use to track reimbursable expenses. Leave the Sales Price blank if you plan to charge the actual mileage because the number of miles will vary from customer to customer. Click **OK** to save the item.

You use the item when you invoice a customer for mileage. The income account tells QuickBooks where to track the income you receive and what to charge for it. The rate can be the exact IRS mileage rate or a different rate that you choose. Whatever rate you enter, it will be multiplied by the actual number of miles that you enter on the invoice.

QUICKTIP

If you don't want to keep track of and charge for actual miles, you can set up the item with a flat rate and call it something like Delivery Charges. Leave the **This Item Is Used in Assemblies or Is a Reimbursable Charge** check box unchecked.

Entering Miles Driven

Every time you use a company vehicle, you can track the miles to get reimbursed by a customer or to log miles even when not billable.

To enter miles driven, follow these steps:

1. Go to the **Company** menu and click **Enter Vehicle Mileage**.

2. From the Vehicle menu, choose the vehicle you drove (or click **<Add New>** to add a new vehicle). See Figure 25.5.

3. Change the dates (QuickBooks automatically enters today's date), if you need to.

4. Type in the Odometer Start and Odometer End readings. QuickBooks figures out the total miles for you. If you forgot to jot them down, you can just type the total miles in the Total Miles field. Keep in mind, though, that your friendly IRS auditor really likes to see odometer readings.

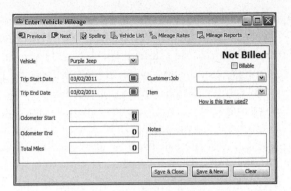

Figure 25.5: *The Enter Vehicle Mileage window.*

5. If you're going to bill a customer for the mileage, click the Billable check box to put a check mark in it. Then choose the customer from the Customer:Job menu and choose the mileage item you created to track the mileage. If the mileage is billable, both the Customer:Job and Item are required.

6. If the mileage isn't billable, make sure the Billable check box is not checked. From the Customer:Job menu, choose the fake customer you created to use for nonbillable tasks in "Setting Up Service Items for Tracking Time," earlier. From the Item menu, choose the mileage item so you can track the nonbillable mileage expense.

7. If you track classes, choose the class.

8. In the Notes box, type an optional description or reason for the mileage.

9. Click **Save & Close** to save and close the Enter Vehicle Mileage window, or click **Save & New** to save and enter more mileage records.

BEHIND THE SCENES

When you mark the mileage as billable, QuickBooks adds the miles to the list of billable expenses for the customer or job. When you later invoice the customer, QuickBooks reminds you that you can add some billable miles to the invoice.

To add mileage charges on an invoice, see Chapter 13.

Generating Mileage Reports

Mileage reports can show you mileage data to help you prepare at tax time or to show to customers.

To generate a mileage report, click **Mileage Reports** in the Enter Vehicle Mileage window; or go to the **Reports** menu, go to **Jobs**, **Time & Mileage**, and choose one of the following mileage reports:

Mileage by Vehicle Summary: Shows the total miles and mileage expense for each vehicle. If you're preparing taxes, you can change the date range to **This Tax Year**, **Last Tax Year**, or **This Tax Year-to-Date**. This report can also tell you how many miles have been put on the vehicle so you can stay on top of servicing, such as a 6,000-mile service.

Mileage by Vehicle Detail: Shows each trip made for each vehicle and includes the trip end date, the total miles for the trip, the mileage rate, and the mileage expense. Double-click a row to open the Enter Vehicle Mileage record for the trip. You can see whether it has been billed (Billed) or not billed (Not Billed), along with the associated customer or job and item.

Mileage by Job Summary: Shows the total miles driven by customer or job, regardless of which vehicle was used. It shows the billable amount for both billed and unbilled mileage records. If you didn't mark the mileage record as Billable or you didn't associate it with an item, the trip doesn't appear on this report.

Mileage by Job Detail: Shows the miles grouped by customer or job, and then shows the individual mileage records. It shows the Billing Status, whether it is Billable or Billed, and the Time End Date, Item, Total Miles, Sales Price, and Amount. This is a good report to generate if a customer has questions and wants to see details. Note that if the sales price and amounts are zero, you didn't associate the mileage record with an item.

The Least You Need to Know

- Track time and mileage so you can get reimbursed by your customers and deduct the expenses at tax time.
- You can record your time spent on a task as you perform it, or you can enter time on weekly timesheets.
- If you have workers who don't have access to your QuickBooks or subcontractors, you can print out a blank timesheet for them to fill out by hand.
- When you mark time and mileage as billable, QuickBooks adds the time and miles to the list of billable expenses for the customer or job. When you later invoice the customer, QuickBooks reminds you that you can add some billable expenses to the invoice.

Recording Owners Equity

In This Chapter

- Understanding owners equity accounts
- Understanding owners draw accounts
- Creating owners equity accounts
- Paying yourself or your partners
- Recording capital investments

You're probably wondering how you get paid. I know I'm not in business only for the fun of it; I need to make some money, too. Paying yourself or your partners is different from paying your employees.

According to the IRS, as a sole proprietor, you're not on your business payroll. Nor are your partners. You cannot write yourself or your partners a check through payroll. What you have is equity in your business, from your or your partner's initial capital investments and from your profits. When you record a profit at the end of the year, the equity of the business increases.

But you might still be wondering how you get paid. You can take money out of the business by drawing on the equity.

About Owners Equity Accounts

A company's equity comes from money invested in your company, including the initial investment and subsequent cash infusions. It also comes from your company's profits.

About Retained Earnings

When you set up a company file, QuickBooks creates an equity account that tracks *retained earnings*. This means that, at the end of the fiscal year, QuickBooks puts any profits (the earnings retained) into this account. At the year-end close, QuickBooks resets all income and expense accounts to zero for the start of the new year.

DEFINITION

Retained earnings are profits from previous accounting periods.

The name of this account changes depending on the type of business you indicated when you set up your company file. For sole proprietorship, the account is called Owners Equity. For a single-member LLC, the account is called Members Equity. For nonprofits, it's called Unrestricted Net Assets. For all other types, it's called Retained Earnings.

Here's an example of how this works (using small, round numbers):

A business owner creates a balance sheet on the last day of the fiscal year (December 31, in this example) of his first year in business. The retained earnings account has a zero balance because it's the first year of the business, so there were no profits from the previous year. The net income for his current fiscal year was $10,000. On January 1, the first day of his new fiscal year, he creates a balance sheet. This time, the retained earnings account has $10,000 and the net income is zero.

At some point, if the business owner had partners, that $10,000 profit can be distributed among the partners into their individual equity accounts.

QUICKTIP

To see the balance in the retained earnings (or owners equity) account, open the chart of accounts and double-click the account.

About Owners Draw Accounts

Another owners equity account that you might want to create (if QuickBooks hasn't already created it for you) is an *owners draw* account. You use this account to track your withdrawals from the company assets to pay yourself. The draws reduce the company's equity.

If you also want to track your original investments in the company or track a partner's investment, you can create separate equity accounts. See the following section for how to create an equity account.

DEFINITION

An **owners draw** account tracks withdrawals of the company's assets to pay an owner.

Creating Owners Equity Accounts

If you don't see owners draw or capital investment accounts in your chart of accounts, you can create them. You can create as many equity accounts as you need. In a sole proprietorship, for example, you might want to create a separate account to track your personal investment of capital, called Capital Investments, and a draw account to record the money you take out.

For partnerships (not corporations), you should create three accounts for each partner/owner. To keep things neat and tidy in your chart of accounts, you could create an "umbrella" owners equity account and create subaccounts for each owner/partner. Create a draw account for each owner/partner to track the withdrawals separately. You'll also want to create an account for each owner/partner to track each person's investments into the company. If you do profit sharing, you'll need to create those as separate accounts as well, sometimes called distribution accounts.

QUICKTIP

Set up co-owners or partners in the Other Names list. Co-owners/partners are not considered employees and are not paid through payroll.

If you're a corporation, talk with your accountant about the accounts you need to set up and what you need to track. This is more complicated than if you're a sole proprietorship or partnership.

Chapter 8 covers creating accounts, so I'll just go over it briefly here.

To create an owners equity account, follow these steps:

1. Press **Ctrl+A** to open the chart of accounts.

2. Press **Ctrl+N** to create a new account.

3. Choose **Equity** as the account type.

4. Type a name for the account and indicate whether it is a subaccount.

5. Fill out the optional fields, if you want.

6. Click **Save & New** to save and create another equity account, or click **Save & Close**.

Recording an Owner's Withdrawal

After creating the draw account(s) (one for each owner, if you're a partnership), you can record withdrawals to pay yourself or to pay a co-owner or partner.

To record a draw, follow these steps:

1. Go to the **Banking** menu and click **Write Checks**, or, on the Home page, click **Write Checks**. The keystroke shortcut is **Ctrl-W**.

2. Make sure the account you want to use to write the check is selected in the Bank Account field.

3. Choose the name of the owner/partner in the **Pay to the Order Of** field.

4. Type the amount of the withdrawal.

5. Click in the **Account** field on the Expenses tab and choose the owner or partner's draw account.

6. Click one of the **Save** options.

Recording Capital Investments

When an owner/partner puts personal money into the business, it is considered a capital investment. You need to keep track of those investments in equity accounts (one for each owner/partner).

To record a capital investment, follow these steps:

1. Go to the **Banking** menu and click **Make Deposits**, or click **Record Deposits** on the Home page.

2. If you see the Payments to Deposit window, click **Cancel** to deposit the investment only.

3. Choose the bank account to deposit to.

4. Click in the **Received From** column and choose the owner/partner's name.

5. Click in the **From Account** column and choose the owner's or partner capital investment account.

6. Press **Tab** until you reach the amount column and enter the investment amount.

7. Click **Save & Close**.

The Least You Need to Know

- A company's equity comes from money invested in your company, including the initial investment and subsequent cash infusions. It also comes from your company's profits.

- To track your withdrawals from the company assets to pay yourself, use an owners draw account. The draws reduce the company's equity.

- Set up co-owners or partners in the Other Names list. Co-owners/partners aren't considered employees and aren't paid through payroll.

- When an owner/partner puts personal money into the business, it is considered a capital investment. You need to keep track of those investments in equity accounts (one for each owner/partner).

Managing Your Company File

In This Chapter

- Backing up and restoring from a backup copy
- Scheduling backups
- Creating and using a portable company file
- Deleting a company file

This chapter talks about managing your company file and includes topics like backing up your file, creating a portable company file, and deleting a company file.

Making Backups

Backing up your company file is pretty important, as you will discover when you count how many times QuickBooks nags you about backing up. You just need to determine how often you want to back up. Some businesses with a lot of transactions may want to back up every day; others do so once a week. That way, when you put your laptop on the top of your car while you're looking for your keys and you end up driving off, you can at least restore the QuickBooks data from your backup copy.

Backing Up

The simplest way to create a backup is to back it up to a USB flash drive or CD. Follow the instructions that came with the drive or computer to insert the device or CD, and then follow these steps:

1. Go to the File menu and click **Create Backup**.

2. In the Create Backup Wizard (shown in Figure 27.1), click **Local Backup**. (The other option, Online Backup, is an extra service for a fee.)

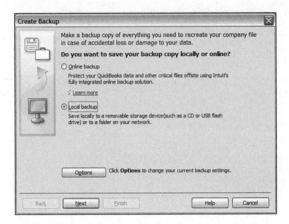

Figure 27.1: *Choose the location of the backup copy.*

3. Click **Next** and set up the options for backing up, as shown in Figure 27.2.

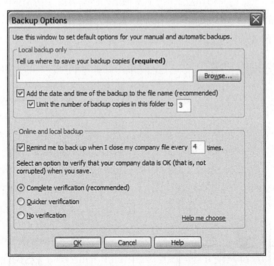

Figure 27.2: *Choose the backup options.*

Browse: Click **Browse** to tell QuickBooks where to back up the file. Choose the USB drive, zip drive, network drive, or CD drive and click **OK**.

Timestamp: Select the check box to add the date and time to the filename of your company file. If you don't select the check box (that is, you don't put a check mark in the box), the backup file is replaced each time you create a backup.

Reminders: Tell QuickBooks how often you want to be nagged to make a backup. Select the check box and indicate how often.

Verification: Choose how you want QuickBooks to verify the backup copy, if at all. You can choose a complete method, which takes longer; a quicker method; or no verification at all.

4. Click **OK**.

5. Click **Save It Now** and then click **Next**.

7. In the Save Backup Copy dialog box, confirm the location to save the file and click **Save**.

8. In the dialog box confirming that a backup was completed, QuickBooks offers to let you try the online backup solution. Click **No, Thanks**, unless you want to try it.

Scheduling Backups

If you want to schedule an automatic backup, follow the steps above through step 5. At step 6, choose either **Save It Now and Schedule Future Backups** or **Only Schedule Future Backups**. Figure 27.3 shows the backup schedule options.

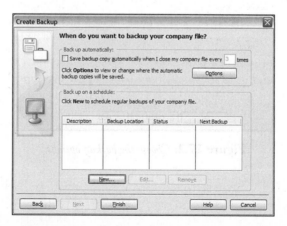

Figure 27.3: *Choose the backup schedule options.*

Back Up Automatically: Click this option to select it and then enter how frequently you want to back up.

Back Up on a Schedule: Click **New** and enter the schedule, as shown in Figure 27.4.

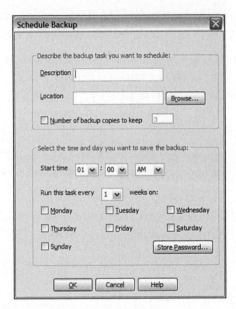

Figure 27.4: *Choose the backup schedule for an automatic, unattended backup.*

Description: Type a name for the schedule, such as USB backup.

Location: Click **Browse** to tell QuickBooks where to back up the file. You can schedule backups only for Zip drives, USB drives, or a network drive; you can't schedule backups for a CD because it takes more steps and can't be completed without attendance.

Number of Backup Copies to Keep: Tell QuickBooks how far back you want to keep backups. If you enter 2, QuickBooks adds a new backup file and removes the oldest backup file.

Date and Time: Choose the start time when you won't be using the computer, such as 1 A.M. Choose the frequency and day of the week. To schedule the backup to run daily, choose **1** for the frequency and then click every day of the week.

Store Password: Click **Store Password** to enter your Windows username and password, and click **OK**. If you don't enter login information, the backup fails because of a Windows permission failure.

Back at the Create Backup Wizard, click **OK** and then click **Finish**.

Note that if you've scheduled a backup, the computer must be on at the time of the backup and the file must not be in use to perform the backup.

Restoring a Backup Copy

Holy cannoli! Your computer's hard drive is fried! Hopefully this never happens to you, but you'll be okay if you made a backup copy of your company file.

You may end up having to buy a new computer and reinstalling QuickBooks on that computer. But after you do, you can restore your company file from the backup copy.

In another scenario, your company file might get corrupted. When that happens, open QuickBooks and restore from backup.

To restore your company file, follow these steps:

1. Go to the **File** menu, go to **Restore Previous Local Backup**, and then choose the backup you want to restore. The Restore wizard appears, as shown in Figure 27.5.

Figure 27.5: *The Restore Wizard.*

2. Click **Next** and tell QuickBooks the location for your file. Confirm the location and click **Save**. Click **Yes** to replace the existing file. QuickBooks wants to be really sure you want to replace it and asks you to physically type **YES** because it first needs to delete the previous version of the file.

3. If you've password-protected your company file, type your password and click **OK**. Click **OK** at the message that your file has been restored successfully.

Hopefully your last backup wasn't too long ago. You'll have to re-create all the transactions that occurred since the last backup.

Creating a Portable Company File

A portable company file is your company file condensed so you can e-mail it or transport it from your office computer to your home computer. Keep in mind that a portable copy is just for moving from one computer to another; it's not meant to be used on two systems because you can't merge data. If you add information to the original company file while a portable one is out in the world, when you restore the file, all the changes you made to the original file will be lost. You can merge changes on an accountant's copy of your file; see Chapter 32 for details.

To create a portable company file, follow these steps:

1. Go to **File** and click **Create Copy**. The Save Copy or Backup window appears, as shown in Figure 27.6.

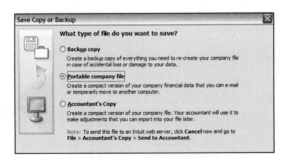

Figure 27.6: *The Save Copy or Backup window with Portable Company File selected*

2. Select **Portable Company File** and click **Next**. Tell QuickBooks where you want to save the file.

3. QuickBooks adds the word "(Portable)" and the extension .qbm to the name of your file. Click **Save** and then click **OK** at the message that appears.

4. Click **OK** when QuickBooks has finished.

Before you can use the portable file on another computer, you must restore it. First, follow the preceding steps above to make the portable company file. To restore it, go to **File** and click **Open** or **Restore Company**. In the window that appears, click **Portable Company File** and then click **Next**. Locate the .qbm file and click Open.

Deleting a Company File

Before you delete a company file, make sure it wasn't the last file QuickBooks had open. Otherwise, when you start QuickBooks the next time, it won't be able to find the file because it automatically opens the last file you had open. Before deleting the company file, open another file that you're not planning to delete, or open the file you plan to delete, go to the **File** menu, and click **Close Company**.

To delete the file in Windows Explorer follow these steps:

1. From the Start menu, navigate to the folder where the company file is stored.

2. Choose the List view to see the files by name. Delete all the files associated with the name of the company file (there might be 4 different files).

To delete the file in QuickBooks, follow these steps:

1. Go to **File** and click **Open** or **Restore Company**.

2. In the window that appears, click **Open a Company File** and click **Next**.

3. In the list of files, right-click the file you want to delete and choose **Delete**. Click **OK** to confirm.

4. In the list of files, open a company file or click **Cancel** to close the dialog box.

That deleted file may continue to haunt you in the "previous" file list. When you choose **Open Previous Company** from the **File** menu, or in the No Company Open window, you see a list of company files. If the file you deleted is listed, choose **Open Previous Company** from the **File** menu and then choose **Set number of previous companies** (the menu item at the bottom of the previous files list). Change the number to 1. Later, if you want more files to be displayed, you can change it to a higher number.

The Least You Need to Know

- Backing up your company file important! The simplest way to create a backup is to back it up to a USB flash drive or CD.

- You can schedule backups to occur automatically during a time you're not using the computer.

- Create a portable company file (a condensed version of your company file) so that you can e-mail it or transport it from your office computer to your home computer.

- If you created a company file to experiment with before creating the actual file, you should delete it so it no longer appears in the list of previously opened files.

How Is Your Business Doing?

In this part, you learn about running reports that help you monitor several key areas of your business. QuickBooks offers reports for all aspects of your business, not just the financials. Part 8 also covers some important tasks you need to perform at year's end. Some minor miscellaneous tasks—such as making a copy of your company file for your accountant to review and making journal entries—are also covered in these chapters.

Chapter 28 provides an overview of reports, setting up report preferences, generating reports, and printing and memorizing reports for re-use.

Chapter 29 covers common reports you're likely to use on a day-to-day basis—such as reports on your sales, customers, and vendors.

Chapter 30 goes over the all-important financial reports—such as profit and loss reports, the balance sheet reports, and a statement of cash flows.

Chapter 31 explains how you can customize reports to suit your needs.

And Chapter 32 helps you prepare for the tasks you need to do at the end of the fiscal and calendar years, including creating a copy of your company file to give to your accountant.

Reports Overview

In This Chapter

- Setting up preferences for reports
- Getting the most out of the Report Center
- Generating a report
- Printing a report to PDF, a file, or your printer
- Memorizing a report

Want a report to track how much chicken feed you've sold over the past week, month, or year? Do you want to compare sales of organic chicken feed with nonorganic feed? QuickBooks can help you track and compare whatever you want. In fact, you have so many reports to choose from, it's almost overwhelming. In this chapter, I give you an overview to simplify them.

About Reports

QuickBooks reports can be classified as summary reports, transaction reports, and list reports. (QuickBooks also creates a few reports in graph format.)

Summary reports summarize and subtotal the data. For example, a summary report can provide totals for each income and expense account.

Transaction reports (known as Detail reports) expand on summary reports by showing each transaction that makes up the subtotal. To continue with the example, a transaction report would show each transaction by income account and each transaction by expense account.

List reports show just what you would expect: lists of your customers, vendors, accounts, items, fixed assets, and so on.

Another type of report is called the QuickReport. Whenever you're displaying a list, such as the Class list or Item list, you can right-click an item in the list and choose **QuickReport**. If you're displaying a customer in the Customer Center, you'll see a QuickReport link. Like ants at a picnic, QuickReports are everywhere.

Setting Report Preferences

Before you start generating reports, you can set preferences that apply to all reports. To display report preferences, go to the **Edit** menu and click **Preferences**. In the left panel, click **Reports & Graphs** and then click the **Company Preferences** tab (see Figure 28.1).

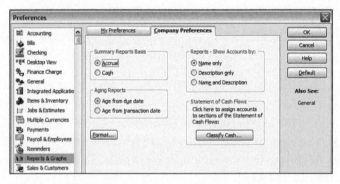

Figure 28.1: *Reports & Graphs preferences.*

The following describes the options for report preferences:

Summary Report Basis: Accrual: If you choose Accrual, summary reports use the data from your transactions as soon as you enter an invoice (even though you don't yet have the cash in hand) or enter a payment (even though you haven't yet paid for the expense). (Chapter 4 talks more about cash and accrual accounting methods.) If you choose Accrual as the preference, you can always change it on an individual report later. See Chapter 31 for details.

Summary Report Basis: Cash: If you choose Cash, summary reports use the data from your transactions as soon as you receive money from customer payments or make an actual payment for your expenses. For example, a cash basis report wouldn't show outstanding invoices as income, or unpaid bills as expenses. If you choose Cash as the preference, you can always change it on an individual report later. See Chapter 31 for details.

Age from Due Date: Choose this option to have QuickBooks start the aging count (how many days overdue) from the due date that appears on an invoice, statement, or bill.

Age from Transaction Date: Choose this option to have QuickBooks start the aging count (how many days overdue) from the date you created the invoice or statement, or received a bill.

Format: Click this button to change the appearance of all reports that you generate. See Figure 28.2 for the options you can change.

Reports Show Accounts By: Choose how you want accounts to be displayed in your reports: by the name of the account, by the descriptions you entered when you created the account, or by both the name and description.

Statement of Cash Flows: QuickBooks automatically uses certain accounts when generating the statement of cash flows report. To change the accounts, talk to your accountant first; then click the **Classify Cash** button.

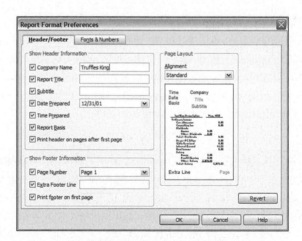

Figure 28.2: *Report Format preferences.*

Click **OK** to save your changes to the Reports & Graphs preferences.

Using the Reports Center

It might seem like QuickBooks has a gazillion reports, but the Report Center does a great job of organizing them.

To open the Report Center, click the **Report Center** icon in the navigation bar, or go to the **Reports** menu and click **Report Center**. Figure 28.3 shows the Report Center.

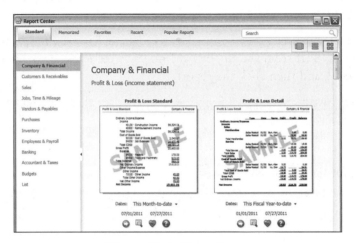

Figure 28.3: *Report Center.*

QuickBooks organizes reports by area in the left panel. Click the area you want to use, and QuickBooks changes the display to show visual representation of the reports. If you prefer to see a list of reports with descriptions, click the **List** icon in the upper-right corner of the Report Center. See Figure 28.4.

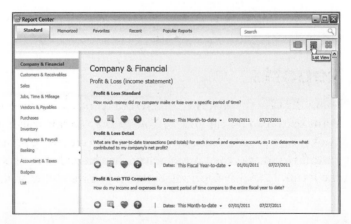

Figure 28.4: *Report Center List view.*

Play around with the display buttons in the upper right to find the best view for you: carousel, list, or grid.

Generating Reports

QuickBooks offers several starting points for generating reports: from the Report Center, from the Reports menu, and from other areas of the program, such as the Customer Center.

To generate a report from the Report Center, double-click the report you want to see. To generate a report from the Reports menu, go to **Reports**, click the reporting area from the menu, and then click the report.

QuickBooks presents a standard report, which you can then customize. Chapter 31 talks about customizing reports.

Zooming In on a Report

When a report is displayed on a screen, you can do some fun stuff with the QuickZoom feature. If you want to check on a transaction or a number on a report, you can zoom in. When you move your pointer over a number or transaction, the pointer changes to a magnifying glass (see Figure 28.5). Double-click to see all the transactions behind that number.

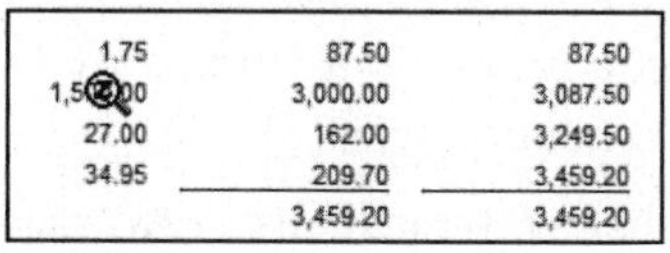

1.75	87.50	87.50
1,5@00	3,000.00	3,087.50
27.00	162.00	3,249.50
34.95	209.70	3,459.20
	3,459.20	3,459.20

Figure 28.5: *Zooming in on a figure.*

Printing Reports

After QuickBooks displays the report on the screen, you can print the report by clicking the **Print** button above the report. You'll see a window where you can set some print options. If you have Adobe Acrobat installed on your computer and you want to print it to PDF to save the forests, select **Printer** and then choose the PDF option from the menu. Click the **Options** button if you want to change the PDF options, or click **Print**. You'll need to indicate a name and where to save the file. Then click **OK**.

Another choice is to print the report to a file (ASCII, comma-delimited, or tab-delimited), which you can then import into a spreadsheet. Select **File** and then choose the file format. Click **Print** to print the report. You'll need to indicate a name and specify where to save the file. Then click **Save**.

Memorizing Reports

When you create a report, make some customizations, and change the format, you may want to keep those changes for future reports so you don't have to re-create them. To do this, you can "memorize" the report. Just click the **Memorize** button when you're finished with your changes. Give the report a name, choose the report category (optional), and click **OK**. To later regenerate the report, go to the **Reports** menu, go to **Memorized Reports**, and then choose the report from there. You get your customized report, without having to choose the customizations again.

The Least You Need to Know

- Before you start generating reports, you can set preferences that apply to all reports, including how to format them.
- Use the Report Center for easy access and visual cues to all QuickBooks reports.
- To view the transactions behind a number on the report, use QuickZoom. Hover over the number and double-click.
- Memorize reports after you make the customizations you want to keep the next time you generate the report.

Generating Day-to-Day Reports

In This Chapter

- Finding out how your sales are doing
- Getting reports on your customers and vendors
- Reporting on banking activities
- Finding voided and deleted transactions

I hate to be a downer, but I recently read about two separate incidents in my area in which the owners (one the owner of a tire company and the other a lawyer) knew little about what was going on in their day-to-day businesses—they relied on an employee to take care of the books and other details. In both cases, the employees were messing around, falsifying transactions, and robbing the owners' hard-earned money. (Not to leave you in suspense—both the offenders were caught.)

If only those owners had checked up on their business regularly, such as by generating reports, perhaps they could have avoided this painful situation.

About Day-to-Day Reports

In addition to the standard financial reports that help you analyze the health of your business, QuickBooks offers a ton of reports that enable you to monitor the tasks and transactions you perform during the day-to-day operation of your business. These include sales reports, vendor reports, and banking reports. The following sections describe these reports by category. Other chapters, such as Chapter 20 on inventory and Chapter 24 on payroll, discuss the relevant reports.

You can customize all these reports, too, as you'll find in Chapter 31.

Sales Reports

QuickBooks supplies several reports based on your sales, including sales by customer, by item, by sales rep, and more. This section explains each type of sales report in more detail.

To generate sales reports, go to the **Reports** menu and click **Sales**.

Sales by Customer Summary summarizes sales income by customer and job, including income from products, services, and other charge items from invoices or sales receipts. This doesn't include sales tax collected or income from reimbursed expenses.

Sales by Customer Detail lists sales transactions for each customer.

Sales by Item Summary summarizes sales, both by dollar amounts and by number of items, subtotaled by item.

Sales by Item Detail lists each sales transaction by item (product or service).

Sales by Rep Summary summarizes sales by sales reps, including income from products, services, discounts, and other charges. This doesn't include sales tax or reimbursable expenses.

Sales by Rep Detail lists each sales transaction by sales reps, including income from products, services, discounts, and other charges. This doesn't include sales tax or reimbursable expenses.

Sales by Ship To Address lists each sales transaction by the address it was shipped to.

Pending Sales lists all invoices, cash sales, and credit memos that are marked as pending.

Sales Graph shows sales income in a bar graph or pie chart for the time period you specify.

Customer Reports

QuickBooks supplies several reports on your customers, some of which you learned about in Chapter 15. This section explains each type of customer report in more detail.

To generate customer reports, go to the **Reports** menu and click **Customers & Receivables**.

A/R Aging Summary summarizes when payments are (or were) due, subtotaled by customer.

A/R Aging Detail lists each unpaid invoice and statement charge, grouped and subtotaled by due date. If an invoice or statement charge is overdue, the Aging column shows the number of days past due.

Customer Balance Summary shows balances for customers with unpaid balances, grouped by customer and job.

Customer Balance Detail shows all customer transactions, grouped by customer and job. The totals in the Balance column are the unpaid balances for each customer and job. A total of $0.00 means that the customer has no unpaid balance.

Open Invoices lists each unpaid invoice and statement charge, grouped and subtotaled by customer and job.

Collections Report displays which invoices or statement charges are overdue, grouped by customer and job, along with customer contact names and phone numbers.

Accounts Receivable Graph displays a graph showing accounts receivable by aging period.

Unbilled Costs by Job shows any outstanding reimbursed expenses that have not yet been charged back to the customer.

Average Days to Pay shows how long it takes, on average, for each customer to pay you.

Transaction List by Customer lists all the transactions by the date range you specify for each customer.

Customer Contact List lists all customers alphabetically and includes contact, phone numbers, address, and current open balance.

Customer Phone List lists all customers alphabetically and their phone numbers.

Item Price List lists all of your items and shows the price and preferred vendor.

Vendor Reports

QuickBooks supplies several reports on your vendors, including balances you owe to vendors and vendor aging reports. This section explains each type of vendor report in more detail.

To generate vendor reports, go to the **Reports** menu and click **Vendors & Payables**.

A/P Aging Summary summarizes the aging status of unpaid bills in your A/P account, subtotaled by vendor.

A/R Aging Detail lists each unpaid bill, subtotaled by aging period. This tells you the number of days a bill is overdue.

Vendor Balance Summary shows balances for all open vendor bills, with no end date.

Vendor Balance Detail shows all vendor transactions, subtotaled by vendor. The total for a vendor is the vendor's unpaid balance. A total of $0.00 means that you do not owe this vendor any money.

Accounts Payable Graph displays a graph showing how much you owe vendors by aging period and the percentages you owe by vendor.

Unpaid Bills Detail lists each unpaid bill, subtotaled by vendor.

Transaction List by Vendor lists all the transactions by the date range you specify for each vendor.

1099 Summary summarizes your 1099 payments to your 1099 vendors. This helps when filling out tax forms.

1099 Detail lists each transaction that contributes to a 1099 vendor's total.

Banking Reports

QuickBooks supplies several reports on your banking activities. This is an area of reporting that you may want to keep a close eye on, to catch fraud before it's too late. This section explains each type of banking report in more detail.

To generate banking reports, go to the **Reports** menu and click **Banking**.

Deposit Detail shows detailed information on each bank deposit and the source of the payments.

Check Detail shows detailed information on each check, including the expense accounts affected by the check. It shows all the different types of checks you've written—paychecks, bill payment checks, payroll liability checks, and so on.

Missing Checks lists checks in a bank account by number and identifies missing and duplicate numbers.

Reconciliation Discrepancy shows which cleared transactions have been modified since you last reconciled the account.

Previous Reconciliation lists which transactions were cleared in a prior reconciliation.

Voided and Deleted Transactions Reports

These reports are grouped with Accountant & Taxes reports (which are covered in Chapter 32), but I'm separating them out because you might want to keep an eye on these types of transactions if you're not the only person with access to your company file.

To generate these reports, go to the **Reports** menu and click **Accountant & Taxes**. Then choose the report type.

Voided/Deleted Transactions Summary shows which transactions have been voided or deleted.

Voided/Deleted Transactions Detail shows a detailed history of each voided or deleted transaction.

The Least You Need to Know

- Use sales reports to find out how your business is doing. Track sales by customer, product or service, sales rep, and more.
- Customer and vendor reports help you stay on top of customers who owe you money and vendors you owe money to.
- Use banking and voided/deleted transaction reports to keep a close eye on all your business transactions.
- Some report categories include graphs, which can provide you with a quick, visual overview.

Understanding Your Financials

In This Chapter

- Determining the profit (or loss) of your business
- Generating a balance sheet
- Understanding the statement of cash flow
- Generating a cash flow report

To keep an eye on whether your business is financially on the right track, you can generate financial reports. Hopefully, your reports will show that you're making a profit. Chapter 4 talks in general about these financial statements, so I won't go into too much detail here; instead, we focus here on simply generating these reports.

You'll also need these reports if you ever want to apply for a loan or line of credit.

About the Profit and Loss Report

If you want to see whether you're making any money, you need to run the profit and loss report. It's also called the *P&L* for short—and just to confuse things more, sometimes people refer to it as an *income statement*. This report shows whether you're operating with a loss or a profit. Most businesses run this report monthly or more, just to stay on top of things.

You can create a standard summary report or a detail report, as explained below.

The standard P&L Report summarizes your income and expenses for the date range you specify. If you track inventory, the report also shows numbers from your COGS (Cost of Goods Sold) account. Bottom line, it tells you your net income (profit) or net loss (loss).

To generate a standard P&L report, go to the **Reports** menu, go to **Company & Financials**, and choose **Profit & Loss Standard**. This report lists and totals your income, lists your cost of goods sold (if you track inventory), and subtracts the COGS amount from your income total to get your gross profit. Then the report lists and totals all your expenses. Your net profit (or loss) is the difference between your expenses and your gross profit.

You can change the date range that the report shows. QuickBooks initially displays the current month-to-date. You can change the date range by clicking the arrow next to the Date menu. Figure 30.1 shows your date range options.

Figure 30.1: *Changing the date range options.*

QuickBooks offers several flavors of profit and loss reports in addition to the standard P&L; each one is described briefly here.

Profit & Loss Detail shows you year-to-date transactions (instead of totals only, as in the standard P&L report) for every income and expense account. Use this report if you want to check how the standard P&L came up with those numbers—but beware, it's a long and cumbersome report. The standard P&L is best for getting your net income (or loss).

Profit & Loss YTD Comparison compares your year-to-date (YTD) totals (based on your fiscal year) with the income and expenses for the current month. You can tell whether you're operating at a profit or loss this month, and you can compare this month's performance against your profit or loss for the fiscal year.

Profit & Loss Prev Year Comparison compares the current month's profit or loss with the same month last year. It shows the difference in both dollar amounts and percentage. After you've been working in QuickBooks for a year, this might be one of your favorite reports.

Profit & Loss By Job shows how much you're making or losing on each job, subtotaled by income or expense accounts. This way, you can figure out where the money comes from and where it goes. Only the transactions that have been assigned to a job appear on this report, so it's not a report to use to find your net income (loss) overall.

Profit & Loss By Class shows how much you're making or losing by class. (Remember classes? They let you segment your business by location or department.) The classes are subtotaled by income or expense accounts so you can figure out where the money comes from and where it goes. Only the transactions that have been assigned to a class appear on this report, so it's not a report to use to find your net income (loss) overall.

Profit & Loss By Unclassified shows you transaction totals that haven't been assigned to a class. In fact, that is why this report is useful—you can keep zooming in until you open a transaction, and then you can assign it to a class, if desired.

About the Balance Sheet Report

The balance sheet report shows you an overall picture of the health of your business finances as of a certain date. It basically shows you how much your company is worth. To calculate your equity (net worth), the report subtracts your liabilities (money you owe) from your assets. To calculate your total assets, the report subtracts your liabilities from your equity. (See Chapter 4 for more information.)

To generate a standard Balance Sheet report, go to the **Reports** menu, go to **Company & Financials**, and choose **Balance Sheet Standard**.

You can change the date range that the report shows. QuickBooks initially displays the fiscal year-to-date. You can change the "as of" date by choosing a new date from the calendar, or you can change the date range by clicking the arrow next to the Date menu. Figure 30.1 shows you the date range options you can choose.

QuickBooks offers several flavors of balance sheet reports besides the standard report; each one is described briefly here.

Balance Sheet Detail shows you all the transactions in each balance sheet account (see Chapter 4 for a reminder). It shows the balance for each account for the current month-to-date. This report can get very long. The Balance Sheet Standard report shows you basically what you need to know.

Balance Sheet Summary shows less detail than the Balance Sheet Standard report. It lists totals for each type of account but doesn't show the balances of every account. For example, instead of listing the balances for all your bank accounts, it shows the total balance. You must generate a standard balance sheet report to see individual account balances.

Balance Sheet Prev Year Comparison compares the worth of your business compared to the same period one year ago. It shows the difference in both dollar amounts and percentage.

About the Statement of Cash Flows

Cash flow reports show you the cash coming in (called cash inflow) from profits and the cash spent (called cash outflow) during a specified time period. What is this good for? Even though the balance sheet might show a healthy net worth, sometimes it may feel like you have no cash to pay bills. Cash flow reports are good for pinpointing the actual cash flowing in and out of your business, whereas the balance sheet reports include things like your fixed assets, which are easily converted to cash.

QuickBooks has two types of cash flow reports: Statement of Cash Flows and Cash Flow Forecast.

To generate cash flow reports, go to the **Reports** menu, go to **Company & Financials**, and choose either **Statement of Cash Flows** or **Cash Flow Forecast**.

The **Statement of Cash Flow** report shows your cash position over a period of time. It shows the amount of cash earned from profit, where you received additional cash, and where your cash was spent. These appear on the report as "Operating Activities," "Investing Activities," and "Financing Activities." You probably need to generate this report only for a bank or a potential buyer.

The **Cash Flow Forecast** report helps you figure out how much cash you'll have by projecting your cash coming in and cash going out, along with your bank account balances.

The Least You Need to Know

- Summary reports show you high-level totals, and detail reports break down those totals to show each individual transaction.

- Use the standard P&L report often to track whether your business is making or losing money.

- Balance sheet reports give you an overall picture of the health of your business finances as of a certain date. They basically show you how much your company is worth.

- The cash flow reports are useful when applying for a loan or selling your business. Your accountant will also want to generate these reports at year's end.

Customizing Reports

In This Chapter

- Customizing dates and columns on preset reports
- Filtering the report to remove things you don't want to report on
- Changing the header, footer, and font on a report
- Saving a customized report for later use

In addition to providing reports on every conceivable aspect of your business, QuickBooks offers a ton of ways you can customize them. When you get your reports just the way you want them, you can have QuickBooks memorize them so you can generate them again quickly.

Customizing Reports

What you can customize in a report depends on the type of report you're generating, but the display options for all summary reports are similar and the display options for detail reports are similar.

You can also filter a report to narrow what is displayed. Filtering works the same for both summary and detail reports.

Changing Display Options for Summary Reports

Summary reports group transactions and show a single total for each group. For example, a vendor summary report groups individual transactions for each vendor and shows the total of all that vendor's transactions. Summary reports don't show each individual transaction.

To customize a summary report, click the **Customize Report** button at the top left of the report. Figure 31.1 shows the Modify Report window for a Profit and Loss report. Not all summary reports have all the options; some might have a subset of those shown.

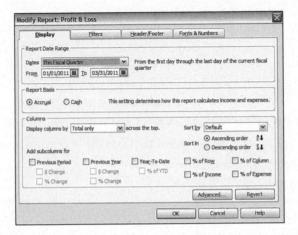

Figure 31.1: *Choose options to change what the report shows.*

The basic display options for summary reports are as follows:

Dates: Sets the date range to show in the report. Choose a range from the menu or select dates in the From and To fields for a custom date range.

Report Basis: Determines how QuickBooks calculates income and expenses on the report. (See Chapter 4 for more about cash and accrual accounting methods.) Choose **Cash** to base calculations on the date the cash is exchanged. Choose **Accrual** to base income calculations on the date you invoiced a customer, and expense calculations on the date you entered a bill.

Columns: Groups subtotal amounts in columns by time period or other settings, such as vendor, item type, customer type, and more. As an example, if you choose Year, the report displays separate columns for each year, within the date range for the report. So if your date range consists of more than one year, you would see a column for each year. If you choose Vendor, the report displays a column for each vendor.

Sort By: Determines the column to sort by. Your choices depend on the type of report, and not all reports can be sorted. If you don't see a Sort By menu, the report can't be sorted.

Sort In: Determines the sort order: ascending (A to Z) or descending (Z to A).

Add Subcolumns For: Adds subcolumns that show time periods and changes in amounts or percentage. Put a check mark in the check box to see the column in the report. For the Previous Period and Previous Year columns, you can also show $ Change or % Change. For a Year-to-Date column, you can show % of YTD.

Additional Columns: Adds columns that show percentages of the total. % of Column shows the percentage that the amount in the row contributes to the total of all amounts in the column. % of Row shows what percent one figure in the row on the report contributed to the total of all amounts in the row. % of Income shows the percentage the amount in the row contributes to the total of all your income. % of Expense shows the percentage the amount in the row contributes to the total of all your expenses.

The % of Row and % of Column can be pretty tricky to grasp—at least, it was a brain twister for me. So here's an example of % of Column that I hope will make it clearer. Let's say you have two sales reps that you want to compare. You can see what percentage each sales rep contributes to your total income for a given time period. By adding a % of Column to the report, you see the rep's percentage of the total, as shown in Figure 31.2.

Sales by Rep Summary		
March 2011		
	Mar 11	% of Column
Diesel Anderson	3,845.20	66.1%
Flora Turner	1,198.50	20.6%
No sales rep	774.50	13.3%
TOTAL	5,818.20	100.0%

Figure 31.2: *The % of Column shows clearly who is the stronger sales rep in terms of sales.*

And here's an example of % of Row. Let's say you run a nonprofit, after-school theater group and you need to find out what percentage overhead is of your total expenses. You created three classes for Overhead, Fundraising, and Programs. To see the percentage of overhead, create a Profit & Loss by Class report. By adding a % of Row to the report, you can see the percentage of the total expenses that each class represents.

Changing Display Options for Detail Reports

Detail reports show all the transactions behind the amounts on the report. To customize a detail report, click the **Customize Report** button at the top left of the report. Figure 31.3 shows the Modify Report window for a Profit and Loss report. Not all detail reports have all the options; some might have a subset of those shown.

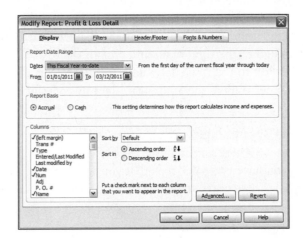

Figure 31.3: *Choose options to change what the report shows.*

The Report Date Range and Report Basis are the same for both summary and detail reports, so I won't repeat those here. The basic display options for columns detail reports are as follows:

Columns: Lists all the columns that can be shown in the report. To add a column, click it to put a check mark next to it; to remove a column, click a check mark to remove it. On some detail reports, you can select to display the Debit and Credit columns and then remove the Amount column.

Sort By: Determines the column to sort by. As you add or remove columns, the Sort By menu changes to reflect the columns you selected to show. Not all reports can be sorted. If you don't see a Sort By menu, the report can't be sorted.

Sort In: Determines the sort order: ascending (A to Z) or descending (Z to A).

Total By: Groups and subtotals transactions. Not all reports have a Total By menu.

QUICKTIP

If a detail report has too many columns and is too wide for your screen, hide any unnecessary columns, including **(Left Margin)** to remove the space created by the margin or **Memo**.

Choosing Advanced Options

Several reports have additional options that tell QuickBooks which data to include in the report. If the report you're working with has an Advanced button on the Display tab of the Modify Report window, you can set additional options. Figure 31.4 shows some typical advanced options.

Figure 31.4: *Choose options to tell QuickBooks which data to include in the report.*

The Advanced Options window varies based on the type of report. Depending on the type of report you are working on, some of the following options might not be valid:

Display Rows: Specifies which rows to include or exclude, based on financial activity during the selected date range. Choose **Active** to include only rows that have some financial activity; this also includes rows with amounts of $0.00. Choose **All** to include all rows, both those with and those without financial activity. Choose **Nonzero** to exclude rows with amounts of $0.00.

Display Columns: Specifies which columns to include or exclude, based on financial activity during the selected date range. Choose **Active** to include only columns that have some financial activity; this also includes columns with amounts of $0.00. Choose **All** to include all rows, both those with and those without financial activity. Choose **Nonzero** to exclude columns with amounts of $0.00.

Reporting Calendar: Specifies the month to use as the first month for the report. Choose **Fiscal Year** to base the report from the first month of your fiscal year. If your fiscal year starts in April and you choose First Fiscal Quarter from the Date

Range menu on the report, QuickBooks shows the data from April, May, and June. Choose **Calendar Year** to start the year from January. Choose **Tax Year** to start with the first month of your company's tax year. (You entered your fiscal year and tax year information during the EasyStep interview, but if you need to change it at any point, go to the **Company** menu and choose **Company Information**. If you used Express Start to set up your company file, QuickBooks assumed your fiscal year and tax year start in January.)

Include: Tells QuickBooks which accounts to use for the detail transaction report. Choose **All** to include all accounts, even if the account had no transaction activity during the date range of the report. Choose **In Use** to include only the accounts that had transaction activity during the date range of the report.

Open Balance/Aging: Tells QuickBooks how to determine a customer's balance in aging reports. Choose **Current** to show the customer's open balance as of today, including payments received through today's date. Choose **As of Report Date** to show the customer's open balance as of the ending date of the report; this doesn't include payments received after the ending date of the report.

Filtering Reports

When you want to restrict what the report shows, you can filter it. When you choose a report, QuickBooks prepares a predefined report, but it might show more than you need. You can apply filters one at a time or combine them.

To open the Filters tab, click the **Customize Report** button at the top left of the report. In the Modify Report window, click the **Filters** tab, as shown in Figure 31.5.

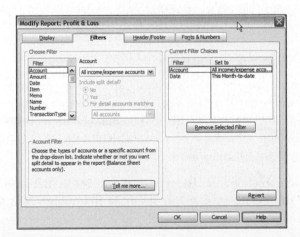

Figure 31.5: *Choose the filters to use to restrict what the report shows.*

QuickBooks has too many filters to cover in this chapter. Basically, you click a filter in the Filters list. As you click a filter, the options just for that filter appear to the right of the Filters list. To get an explanation of the options for each filter, click the filter, read the brief description below the Filter list, and then click **Tell Me More** to learn more about the filter. After you set options for a filter, press **Tab**; the selected filter moves to the right of the window, to the area called Current Filter Choices. To remove a filter, click it in the Current Filter Choices list and click **Remove Selected Filter**. When you've selected the filters for the report, click **OK** to see the report.

Figure 31.6 shows how the options change after you select a filter.

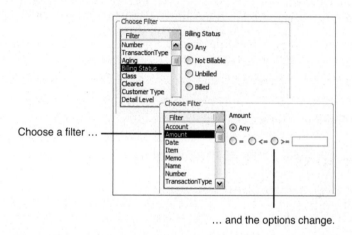

Choose a filter ...

... and the options change.

Figure 31.6: *When you select a filter, options just for that filter are displayed.*

Not all filters are available in every report or make sense to use in the report. Some rainy afternoon, spend some quality time with QuickBooks filters to get to know them. Some of the less obvious filter options are as follows:

Account: Limits the report to certain accounts. You can choose to show all accounts, more than one account, all accounts of a certain type (like bank accounts), or individual accounts (like Savings or Office Supplies).

Amount: Limits transactions that fall within the amount you specify. Select **Any** to show any amount. Alternatively, select = (equals), <= (less than or equal to), or >= (greater than or equal to) and then type in the amount.

Aging: Limits transactions on the basis of aging, meaning the number of days that an invoice or bill is past due. Select **Any** to show all overdue invoices or bills.

Alternatively, select = (equals), <= (less than or equal to), or >= (greater than or equal to) and then type in the amount.

Billing Status: Limits the report to show only customers with the billing status you select. For example, you can show only customers that are Unbilled.

Detail Level: Shows or hides the detail lines (line items on an invoice or expense account splits on checks) on detail transaction reports. Choose **All** to include all details for each transaction in the report. Choose **Summary Only** to hide all details and show only totals. Choose **All Except Summary** to show the detail lines for each transaction without the transaction totals.

FOB: Shows only the product sales shipped from a particular location, if you use F.O.B. (which is the location from which you ship products) on your forms.

Item: Limits the report to certain items. You can choose to show all items, more than one item, all items of a certain type (like service items), or individual accounts (like Consulting).

Memo: Limits the transactions based on the content of the Memo field. For example, if you consistently added a word or phrase in the memo of your invoices for "catering labor," you could limit a sales report to show only the invoices that have "catering labor" in the Memo field.

Name: Limits the report to show only the names you select. This, along with some of the other Name filters for the address (such as Name Zip), is useful for creating a customer contact list report, which you can then export to use print mailing labels for a mailing targeted for that zip code.

Number: Limits the report by the number(s) of transactions. You can show a single invoice or check number, for example, or a range of numbers, such as invoices numbered 1,000 to 1,500. To limit to a single number, type the number in the first field and leave the second field blank.

Posting Status: Limits the report based on whether the transactions are posting transactions. For example, estimates, pending sales, and purchase orders are nonposting transactions. To see only nonposting transactions, choose **Nonposting**; to see only posting transactions, choose **Posting**.

Printing Status: Limits the report based on whether the transactions have been printed. Use this filter along with the Transaction Type filter on a Check Detail report to see, for example, all the checks you need to print.

Received: Limits a purchase order report to show purchase orders that are open (not yet received) or closed (received). If you select **Either**, QuickBooks shows both open and closed purchase orders.

Changing Headers and Footers

If you don't like what QuickBooks displays in the header and footer of a report, you can change it. For example, if you don't want people to know you were up until 3:22 A.M. working on the report, you can remove the time the report was prepared. You can also change the alignment (left, center, right) of the items displayed in the header and footer.

To open the Headers/Footers tab, click the **Customize Report** button at the top left of the report. In the Modify Report window, click the **Header/Footer** tab, as shown in Figure 31.7.

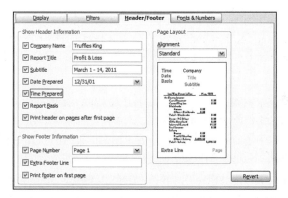

Figure 31.7: *Change the header and footer that appears on the report.*

To remove a header or footer item from the report display, click in the check box to remove the check mark. Note that the Date Prepared option doesn't show the date that will be used; it just shows the format of the date. Choose the format you want from the menu.

In the Page Layout section of the tab, choose how you want the header and footer aligned. Click **OK** to save the changes.

Changing Fonts and Numbers

If you don't like the boring fonts that QuickBooks uses in the reports, you can change them for different elements in the report. For example, you can choose to display the Company Name in an extra fancy font. But you don't want to go overboard changing the fonts for all the elements, or else the report could become difficult to read. If you make a hot mess using too many fonts, you can always click **Revert** in the Fonts & Numbers tab.

To open the Headers/Footers tab, click the **Customize Report** button at the top left of the report. In the Modify Report window, click the **Fonts & Numbers** tab, as shown in Figure 31.8.

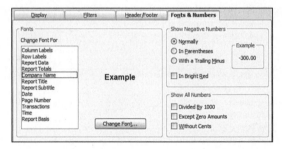

Figure 31.8: *Change the font and number style for the report.*

To change the font for a particular element in the report, click the element and then click **Change Font**. Figure 31.9 shows the Fonts window. Change the font information and click **OK**. When you see the message Change Related Fonts?, click **No**.

In the Show Negative Numbers section of the Fonts & Numbers tab, select how you want negative numbers to be displayed. You can also select how you want to display all numbers. **Divided by 1,000** is useful if you're lucky enough to have numbers with seven or eight digits. **Without Cents** removes the decimal point and cents in figures; QuickBooks rounds the cents to the nearest dollar.

Figure 31.9: *Choose the font, style, size, color, and effect for the selected element.*

Moving Report Columns

When you display a report, you can rearrange the columns on detail transaction and list reports (you can't rearrange columns on summary reports). With the report displayed on the screen, position the mouse pointer over the name of the column. When you see the hand icon, drag the column to where you want it to go. You'll see a red arrow for placement, as shown in Figure 31.10. Release the mouse button to place the column.

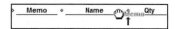

Figure 31.10: *Rearrange columns on transaction and list reports.*

Saving Reports You've Customized

After you create the perfect report, you can save it so you don't have to go back and redo all the customizations you've made. QuickBooks calls saving the report "memorizing." QuickBooks saves all the changes made in the Modify Report window, as well as the rearrangement of columns, if any. After you create the report with all your customization, click the **Memorize** button at the top of the report (next to the Modify Report button). Give the report a name (each memorized report must have a unique name). To save the report as part of a group (this keeps the Memorized Reports menu organized), click the **Save in Memorized Report Group** check box and then choose the report group. Click **OK**.

The next time you use the memorized report, QuickBooks uses all your customizations, but uses the most recent financial data.

To use a memorized report, go to the **Reports** menu, click **Memorized Reports**, go to the group (if you saved the report in a group), and then click the report name.

QUICKTIP

Memorizing a report saves the report formatting, not the report data. To save the actual data, you can export it to Microsoft Excel or .csv file (click the Excel button), or save it as a PDF (on the **File** menu).

Processing Multiple Reports

If you're doing month-end or year-end reports for review, you can save time by processing several reports at the same time. Go to **Reports** and click **Process Multiple Reports**. In the window that appears, check the reports you want and QuickBooks generates them and displays them all at once.

The Least You Need to Know

- Customize a report to format it and make it display exactly the data you want.
- When you want to restrict what the report shows, you can filter it.
- You can change how a report looks, including the header and footer information, the fonts used, and how numbers are displayed.
- After you create the perfect report, you can save it so you don't have to go back and redo all the customizations you've made. QuickBooks calls saving the report "memorizing."

Performing Year-End Tasks

In This Chapter

- Performing fiscal year-end tasks
- Performing calendar year-end tasks
- Making year-end journal entries
- Creating a copy of your file for your accountant to review
- Closing the books

That year went by way too quickly, didn't it? Now it's the end of your fiscal year. But don't get too excited and gung ho about the next year; you still have a bunch of stuff to do to close out the year. There are lots of terms for this: closing out the year, closing the books, and year-end close. QuickBooks doesn't require that you close the books. You're not off the hook, though. You still need to complete some tasks before and after the end of the fiscal year, as well as the end of the calendar year. That's what this chapter is all about.

Here's a little disclaimer: ask your accountant what year-end tasks you should do. Your accountant knows your business and can help you avoid potentially serious mistakes. In fact, I recommend handing over all year-end tasks and tax preparation to your accountant.

Fiscal Year-End Tasks

At the end of your fiscal year (which could be the end of the calendar year), you should go over your year-end reports, make any corrections or adjustments to transactions, and prepare for tax time. This section covers some of the basic tasks you'll need to perform.

Checking Reports Before Fiscal Year End

One report you should check before the end of your fiscal year is the Balance Sheet report. To generate the balance sheet, go to **Reports**, go to **Company & Financial**, and click **Balance Sheet Standard**. Check in the Dates field to make sure the report represents the correct fiscal year. (If you're running this report before the end of the fiscal year, choose **This Fiscal Year-to-Date**. If it's after the end of the fiscal year, choose **Last Fiscal Year**.)

Under Other Current Liabilities (see Figure 32.1), check to see whether there are any outstanding payroll liabilities, and pay them before the end of the fiscal year. Same with sales tax liabilities. If you have any outstanding bills in A/P, pay as many as you can so you can take the deduction in the current fiscal year.

```
LIABILITIES & EQUITY
   Liabilities
      Current Liabilities
         Accounts Payable
            Accounts Payable              624.00
            Total Accounts Payable    ▶   624.00 ◀

         Credit Cards
            Business Credit              345.00
            Total Credit Cards           345.00

         Other Current Liabilities
            Payroll Liabilities          243.75
            Sales Tax Payable             31.17
            Total Other Current Liabilities   274.92

      Total Current Liabilities       1,243.92

   Total Liabilities                  1,243.92
```

Figure 32.1: *Review the balance sheet before the end of your fiscal year. The liabilities section is shown here.*

Another report to generate close to the end of your fiscal year is the trial balance. To generate the balance sheet, go to **Reports**, go to **Accountant & Taxes**, and click **Trial Balance**. In the Dates field, choose **This Fiscal Year-to-Date**. At the bottom of the report, you'll see the Ask My Accountant account. If you've selected that account, you'll see the total amount of all transactions that you assigned to Ask My Accountant. Double-click the amount to see a report listing all the transactions you weren't sure which account to assign them to. Talk with your accountant to get the transactions assigned to the correct accounts.

Reconciling Accounts After Fiscal Year End

After you get your bank statements, in the month following the end of your fiscal year (January, if your fiscal year ends in December), reconcile your bank accounts and credit card accounts. Go over the registers to see if any checks you wrote never got cashed or if checks you received never cleared the bank.

Check your petty cash register to see if all transactions have been entered and balanced.

Taking Inventory

At the end of the year, do a physical count of your inventory and make adjustments to account for discrepancies. Chapter 20 talks about counting inventory. To figure out the inventory count as of the last day of your fiscal year (assuming that you were unable to count inventory after the last day of your fiscal year), adjust for the number of items sold and purchased since the end of the previous year. Date the inventory adjustment the last day of the fiscal year.

Let's say a boutique hardware store took a count of the knob inventory and found 113 fish-shaped ceramic knobs. (To keep it simple, this example uses only one product.) The count was taken on January 12. Between January 1 and January 12, the store sold 31 fish-shaped knobs and received 10 more into inventory. To get the year-end count, add the amount sold since January 1 to the physical count and subtract the amount received. In this example, the count for the fish knobs as of the last day of the fiscal year was 134.

Generating Financial Reports

Financial reports show you the health of your business. Chapter 30 covered these reports in detail. You'll want to generate these reports at the end of your fiscal year and review them to catch any glaring errors or inconsistencies. You (or your accountant) can try to fix those and make adjustments. If you do end up making adjustments, generate the reports again to ensure you have the accurate numbers.

To create the reports to show data for your fiscal year, go to Reports, choose the report category, and then choose the report. From the **Dates** menu, choose **Last Fiscal Year** (assuming that you're generating the report after your fiscal year closes). Figure 32.2 shows the Dates menu.

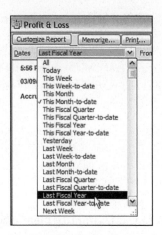

Figure 32.2: *Choose Last Fiscal Year to see the report for the fiscal year that just ended.*

You should generate the following reports after the end of your fiscal year:

Trial Balance: Generate this report the day after the end of your fiscal year. Check to see that the income and expense accounts have a zero balance.

Profit & Loss Standard: Shows the net income for the fiscal year. It shows subtotals for your income and expense accounts. At the bottom of the report is your net income (or loss) for the fiscal year. If you see any suspicious numbers, track down the problem and fix it or make a journal entry (described in the following section). After fixing any errors, run the report again and keep it with a copy of your tax return for your records.

Balance Sheet Standard: After reconciling and verifying your balance sheet accounts, run this report to see how much your business is worth (your business's equity). The business equity includes the net income (or loss) for the fiscal year. Verify that this year's Retained Earnings equals last year's beginning retained earnings plus last year's profit or loss (net income). If they don't match, maybe you inadvertently changed a prior-year transaction, deleted a transaction, or added a new transaction to that year. This could easily be caused by a typo in typing the year. To find offending transactions, run the **Audit Trail** and **Voided/Deleted Transactions** reports in **Accountant & Taxes**. After you fix any errors, run the report again and keep it with a copy of your tax return for your records.

Making Year-End Journal Entries

After inspecting your reports and accounts for potential errors, you may find that you need to make an adjustment. Some adjustments are made using what's called a *journal entry*. If the debit/credit idea messes with your mind, leave journal entries to your accountant.

> **DEFINITION**
>
> A **journal entry** comes from the old-fashioned method of accounting in which accountants used general ledgers. It is also called general journal entry.

To make a journal entry, go to the **Company** menu and click **Make General Journal Entries**. Read the message that appears and click **OK**. Figure 32.3 shows the journal entry window.

Most of the time, you don't need to worry about making journal entries, but in the following cases, you have no choice:

Splitting up an account: If you want to change the way an account is set up, such as break one account into two (or more) accounts, you need to use journal entries. For example, let's say a retail cookware store originally sold only kitchen equipment, cookbooks, and linens, and tracked the income in a Product Sales Income account. Later, they branched out and started offering cooking classes. Now they want to track the cooking class income separately. To do this, make a journal entry to debit the Product Sales Income account for the amount that should now go in the new Cooking Class Income account. Credit the Cooking Class Income account the same amount, as shown in Figure 32.3.

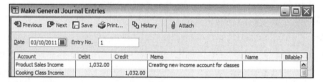

Figure 32.3: *Use a journal entry to reassign income or expense accounts.*

If the account was an expense account, you would credit the initial expense account by the amount you want to put in the new account and debit the new account with the same amount.

QUICKTIP

After splitting out an account into a new account, go back to the items assigned to the old account and reassign them to the new account, as appropriate.

Income or expense incorrectly assigned: If you assigned an expense to the wrong expense account, use a journal entry to fix it. For example, maybe you assigned your phone bill to the Utilities expense account instead of the Telephone expense account. In this case, you would credit the Utilities expense account by the amount you want to put in the Telephone account and debit the Telephone account with the same amount. If you use classes, this same method works if you assigned the incorrect class.

End-of-year transactions: Your accountant will probably make several journal entries at the end of the year, so you don't have to worry about them. The journal entries might adjust for prepaid expenses and adjust for cash versus accrual. Just don't be surprised if you see general journal type transactions on reports or in registers.

Depreciation: This is probably best left to your accountant, but you can use a journal entry to record depreciation. A fixed asset, such as a vehicle or piece of equipment, loses value as it gets older, and depreciation tracks the current value. Usually you enter depreciation at the end of the year so you can track it for your tax return. QuickBooks probably set up a Depreciation Expense account for you, but if you don't see it, set one up. You'll also need a fixed asset account for each asset you want to depreciate, as well as an accumulated depreciation account for each asset. See? It gets complicated. To record the depreciation, create a debit (increase) for the Depreciation Expense account and create a credit (decrease) for the fixed asset's accumulated depreciation account. According to IRS rules, the debit account must be an expense account used for depreciation, and the credit account must be a fixed asset account. When recording a depreciation at the end of the year, date the transaction the last day of your fiscal year.

QUICKTIP

Create a main fixed asset account for each category of fixed asset, such as Computer Equipment, Vehicles, and Office Furniture. Group like assets under the main category: Laptop, iPad, and Desktop could be subaccounts under Computer Equipment.

To view the general journal to see all the journal entries, click **Reports**, click **Accountant & Taxes**, and then click **Journal**.

Calendar Year-End Tasks

The main tasks to do at the end of the calendar year have to do with taxes. You'll need to create and file payroll forms and generate tax-preparation reports to help you prepare your taxes.

Performing Payroll Tasks

I talk about payroll in Chapter 24, so here's just a checklist of tasks you need to do at the end of the year:

- Generate and print W2/W3 forms to document the annual payments per employee.

- Generate and print 1099 forms, if you employ subcontractors (1099 vendors).

- Check to see whether you have any payroll tax liabilities by generating a Payroll Liability report, and set the date range for the entire year. Check to see if you have a balance due.

- Prepare the end-of-quarter Form 941 or 944, even if you don't owe. The tax agencies want a quarterly reconciliation. See "Preparing Tax Forms" in Chapter 24.

- Prepare the 940 (FUTA) form, which must be filed annually.

NUMBERS HAPPEN

Get help from your accountant when preparing for year-end close, especially with payroll, because things can get tricky. You don't want to mess with tax authorities.

Generating Tax Reports

QuickBooks provides three reports that can help you fill out your tax forms. In addition, you can generate several reports to see your fiscal year financials, which businesses can submit with their tax returns.

QUICKTIP

Before generating your tax reports, run the Income Tax Preparation report to assign tax lines to accounts listed as <Unassigned>. Double-click an account and assign the tax line.

To generate reports for tax preparation, go to **Reports**, go to **Accountant & Taxes**, and click one of the three income tax–related reports at the bottom of the menu. By default, the report covers **Last Tax Year**. Change the date if you want to see a different time period. The reports are as follows:

Income Tax Preparation: Run this report before generating the other tax reports. This report shows all the accounts you've set up and the tax lines associated with them. If you see <Unassigned> in the Tax Line column, double-click the name of the account. This opens the Edit Account window. From the Tax Line Mapping menu, choose the tax line to assign to it. The tax lines come from the tax form you chose during the initial setup of your company file.

Income Tax Summary: Shows the amounts assigned to each tax line in the tax form you chose. See Figure 32.4 for an example.

Schedule C	
Gross receipts or sales	5,446.75
Other business income	6.58
Advertising	240.00
Car and truck expenses	428.74
Depletion	575.00
Interest expense, other	595.42
Office expenses	170.76
Repairs and maintenance	175.00
Utilities	611.90
Materials/supplies, COGS	2,365.80
Tax Line Unassigned (balance sheet)	1,439.27
Tax Line Unassigned (income/expense) ▶	-649.06 ◀

Figure 32.4: *Use the Income Tax Summary report to help fill out your tax forms.*

Income Tax Detail: Shows the individual transactions that make up the total amounts assigned to each tax line, as shown in the summary report.

Creating an Accountant's Review Copy

At the end of the year (or any time of year, actually), your accountant may want to review your "books." You can save a version of your company file that your accountant can use while you continue to work in your company file. When you get the file back from your accountant, you can merge the changes back into your company file.

Choosing the Dividing Date

Before you create the accountant's version, figure out with your accountant what the dividing date should be. You will be able to continue working in the file and adding transactions after that date, but there are a few things you shouldn't do. You can't add or change transactions dated earlier than that date. You can't edit, merge, or add sub-accounts to existing accounts, or make an existing account inactive. You can't delete or merge list items. And although you can reconcile an account, it's probably not a good idea, in case your accountant has undone a prior reconciliation that may affect future reconciliations. Also, you can't process payroll if there's a payroll transaction dated before the dividing date.

A logical dividing date is the end of a fiscal period or end of a month, plus a couple weeks after that date. This gives your accountant a little leeway for moving transactions between periods.

Sending the File

You can send the file to your accountant in two ways. You can save the file to a disc or flash drive, or you can upload the file to a QuickBooks server (if your accountant subscribes to that service).

To save the accountant's copy to a disc or flash drive, go to **File**, go to **Accountant's Copy**, and click **Save File**. The option **Accountant's Copy** should be selected; if not, select it. Click **Next**. On the Dividing Date window (see Figure 32.5), choose one of the options QuickBooks suggests or click **Custom** to enter the date. Click **Next** and choose where you want to save the file: the flash drive, disc, or desktop. (QuickBooks suggests a name for the file that includes the date and time, and it's a good idea to keep that name.) If the file is small enough, you may be able to e-mail it to your accountant. Otherwise, send it by snail mail or hand-deliver it.

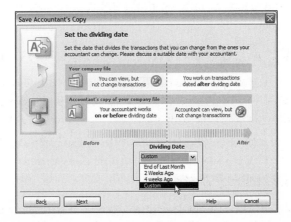

Figure 32.5: *Choose the date you and your accountant agreed to be the dividing date.*

A couple of limitations apply to sending the accountant's copy to the QuickBooks server. The company file must be smaller than 200MB, and you must have a fast Internet connection speed (dial-up just won't cut it).

To save the accountant's copy to the QuickBooks server, go to **File**, go to **Accountant's Copy**, and click **Send to Accountant.** Click **Next**. On the Dividing Date window (see Figure 32.5), choose one of the options QuickBooks suggests or click **Custom** to enter the date. Click **Next**. Type in your accountant's e-mail address two times, type your name and e-mail (if not already supplied by QuickBooks), and click **Next**. The next window asks you to create a password for downloading the file. This isn't the Admin password you may have set up in the EasyStep Interview. The password you enter in this window must be seven characters or more and must include at least one number and at least one capital letter. Type the password twice and then type an optional note to your accountant (but don't put the password in the note). Click **Send**. The process may take up to 15 minutes. Don't quit QuickBooks until the file transfer has completed.

Click **OK** at the message that the file has been uploaded successfully. QuickBooks sends a message to your accountant that includes a link to download the file.

If QuickBooks is unable to upload the file, first try sending it again. If there's still a problem, check your firewall settings or your Internet connection. Alternatively, you can save the accountant's copy to a flash drive or disc.

If you created an Admin password for your company file, be sure to tell your accountant what the password is so he can open the file.

Importing Your Accountant's Changes

When your accountant is finished reviewing your books, you can import the changes into your company file. The file created with your accountant's changes contains only the changes; it doesn't include your complete company file, so it's small enough that your accountant will probably just e-mail it to you. The file has the extension .qby, and it can be imported only into your company file; QuickBooks encrypts the file, and it's safe to send via e-mail.

To import the changes, open your company file in QuickBooks. Go to the File menu, go to Accountant's Copy, and click either **Import Accountant's Changes from File** or **Import Accountant's Changes from Web**. Locate the **.qby** file your accountant sent you, and click **Open** (or download the file from the server).

Review the changes. To keep a record of the changes made, either click **Print** to print a paper copy or click **Save As PDF**. If you agree with the changes, click **Incorporate Accountant's Changes**. (If you don't agree, click **Close** and read the following paragraph for what to do.) Click **OK** to close the window. QuickBooks prompts you to make a backup of your company file. Review the changes again to see if your accountant's changes conflict with anything. QuickBooks explains any conflict and offers suggestions on what you should do. When finished, click **Close**. QuickBooks asks if you want to set a closing date and password. Closing the books has pros and cons, so read the following section. Click **Yes** or **No** as appropriate.

If you didn't agree with your accountant's changes, or if the accountant didn't find anything that needed to be changed, you can cancel the accountant's copy to remove the restrictions. To do this (with your accountant's blessing), go to **File**, go to **Accountant's Copy**, and click **Remove Restrictions**. Click **Yes** to confirm and then click **OK**.

Closing the Books

Closing the books is an accounting practice that ensures that transactions do not change after your taxes have been filed. Once the books are closed, no one (without the password set when you close the books) can change or add transactions dated on or before the close date. Books are usually closed a few months after the end of the fiscal year.

To close your books, go to the **Company** menu and click **Set Closing Date**. This takes you to Accounting preferences. Click **Set Date/Password**. Enter the date for the closing, which is likely the last date of the fiscal year. It is highly recommended that you set a password so that only people who know the password can make changes to the closed books. Click **OK** to save the closing date.

The Least You Need to Know

- At the end of your fiscal year, go over your year-end reports, make any corrections or adjustments to transactions, and prepare for tax time.
- QuickBooks provides three reports that can help you fill out your tax forms and other reports on your financials to submit with your tax returns.

- You can save a version of your company file so your accountant can review it while you continue to work in your company file. When you get the file back, merge the changes into your company file.

- Closing the books is an accounting practice that ensures that transactions do not change after your taxes have been filed.

Glossary

account   QuickBooks has accounts such as checking and savings, as well as income and expense accounts used to categorize your transactions. The chart of accounts lists all your accounts.

accounting period   The time period covered by financial reports, such as a Profit and Loss report.

accounts payable   (Abbreviated as A/P) The account that tracks the money your business owes to others: vendors, contractors, suppliers, and consultants. Other accounts track items like loans and mortgages.

accounts receivable   (Abbreviated as A/R) The account that tracks money owed to you from sales you've made that haven't yet been paid for.

accrual basis   An accounting method in which you report income as soon as you invoice a customer instead of when you actually receive the money. You report expenses when you receive a bill, not when you pay the bill.

accrued expenses   Expenses that you have incurred but not yet paid, such as taxes and payroll.

accrued income   Income that you have earned but not yet received.

adjusting entry   Accounting entries made at the end of an accounting period, used to adjust for errors and for depreciation. Also known as *closing entries.*

aging   When invoices get old, just like people, it's called aging. The aging reports show across all open invoices how much money is due, how much is overdue, and how many days it's overdue.

average cost   Method that calculates the value of inventory based on the price of each inventory item divided by the number of those items in stock. QuickBooks uses the average cost method.

assets   Items your company owns that have value, such as cash, equipment, and supplies. QuickBooks records two types of assets: current assets and fixed assets.

audit trail   A record of all the additions, deletions, and modifications made to transactions in your company file. The audit trail is used to trace changes and track down possible fraud.

backup   A copy of your company file that you have "backed up" to store on another computer, flash drive, or CD, in case of computer breakdown or other situation. If that happens, you can restore the backup.

balance sheet   The primary financial statement that shows your business assets, liabilities, and equity at a point in time.

balance sheet accounts   Includes items you own and the debts you owe. What you own includes assets, bank accounts, buildings, and money that people owe you; debts include liabilities such as credit cards or loans from banks. Equity accounts are also included in the balance sheet.

balance sheet report   One of three primary financial reports of a business. Shows you an overall picture of the health of your business finances as of a certain date. It basically shows you how much your company is worth.

bank account register   A list of transactions, much like the paper register of your checkbook. Can be a checking, savings, money market, or petty cash account.

billing statement   (Also called a statement) Lists the charges a customer has accumulated over a period of time.

capital investment   Personal money an owner or partner puts into the business. These investments are tracked in equity accounts (one for each owner/partner).

cash basis   An accounting method in which you report income when you receive a payment instead of when you bill a customer. You report expenses when you pay bills.

cash flow   Represents the cash coming in (called cash inflow) from profits and the cash spent (called cash outflow) during a specified time period.

chart of accounts   A list of all your accounts and their balances.

classes   Used to classify your transactions by segments of your business—for example, by department, location, service, or product lines. Then you can track the segment's income and expenses.

company file   A QuickBooks file that stores financial information for a single business. QuickBooks company files have the .qbw extension.

company snapshot   A view into your company within QuickBooks to see real-time company information and perform tasks from a single place. Includes tabs for Company, Payments, and Customers.

cost of goods sold   The cost of your products and materials held in inventory and later sold.

Cost of Goods Sold account   The account that tracks how much you paid for items (the cost) that you had in inventory and then sold.

credit   In accounting, a credit (along with a debit) represents an increase or decrease in accounts. A credit decreases asset and expense accounts; a debit increases liability and income accounts. In traditional, double-entry accounting, the total of debits must equal the total of credits—that is, the "books must balance." See also *debit*.

credit memo   Similar to an invoice, but reduces the customer's balance. (For example, the customer cancelled the sale, overpaid, or returned something.)

current assets   Assets that you plan to use up within a year or that can be converted to cash within one year. This also includes "cash" in your checking and savings accounts and any money your customers owe you.

current liabilities   Debts that you must pay within one year.

customer   Used loosely to apply to all kinds of situations—your business may refer to them as clients, patients, collectors, club members, donors, visitors, and so on. See also *job*.

customer type   Provides a way for you to group or categorize your customers, to help you analyze different segments of your business.

debit   In accounting, a debit (along with a credit) represents an increase or decrease in accounts. A debit decreases liability and income accounts, and it increases asset and expense accounts. See also *credit*.

depreciation   Used to expense the price of a fixed asset over time (and not just the year in which it was purchased), since fixed assets generally have long-term value when operating a business.

detail report   A report in QuickBooks that shows the individual transactions from which QuickBooks calculated each total. For example, if the total of an office supplies expense account is $453.27, a detail report would show all the transactions that made up that $453.27. Detail reports are also called transaction reports. See also *summary report*.

double-entry accounting   Every accounting transaction has two sides: where the money comes from and where the money goes. All transaction entries must be in balance. The two sides of a transaction are called debit and credit. Every transaction has a debit and a credit.

double-sided item   An item you set up that can be used on both purchase orders and sales forms.

estimate   A form in QuickBooks that you can use to itemize work for a project or products to sell to a customer. This gives the customer an idea of the cost before committing. Also known as a *bid* or *proposal*.

equity   The net worth of a company. This is the difference between your liabilities (what you owe) and your assets (what you have). Equity comes from money you or a partner invests in the company and from the profits you make.

expense   Money spent to run your business.

filters   Used to restrict what's shown in a QuickBooks report. For example, you can limit a vendor report to show only certain vendors instead of all vendors; QuickBooks then excludes all other vendors.

finance charges   Extra fees charged for a customer's overdue balance.

fiscal year   A 12-month period used for calculating your company's yearly financial reports. People usually choose January as the start of the fiscal year, to match the income tax year.

fixed asset   Equipment, furniture, buildings, and vehicles purchased for use in your business to generate income. These are assets that you do not expect to sell, but that will depreciate over the life of the asset. Land is also considered a fixed asset but is not depreciable.

F.O.B.   The location an order is shipped from and the point at which the package becomes the customer's responsibility. Also known as *Freight on Board* and *Free on Board*.

general journal   An entry form in QuickBooks used mostly by accountants to enter transactions using the traditional system of debits and credits.

gross margin   Profit from taking the sales price of items you sell and subtracting the cost of goods sold. Also known as *gross profit*.

income   Money that comes into the company through the sale of products or services, or from investments. Also known as *revenue*.

inventory   Products and materials you have on hand to sell to your customers.

inventory part   Represents items that you buy and store on your shelves before selling.

invoice   A form you fill out to record the amounts and costs of products or services that you sell to a customer, along with other items, such as shipping, taxes, discounts, and so on.

item receipt   Tracks inventory that you receive without a bill. Convert the item receipt into a bill when you actually receive the bill from the vendor.

items   Represent what you sell, buy, or resell in the course of doing business, such as products or services. Items can also include other line items that would appear on an invoice or sales receipt or purchase order, such as shipping, discounts, sales tax, and other charges.

job   Refers to projects and must be associated with a customer. If you're a building contractor and are remodeling a house, you could create jobs for each phase of the project—for example, Kitchen Remodel and Master Bath Remodel.

journal entry   Comes from the old-fashioned method of accounting. It represents either the credit side of a transaction or the debit side. The credit and debit must balance out to zero. Also called *general journal entry*.

liability   Represents the amounts you owe.

long-term liabilities   Liabilities that are not due within a year.

memorized report   A report that you have modified and saved so that you can reuse it at a later date.

memorized transaction   A transaction that occurs frequently or on a regular basis (with a similar payee and amount) that you can save and reuse. Useful for saving time when entering the transaction.

net income   Represents revenue minus expenses. Net income on the balance sheet may be a positive or negative number; it depends on the sum of the net income for all periods for that fiscal year. See also *net loss* and *net profit*.

net loss   When net income is a negative number; this shows that you lost money running your business for the period.

net profit   When net income is a positive number; this shows that you actually made some money and earned a profit.

noninventory part   Represents an item that you purchase but do not sell, or that you purchase on behalf of a customer and immediately resell (it doesn't sit on your shelves in stock).

nonposting account   Accounts that don't affect income, expense, or balance sheet accounts. Estimates and purchase orders are nonposting accounts.

owners draw account   An account that tracks withdrawals of the company's assets to pay an owner. The draws reduce the company's equity.

owners equity   Represents the total value an owner has in the company. Owner equity is equal to the business assets minus liabilities.

payables   Money you owe to vendors or suppliers.

payroll items   Track compensation, tax, and deduction amounts on a paycheck and accumulate year-to-date wage and tax amounts for each employee, as well as items used when making a payroll tax payment.

payroll liabilities account   Tracks the federal, state, and local withholding taxes deducted from your employee paychecks, as well as Social Security and Medicare.

petty cash   Money you use for small business-related expenses.

physical inventory   Process of counting inventory you have in stock at the end of an accounting period.

portable company file   Your company file condensed so that you can e-mail it or transport it from one computer to another.

post   In accounting, a verb that basically means to record the transaction to an account.

prepaid expenses   Expenses paid for before they are used—for example, insurance and rent.

preferences   Used in QuickBooks to turn features on or off and to customize QuickBooks to fit the way you like to work.

price levels   Use these to easily apply different rates on sales receipts and invoices so that you don't have to manually figure out the percentage increase or decrease.

product business   A business that primarily sells goods instead of services.

Profit and Loss report   One of three primary financial reports of a business. Shows your profits and losses over time. This report shows whether you are operating with a loss or a profit. Most businesses run this report at least monthly. Also called an *income statement.*

QuickBooks Centers   QuickBooks organizes the key areas of your business into "centers." All information is easily accessible from here. Centers are set up for Customers & Jobs, Vendors, Employees, and Reports. In addition, Customers Center has a Collections Center.

receivables   Money that your customers owe you.

reconciling   Process of comparing the financial institution's records with your own to make sure they're in agreement.

recurring transaction   Transactions that occur frequently or on a regular basis that are similar (with the same payee and a similar amount), such as Internet expenses. See also *memorized transaction.*

register   A list of transactions, much like the paper register of your checkbook. All accounts have a register in QuickBooks, except income and expense accounts.

reimbursable expenses   Expenses incurred during the course of a job that you can charge back to the customer.

Reminder list   A list in QuickBooks that reminds you when it's time to pay bills; print invoices, purchase orders, and checks; deposit money; enter memorized transactions; pay overdue invoices; and more.

reminder statement   Summarizes a customer's account with your company by listing recent invoices, credit memos, and payments received. Used to remind customers of overdue balances.

retail store   A business, such as a hair salon or hobby store, that sells products or services directly to customers in the business establishment.

retained earnings   Profits from previous accounting periods. QuickBooks creates an equity account that tracks retained earnings. Retained earnings represent the amount of accumulated profits that haven't yet been distributed to owners/partners.

sales receipt   A form you use when you make a sale and receive the full payment at the time of the sale.

sales tax codes   Codes QuickBooks uses to determine your taxable and nontaxable customers.

sales tax group item   In some states, you may have to charge city or county taxes in addition to state taxes. You can group these taxes so the customer sees only one tax line on an invoice or sales receipt.

service business   A business that sells primarily services instead of products.

sole proprietorship   A business that has only one person as the owner.

standard check   A business-sized check printed three per page without a stub.

statement charges   Amounts you charge a customer for any services performed.

statement of cash flows   One of three primary financial reports of a business. It shows how your cash position changed over a period of time, including the amount of cash earned from profit, where you received additional cash, and where your cash was spent. See also *balance sheet report* and *Profit & Loss report*.

subaccounts   Used to break down a larger, more general account into smaller, more specific accounts. Subaccounts are useful for getting more detail in income and expense accounts. For example, Automobile could be the parent account, and Fuel, Insurance, and Repairs could be subaccounts.

subitems   Used to break down a more general item into a hierarchy of items. Useful for grouping information about similar items in sales reports and graphs. For example, if you sell building supplies, Lumber could be a parent item and Decking, Trim, and Rough could be subitems.

summary report   A report in QuickBooks that groups transactions into a single total. For example, if you had four transactions for computer repairs during the time period of the report, a summary report would show the total of all four transactions, not the individual transactions themselves. See also *detail report*.

terms   A shorthand way of describing the time frame when you expect to receive payment from a customer, or when a vendor expects to receive payment from you.

trial balance   A report that adds up all the debits and credits, to make sure debits equal credits.

undeposited funds account   An account that QuickBooks adds to your chart of accounts to keep track of funds you've received but not yet deposited.

vendor   Anyone, except your employees, you pay money to in the course of running your business. Vendors can be subcontractors, your landlord, your cleaning service, utility companies, tax agencies, or suppliers.

voucher check   A check printed on a full page. The check portion at the top tears off, and the remaining portion shows the details of the check. Also known as *vendor checks* or *payroll checks*.

wallet check   A check that's the size of a personal bank check. For printing, each page holds three wallet-sized checks with a detachable stub for each check.

wholesale business   A business that typically contracts with the manufacturer to distribute the products on behalf of the manufacturer to the retailers. Products are sold at a discount. A wholesale business usually does not sell to individual customers.

Resources

When learning and working with QuickBooks Pro, you may come across some features that fall beyond the scope of this book. This appendix talks about some of the resources available to you.

QuickBooks Help

QuickBooks Help provides a thorough explanation of using all the features in QuickBooks. No matter where you are in QuickBooks, you can press **F1** or choose **QuickBooks Help** from the Help menu. Also, when you see a blue question mark anywhere in QuickBooks, clicking it takes you to QuickBooks Help.

QuickBooks Help has two tabs: Relevant Topics and Search. The Relevant Topics tab lists help topics that match where you are currently in the program. So if you're in the Customer Center, QuickBooks Help lists topics related to it. The contents of the Relevant Topics tab change depending on where you are in the program. The Search tab lets you find topics by typing in a word or phrase. For example, if you want to learn more about invoices, type "invoices" to see a list of topics that touch on invoices. If you want to print the topic that's currently displayed, click the **Print Topic** icon. You can use the Back and Forward arrows like breadcrumbs that take you step by step the way you came.

QuickBooks Live Community

At the top of the Help panel, you'll see a Live Community tab. Click this tab to go online to ask questions or provide answers to the online community of QuickBooks users.

The QuickBooks Help Menu

The Help menu provides you with many resources to help you learn more about QuickBooks (see Figure A.1). A few of these menu items are described here.

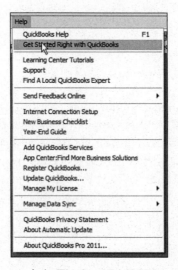

Figure A.1: *The QuickBooks Help menu.*

Get Started Right with QuickBooks takes you online so that you can make an appointment with a member of the QuickBooks Expert team who can help with various setup tasks.

Learning Center Tutorials displays the Learning Center, where you can watch video tutorials that walk you through various features of QuickBooks.

Support takes you online to the Support page, where you can read common questions and answers or get help with an error message.

There's also a handy **Year End Guide** and a **New Business Checklist**. You can also learn about any QuickBooks add-on services, such as payroll or a merchant account.

The QuickBooks ProAdvisor Program

Certified QuickBooks ProAdvisors are typically CPAs, bookkeepers, small business advisors, QuickBooks consultants, or accountants who work with small businesses every day. They can offer guidance on everything from setting up QuickBooks to mastering advanced features. To find a ProAdvisor in your area, go to the **Help** menu and click **Find a Local QuickBooks Expert**.

QuickBooks Sample Files

QuickBooks includes sample company files that you can use to get ideas on how other companies use QuickBooks. One sample file shows a company that provides primarily landscaping services and the other sample file is a construction company that provides services, keeps inventory, and sells products. You can play around with the data, make transactions, and create reports, just to get some hands-on practice. However, these files are not meant to be used as a basis for your company file; don't use them to start entering your own data, because these files are limited and are to be used simply for practice. You must create your own company file to store your accounting data

The QuickBooks Payroll Solutions

QuickBooks offers several different fee-based payroll solutions that take the hard work out of doing payroll. To check them out, go to: payroll.intuit.com/.

Outside Intuit

For help outside Intuit, you'll find a user forum at www.quickbooksusers.com.

And if you're starting to get excited about accounting, check out *The Complete Idiot's Guide to Accounting*, by Lita Epstein and Shellie L. Moore.

Index

Numbers

D

E

M

N

O

T